MOST
TALKATIVE

MOST TALKATIVE

Stories from the front lines of pop culture ☺

ANDY COHEN

HENRY HOLT AND COMPANY
NEW YORK

Henry Holt and Company, LLC
Publishers since 1866
175 Fifth Avenue
New York, New York 10010
www.henryholt.com

Henry Holt® and 🄷® are registered trademarks of Henry Holt and Company, LLC.

Library of Congress Cataloging-in-Publication Data

Cohen, Andy, 1968–
    Most talkative : stories from the front lines of pop culture / Andy Cohen. — 1st ed.
      p. cm.
    ISBN 978-0-8050-9583-8
  1. Cohen, Andy, 1968–   2. Television personalities—United States—Biography.
3. Television broadcasting—United States—Biography.   4. Executives—United States—
Biography.   I. Title.
    PN1992.4.C66A3 2012
    791.45092—dc23
          2012001843

First Edition 2012

Designed by Meryl Sussman Levavi

Printed in the United States of America

1 3 5 7 9 10 8 6 4 2

This book is dedicated to the strong women in my life:

first and foremost my mom, Evelyn Cohen, and all those

in these pages and each and every Housewife.

And of course Madonna. Just because.

CONTENTS

MOST
TALKATIVE

MY DATE WITH
SUSAN LUCCI

'm standing on the corner of Sixty-seventh and Columbus Avenue in Manhattan waiting for a meeting that will change my life. It's December 11, 1987. I'm nineteen years old and about to have my first encounter with a celebrity. Not just any celebrity. The Queen of Daytime, and my first diva: Susan Lucci.

I fell in love with Erica Kane the summer before my freshman year of high school. Like all red-blooded teen American boys, I'd come home from water polo practice and eat a box of Entenmann's Pop'Ems donut holes in front of the TV while obsessively fawning over *All My Children* and Erica, her clothes, and her narcissistic attitude. My sister Em and I even got my mom into the show. Which was a coup because Evelyn Cohen doesn't suffer fools: She gets the *New York Times*—not *Soap Opera Digest*—delivered to our house in

St. Louis. And in general, Jewish women don't tend to sit around watching soaps. Don't ask me why.

Dinner "conversation" at the Cohens' meant my sister, mom, and I relaying in brutal detail the day's events in a state of amplified hysteria, while my father listened to his own smooth jazz station in his head. After dinner, my dad would rejoin the living, and I would inevitably hear the three words I dreaded more than anything else: "Wanna play catch?"

No, I did *not* want to play catch. Ever.

I would turn to my mom for a reprieve, who would instead give me a look that was simultaneously threatening and begging. "Just humor your father and go TOSS THE DAMN BALL!" I got out of it most times by just making a run for it and sliding into my home base, in front of the TV.

Susan Lucci was the biggest star in the daytime galaxy, and she served it up hot and fresh and chic five days a week. Before there was Joan Collins's Alexis Morrell Carrington Colby Dexter Rowan on *Dynasty*, there was Erica Kane Martin Brent Cudahy Chandler Montgomery Montgomery Chandler Marick Marick Montgomery on *All My Children*.

A few months earlier, the professor in my Boston University news writing and reporting class assigned us a feature story and challenged us to nab an interview with one of our idols. He said if we got someone good, we could get our article published in the BU newspaper. Finally, my ticket to something big—a byline— and a chance to meet and interview one of my two idols: Susan Lucci or Sam Donaldson.

I didn't say Sam Donaldson just to impress my professor, either. I really loved him. During the Reagan years, he was the only member of the White House press corps who actually asked the man a direct question and held him accountable. (To this day, when I'm interviewing someone, I try to channel Sam. Of course, today my hardest-hitting interviews are usually with Real Housewives.) My admiration for Donaldson aside, when you give yourself two celebrity options on an assignment like this, you can bet that the one without the weird hair system is going to win every time.

I wrote Lucci's publicist an impassioned declaration of love, which secured me an interview, which was then postponed . . . multiple times . . . until this day. Fearful that I was one more postponement away from cancellation, I woke up at 7 a.m. and began calling that publicist's office to nail down the details and get my instructions for the day. All I knew was that I was supposed to meet Susan Lucci. The rest was a mystery, and I wanted it solved. I dialed and dialed and the phone rang and rang. By 9 a.m. I was convinced this interview, like the others, wasn't going to happen. But I was already in New York City! I couldn't go home empty-handed. Ruefully, I decided that Sam Donaldson's publicist never would have blown me off, if Sam Donaldson indeed even had a publicist. Probably not. Sam Donaldson was too down-to-earth, and there's no way a publicist would have just let that hair thing go.

Three hours after I'd begun, I deliberately punched in the now memorized sequence of numbers in a last-ditch effort. One ring. Two rings. Three, four, five, six, seven . . . and then someone, an assistant I guess, finally picked up. I was told to report to the ABC studios on the Upper West Side at 12:30. And that's how I learned that people in New York don't start working until 10 a.m. How cushy.

I get momentarily dizzy when I see the marquee that says, "In Pine Valley, Anything Can Happen." Of course, I've arrived outside the studio an hour early wearing bar mitzvah attire: button-down, paisley tie, sport jacket, and a trench coat that could have been from the Mini–Dan Rather Collection. My hair is more awkward than normal, as I'm in the midst of growing it out to Deadhead perfection. I tamed the Jewfro when I woke up, but its stability is threatened by the humidity of an unseasonably warm December day.

But I haven't shown up with sixty minutes to spare just to stand around and gawk like a tourist. I have something else on my agenda. In addition to the Lucci interview, I'm working on a creative writing paper examining whether Pine Valley is an accurate representation of society. (Just the sort of deep topic my parents expected me to be exploring when they signed my enormous BU tuition check.) I've brought my tape recorder to nab on-the-street interviews with actors from the show.

Occasionally a Pine Valley "resident" walks out of the stage door and I first internally freak out ("OMG IT'S CLIFF!"), then attack them with my recorder. I see myself as a Sam Donaldson type; they probably see me as a John Hinckley Jr. type.

"IS PINE VALLEY AN ACCURATE REFLECTION OF SOCIETY?!" I yell at every familiar face in a high-pitched panic. They are all initially terrified and must take a moment to process what is happening: overly hyper kid with tape recorder and 'fro yelling stupid question. Once they realize I'm probably not going to shoot any of them to impress Jodie Foster, I get quick interviews with "Donna," "Cliff," "Ross," "Travis" (who has dried shaving cream on his ear), and even the man who plays Palmer's butler, "Jasper." Their answers are gripping—"Not really." "No." "Maybe."

At 12:30, euphoric after my journalistic ramp-up to the main event, I walk into the building and announce that I'm there as a guest of Ms. Lucci. "Susan Lucci," I say, triumphantly. "I am Andrew Cohen and I am here to see Susan Lucci."

The guard nonchalantly mumbles into a microphone, and his voice crackles over a loudspeaker, "Susan Lucci, guest in the lobby." I am stunned at his informality and offended by his lack of respect when summoning the actress who plays Erica Kane.

I wait in terror, convinced that something, yet again, will go awry: I've gotten the day wrong, or Ms. Lucci's changed her mind. Or it could go exactly as I'd imagined—a minion would appear to spirit me away to Erica Kane's penthouse lair. After a couple of minutes, the double doors open, and she glides toward me. Susan Lucci. Radiant. Confident. Really, really small. Like, child-sized, even. My moment of disconcertion at how this person who is larger than life to me could be so alarmingly pint-sized is short-lived, as she opens her mouth to speak.

"You must be Andrew," she coos.

She is wearing a red knit dress, red hoop earrings, black heels, a full-length mink coat, and massive sunglasses. Her hair is teased three stories high: a masterpiece of eighties glamour and engineering.

I finally stammer out something that sounds like "HI!"

"Well, I hope you like Mexican food, Andrew, because I'm taking you to lunch," she purrs.

In fact, I hate Mexican food. I have a lifelong aversion to beans, and I wanted to see the studio. On the other hand: Susan Lucci and I are going to lunch? On a date? *¡Me gusta!*

"Oh my god, I *looooove* Mexican food!" I scream.

The publicist shows up just as we're walking out of the building. She's tall, wearing a butter-leather jacket, with frosted hair pulled back, a smoker's voice, and an air of cosmopolitan authority. We walk a few blocks to a restaurant called Santa Fe. On the way, some nutbag on the street asks Lucci if she received his card.

"Your card?" she asks. She seems concerned. "Oh nooo, I didn't! I'll check with the guard," she says very sincerely, turning to me with a wink. She and I know she'll not be checking with the guard. I'm in on the joke with Susan—on the inside of inside. I marvel at her ability to be tolerant and kind with this weirdo, making him feel as if he really matters to her, treating him as nicely as she's treating me. As we get further down the street, a guy in a truck yells, "Erica Kane! We love you!" She waves. I imagine little cartoon birds fluttering down to pick up the hem of her mink coat so it doesn't drag on the ground.

At the restaurant, we sit down at the table, and Susan and her publicist start talking quietly about a photo shoot that's coming up, and Susan says that ABC "has finally gotten it right." *Susan is happy.* I can't believe how super-confidential their convo feels. There is a business behind this soap I've spent my life ogling from my seat on a sofa in the middle of the country, and it is fascinating. I zero in on what Susan said about ABC "finally getting it right." What was wrong before? I wonder. Was Susan unhappy with ABC? Perhaps, as our friendship deepens, she will learn that she can trust me enough to confide in me regarding these matters. Strictly off the record, of course.

By the time they remember I'm there and turn to me, I'm convinced that my hair has expanded at least an inch in diameter since Sixty-seventh Street.

They ask me about my major, my goals. I am absolutely bullish on my future, and tell them *awwwwllllll* about it, while they sit there, nodding patiently, smiling patiently, and agreeing patiently. I tell them that I'm a sophomore Broadcast Journalism major and I want to be the next Dan Rather. Then, hearing myself say that and realizing that Dan Rather barely ever goes through an interview blathering about his hopes and dreams, I abruptly start reading from a list of questions I've prepared about Erica Kane:

"Is Erica modeled after Kate in *Taming of the Shrew*?"

"How will the pregnancy story line affect her?"

"Who is the love of Erica's life?"

(These are all perfectly fine questions. What I won't know until years later when I re-listen to the interview—yes, I recorded every word—is that I interrupt her every answer to tell her what my mother and I think will happen. In fact, I talk about my mother constantly. Thank God, I got over THAT! My mother would hate it.)

The waiter comes. Lucci orders a cheese enchilada and a chicken enchilada. Her publicist orders the same. I order a beef taco, and, feeling very capable and adult, I firmly tell the waiter that I do not want any beans on the plate whatsoever, and the waiter does not question my decision.

Emboldened, I turn to Susan and ask her the worst thing Erica ever did. She says, "Kill Kent."

"BUT THAT WAS A MISTAKE!" I scream.

She giggles. "This is a man I can talk to!"

Susan Lucci called me a man.

We get into a great conversational rhythm. It's a real interview. I ask about the red knit dress she's wearing. It is her own, not Erica's, she says. I lament the injustice of her eight Emmy losses and question the legitimacy of the Daytime Emmy judges. She is humble and grateful, as though it is her first time discussing this travesty. Near the end of the interview, I ask her what her salary is. And quickly apologize, telling her my professor made me ask. (Asking a difficult question while simultaneously apologizing is a skill I will implement twenty years later with the Housewives.) I feel so triumphant about asking the question that it doesn't register that she never answered.

When all the enchiladas have been consumed and all of the questions have been asked, I give her a BU sweatshirt and she carries on like I've presented her with a diamond ring. "Oh, Andrew, you couldn't have brought me anything better. It is so soft! I can't get over how soft it is. I love sweatshirts!"

In my letter, I may have promised the publicist that this would be a cover story in the BU *Free Press*, not what it really is: an assignment for a class that I'll pitch to the paper. But post-lunch, feeling chummy and in the club, I am comfortable clarifying that the feature is not exactly locked. That comfort curdles, however, when the reaction on the publicist's face indicates this is the number one most wrong thing to say. Yet I can't stop myself, next telling them, "I'm such a huge fan that I probably would have lied about the story altogether just to get a seat at a table with Susan Lucci!" I'm a runaway train of misdirected enthusiasm and late-blooming honesty.

The publicist's face only grows more contorted.

I quickly change my story. "This is a guaranteed cover!" I assure them. Amazingly enough, this seems to get things back on track. They in turn assure me that they can provide "color art," which is a magical-sounding phrase that I later learn means "We'll send some slides to the paper." (The piece will eventually run in the *Daily Free Press*, saving me from my white lie.)

The check arrives. Susan and her publicist compliment me for being well prepared, and I realize our time together is coming to an end. I begin angling to go back to the set with them. Susan tells me—sweetly, pityingly, of course—that visits like these are set up months in advance, and it's not going to be possible today.

I'm devastated. I actually might cry. I've waited six years to get on the inside, and just as the door has opened, it's slamming shut again. I keep it together and refocus on Susan's radiance.

She asks where I'm from.

I tell her I grew up outside St. Louis.

"Oh, St. Louis! There are very bright people outside the coasts," she proclaims. Her publicist agrees! At any other time, at any other table, I would have been highly offended and preached from my soapbox about the spirit and intelligence of the Midwestern people, but because Susan Lucci said it, I feel . . . weirdly vindicated. Perhaps the St. Louis tourism bureau could use her words as a tagline—"There are very bright people outside the coasts!"

In front of the restaurant, we take photos and say good-bye. As

I watch Susan Lucci disappear down Sixty-ninth Street, I wonder if I'll ever see her again. I wonder how my life will ever take me back to this place, where I can sit with an idol and talk about something I love. I feel the tears I pushed down moments before welling back up. I don't let them. Instead, I run to a pay phone on Central Park West so I can report the day's news to a string of people. Starting with my mother.

I didn't know it then, but I'd end up working at CBS News and having a front row seat for every pop culture and news-making event of the 1990s, meeting nearly every idol I'd had as a kid. I didn't know I'd go on to be ringleader to a fabulous galaxy of women starring in a real-life soap opera. And I definitely didn't know that this would not be my last encounter with Ms. Lucci. But sadly for me, none of our other meetings would go as well as our first. In the TV business, that's what we call a tease. So, stay tuned.

The bar mitzvah photo. Oy.

ICED TEA

hate hearing about other people's childhoods. Unless you Mackenzie Phillipsed your way through high school, chances are I won't care about your first kiss. I promise this part won't be long and I will try to make it relatively painless, like my childhood itself. And I'm not writing about my first kiss; it was uneventful and with a girl and that's about all you need to know.

I was a good kid, but I've had one Achilles' heel that's stayed with me through the years: talking. I simply could not shut the fuck up—I still can't—and that small issue has gotten me in all sorts of trouble. For instance, my third grade teacher, a rigid old redheaded German battle-ax, was so appalled by the volume (and relentlessness) of my voice that she made my entire class write "Screaming Causes Cancer" fifty times on a piece of paper that we then had to tape to our desks. Now, my mother is a take-no-prisoners kind of woman, a pint-sized fight-for-what's-righter who is often inclined to march somewhere and give somebody the what-for, and when I let that story spill at the dinner table, Evelyn Cohen demanded a next-day sit-down with the Fräulein and the principal. At the meeting, that sour Kraut informed my mother that beyond becalming my loud voice, she should have me reading *The Runaway Train* instead of *The Secret Garden*, a book I loved and read over and over. Then in the next breath she told my mother that my father should be spending more time with me. Mistake.

My mother went into action like this more than a few times. For instance, in high school, I was kicked off the water polo team during our final practice of the season for (guess what?) talking while the coach was giving us a pep talk at the very end of the practice. He dinked my teammate Jeff Goldstein, too, and our parents were furious—at the coach, not us. At dinner that night my mother shrieked at my poor dad: "What are you going to DO about what's happened to YOUR SON?" She wasn't going to be happy until my dad kicked the coach's ass with such conviction that he let me back on the team in his last gasp of breath. But my father failed in his effort to get me reinstated on the team, thus enduring years of ribbing from my mother. "I'm glad you weren't sent to negotiate during the Iranian hostage crisis, Lou. You'd have GIVEN THEM MORE AMERICANS! Are you listening to me???" By the way, it probably bears pointing out that for my part in getting kicked off the team, I suffered no punishment. I was particularly skilled at getting out of punishment, and usually did so by slowly winking at my mom while she was in mid-yell. It stopped working postpuberty, and now pretty much the only winking in my life is from Vicki Gunvalson during *RHOC* reunion shows.

My talking was legendary among my extended family as well. Once I talked for two days straight in the backseat of my uncle Stanley's station wagon as it careened toward the west coast of Florida. I was probably fourteen, on a road trip with my sister Em and our cousins, and in my boredom, I came up with the brilliant idea of using Em's hairbrush, with its clear plastic handle and black bristles, as a microphone into which I did a constant play-by-play of the trip, with no commercial breaks. I sang pretty much every mile marker—"mile marker *two-hun-dred and sev-en*"—from Missouri to Georgia. I did the weather, monitored goings-on in other cars ("Hairy man in pickup truck to our left is picking a winner! Does he have a problem?"), and interviewed the other passengers. I "reported" on various tidbits of information I'd picked up at Camp Nebagamon that summer, like the rumor that Diana Ross was actually a bitch to the other Supremes.

There were plenty of other things I could have done in that car besides broadcast the station wagon news. I had the new Go-Gos cassette and against my mom's orders had brought my favorite book, a history of *I Love Lucy*, which I'd checked out of the public library (again) at the beginning of the summer, each renewal more and more upsetting to my mom. I thought it was great that I was showing an interest in something—even if that something was Lucy's offscreen relationship with Vivian Vance. (According to this book, Lucy demanded that Vivian be twenty pounds heavier than she during the run of the show. That didn't seem like a friendship to me!) My mother had told me she never wanted to see that pink book in my bedroom again. It wasn't pink, it was salmon, but I instinctively resisted the temptation to correct her. After all, I was the boy who, just a few years earlier, used to go door to door in my neighborhood with a broom and ask if I could sweep people's kitchens.

Back to the car trip. I kept on talking. And talking. I honestly thought everyone was enjoying my commentary, until the truth came out at a Ruby Tuesday's off the highway in Georgia. My aunt Judy expressed her displeasure not by saying, "Shut up, stop talking into the hairbrush!"—which I totally would've understood. No. My aunt—my own flesh and blood by marriage—dumped an entire pitcher of iced tea over my head! Okay, maybe she had asked me to shut up for the love of God once or twice before that. But maybe she should've said it more like she meant it. Anyway, I was shocked.

I sat and sulked in the backseat for the rest of the trip to Sarasota. My bitterness was accompanied by a growing panic about the TV situation that awaited us at the condo. Every year before one of these trips I'd make my parents triple-check that there'd be two TVs in our condo, but sometimes the condo owners lied. Here was the awful problem: Not only was my aunt Judy the type of person to douse me with beverages, she was also the type of person to watch *Days of Our Lives*, and my cousin Jodi had inherited that defective gene. *Days* came on at exactly the same time as *All My Children*. How could we watch both our shows when they were on simultaneously? I knew I would be outnumbered, forced to watch a daytime drama of inferior quality, at peak tanning hour, no less. For the life of me, I didn't understand the appeal of *Days*. It was all fantasy and improbable plotlines. I hated NBC soaps. And *Days* looked especially weird to me, like the tape was old or gauzy or something. (You do NOT want to get me started on CBS soaps— so dark!) ABC soaps, in case you care, were bright and urban and smart—at least that's what I preached.

I don't even remember what happened that year when we arrived at the condo. Maybe there were two TVs and everything was fine. Maybe I missed an entire week of *AMC* because I was moping in my room, or because my aunt drugged me with Dramamine even though we were no longer driving. I'm not saying she definitely did, I'm just saying everything is a blank and I wouldn't put it past her.

I do know that I probably spent some time enjoying the company of my cousins, because we were close and we shared a certain passion. Jodi and I wasted a solid year and a half portraying Donny and Marie in her parents' bedroom. We danced in unison routines, performed witty banter, pretended to skate around the room like the Ice Angels, and sang "I'm a Little Bit Country" and "May Tomorrow Be a Perfect Day." Her brother Josh was a drummer and Em played a supporting Osmond. I loved doing impersonations. My specialty was the Reverend Ernest Angley, who wore a white

Lording over the remote in what looks like a moment of deep pubescent rage

suit and a big toupee and healed people. I often took my Reverend Angley act out onto the street and "preached" around the neighborhood. From my perspective it was a big hit, though now I wonder what people thought of the screamy little Jewish boy pretending to be a Bible Belt preacher.

Donny and Marie were perfect brunette Mormon smiling Barbie dolls and I dug their happiness, purity, and glitz. My uncle indulged me, and several times successfully blew my hair straight and parted it in what looked like a cross between Donny and Steve Schiff, the local anchordude on TV.

My devotion to the Osmonds peaked around the time all us kids collected "pics," which were precisely cut celebrity photos curated from *Tiger Beat* and *Teen Beat*. Pic collecting was sport for Emily and Jodi and me while we schlepped all over the Midwest to watch Josh's soccer and baseball games. The pics were mainly of the Charlie's Angels (though I also had a weird fetish for the Captain and Tennille). The electric blond luminescence of Farrah seared through the pictures; flanked by Jaclyn and Kate, she only glowed more. Whenever I got myself into a situation where I was "playing" Charlie's Angels, which was never often enough but always exciting, I would invariably wind up playing one of the brunettes. Always a Kate, never a Farrah.

Back then, each year came to a thrilling biannual climax in what was my very own version of the Super Bowl, *Battle of the Network Stars*. (In case you're wondering, I did have one interest that didn't scream G-A-Y: the St. Louis Cardinals.) *Battle of the Network Stars* was, I now realize, my first reality-show extravaganza, a pop culture Olympiad. It was an incredible gathering of every major TV star of the day—Farrah! Joyce DeWitt! Chachi! Gabe Kaplan! Valerie Bertinelli! Loretta Swit!—all wearing as little as possible (my lifelong appreciation for a fine Speedo and headband can be traced to this moment) and divided into teams by their network affiliations to compete in swim races, tennis, relays, and the infamous tug-of-war. I had a fierce devotion to ABC and was physically ill any time NBC won, which usually occurred under the "leadership" of (in my opinion, very unsportsmanlike) team captain Robert Conrad—probably best known from his roles in *The Wild, Wild West* and Eveready battery commercials. In this pre–*Entertainment Tonight* era, *Battle of the Network Stars* presented something completely original: celebrities being themselves, interacting with other celebrities in inconceivable combinations. (I loved a crossover then, and I still do. When Mork had Fonzie set himself up on a date with Laverne, I'm pretty sure I had an accident in my pants.)

For as much escape and delight as television provided me, there were times when it also became a difficult mirror—and not just when it was off and the glass was dark. I'm talking, of course, about *CHiPs*. When *CHiPs* premiered, I was suddenly all too happy to forswear my hatred of NBC programming. On the surface, this might not seem unusual. After all, *CHiPs* was made expressly for

Letters from Camp Nebagamon, 1978–1983

Dear Mom and Dad,
Today is the first day of camp. I hate going on planes. I threw up on the plane. Boy, was I sick. I don't like this camp so much, but I've only been here 4 hours. Don't show my letters to anyone. Listen to this saying: "When you're hot, you're hot. When you're not, you're not. When you're on the pot, you give it everything you've got." I've got to go to bed.
Love,
Andy

Dear Mom and Dad,
This morning I managed to hold in my crying until I was alone. Every time I go to write a letter to or from you I cry. No one here knows I'm homesick. Every time I write you, I cry. That is how homesick I am. I am in the biggest trauma I have ever been in. I am not going on the trip on the 30th. I don't know why, but I don't want to go on any trip.
Love,
Andy

Andy,
I am very sorry to hear that you are feeling so homesick. I wish you could allow yourself to join into the spirit of things as you have in other years. Don't feel badly about going on the trip. You are absolutely right. If you don't want to go, you don't have to, for whatever reason.
Love,
Mom

Dear Mom,
I think I am having the worst time in the world.
Andy

Get a hold of yourself, Andy!
Love,
Mom

Dear Mom and Dad,
Today, I listened to the Royal Wedding from 5:30 to 8 on the radio. And then saw an update about it and saw Lady Di and Charles get married on TV. Please save the Time Magazine and the Life Magazine for me. If you still have The Globe or the Post, save that for me too. Jodi saved me a clipping from the newspaper about people in the desert who had to drink their own urine.
Love,
Andy

Dear Mom and Dad,
I am so excited about seeing cable. I know you will love it. I want the record Grease. I'm buying it as soon as I get home. One thing I want you to keep is that all-news channel like the one we had in Florida. I love that.
Love,
Andy

Dear Andy,
Imagine my shock when I heard that you called Gramp C collect! Words fail me! After we told you not to do it! That is the end of the phone calls unless you are in the hospital.
Love,
Mom

Dear Mom,
I know that you told me that I could call Grandpa collect and no one else. If I didn't think you had told me I could call him, I wouldn't have called. I know that you said I could call him. I am positive. If I am wrong, I am sorry. I must have misunderstood. But I know I am right.
Love,
Andy

Dear Mom and Dad,
   It's late at night and I cannot sleep. I am very dizzy. This has been going on for some time. The quack says I'm getting up from sleep too quickly. So I'm getting up slowly. No cure! Mom, are you and Mrs. Arkin still alcoholics?
      Love,
      Andy

Andy,
   I certainly hope that you don't have the whole camp thinking Mrs. Arkin and I are alcoholics! I'm not kidding. Now, that isn't funny!
      Love,
      Mom

Dear Mom and Dad,
   I have been practicing my Hebrew a lot, believe it or not. You better order my invitations or it will be late. I want the ones like this, with the name down the side. I don't care what side. What kind of stuff is on the menu for my bar mitzvah? I thought it would be stuff like eggs and bagels and stuff. Send me some candy and tennis balls, I am desperate. I ate two peaches and an orange yesterday. Everyone in town hates Jews.
      Love,
      Andy
   P.S. Have you seen the movie Grease?

Andy,
   Yesterday I ordered the menu for the bar mitzvah and I don't think there's a thing on it that you like. I think I'll order you a big hamburger plate. I'm not kidding. Yesterday I ordered your bar mitzvah invitations. Don't scream across the lake, but I couldn't get the ones with the name down the side because we couldn't fit all the information on them. I'm sure you'll be happy with the ones I bought.
      Love,
      Mom

Dear Mom,
   I love the bar mitzvah invitations, but what kind of pen am I going to use for the thank yous? Will you send me a list of the people who are coming to my bar? I want to see it to check if there is anyone I want on it. After all, whose bar is it?
      Love,
      Andy

To Mom and Dad,
   See Grease for cryin' out loud! See it! Grease is a good movie, so see it! Don't read this letter to anyone!
      Love,
      Andy

Dear Andy,
   All My Children was good today. Angie brought Jesse divorce papers that Les had prepared but she didn't tell Jesse his parents knew. He signed them and then sobbed after she left. Get this one--Nina went to eat with Sam and Steve took Opal for a drink. The sound portion was off for Enid and Liza's mother. And that's it for today, folks.
      Love,
      Mom

Dear Mom and Dad,
   I'm lying here skipping lunch. I wouldn't have eaten even if I'd gone because it is ham. I'm sick with the flu but the quack won't admit me to the infirmary. Everyone here celebrates Christmas. I saw All My Children for about five minutes the other day. I can't believe it! Jenny in X-rated movies? And Opal and Langley? Loving Erica Kane. Today we saw the movie Meatballs.
      Love,
      Andy

boys my age. It had motorcycles, exciting chases, and lots of cop-talk. But for this ten-year-old boy in St. Louis, it had Mr. Erik Estrada. When Emily and Jodi and I were trading pics, I paid special, trancelike attention to any pic of Señor Estrada. He was like Donny Osmond on Mexican steroids with exploding genitalia. Actually he was nothing like Donny, it's just funny to juxtapose them now. Estrada's entire presentation was captivating, his walk, smile, super-white teeth, jet-black hair, and the air of possibility that he was going to completely burst the seams of his tan pantsuit.

The Estrada trance was different from what I felt when I looked at Farrah. She made me feel happy and clean, but he made me feel dirty and excited. I had flashbacks to the way I'd felt in my dad's tennis club locker room. In the back of my mind I knew what was happening, but I didn't really allow myself to go there. I continued to hold out hope that Farrah and I could have a future. In my mind, that was the only real option, anyway. (Well, not marrying Farrah Fawcett—I wasn't that naïve—but marrying a woman. A woman who looked and acted exactly like Farrah Fawcett. And was possibly named at least Farrah, if not Fawcett.)

☺

When I tell people I grew up in St. Louis, their first reaction is usually either Susan Lucci's ("There are very bright people from the Midwest!") or "Oh, I'm so sorry." Here's what: apology not accepted—or needed.

I loved growing up there. Little dramas due to my talkativeness aside, I was in a cocoon of happiness and simplicity, untouched by any real societal or domestic problem (blackouts, race wars, robbery, divorce) that could get in the way of a happy childhood. What I wanted to be was a latchkey kid like I'd seen in after-school specials—that seemed so urban and self-sufficient. A tragedy did come for me in 1978, when my parakeet, Pork Chop, died suddenly while my sister's nasty old bird, Perky, soldiered on for years. I held a funeral, invited all the neighbors, and read a eulogy encouraging mourners to go to the neighborhood candy shop and buy Pork Chop's grieving "master" some sweet nibbles. The only sour note to the whole affair was when Mom took pictures of the entire thing. I was furious. This was a solemn occasion! No paps!

In the rearview mirror, our family life seems like something out of a fifties television show. Em and I were a team, and our biggest arguments may have related to wanting to listen to different records on the massive wooden phonograph (with wicker speakers) that lived in the hallway. How Beaver Cleaver do I sound when I tell you that I even had a freaking paper route when I was ten? I went to office buildings in "downtown" Clayton after school, dragging around a cart with the afternoon edition of the *St. Louis Post-Dispatch*. (Remember the days when big cities had an afternoon paper? Or two competing papers? How much news was there to report? And how did Pork Chop's death not get any coverage?) It bums me out that today it wouldn't even be possible for a ten-year-old to roam city streets the way I did, in my first official news gig. After school I'd usually hang out with my friend Mike Goldman and watch TV and play board games. Sometimes we would tape ourselves playing a board game, then listen to the tape and marvel at how mind-numbingly boring it was. I guess it was our version of early reality radio. My favorite days by far were Wednesdays and Fridays, when our housekeeper, Kattie, came to our house. Okay, weird but true: Kattie's nickname was Blouse, and my sister, cousins, and I call her Blouse to this day. Her moniker came about when we kids, at a very young age, became enraptured to the way she ebulliently pronounced the word "blouse." I'm sure this is funnier if you are listening to the audio edition.

On the days I didn't see her, Blouse and I communicated through notes we left each other in my room. Hers were punctuated everywhere with "Smile" in quotes and parentheses, sometimes both. And when I got them, I did.

> YouR RooM is
> A MesS
> _____
> Please do SomeThing
> Blouse

> Welcome
> Home
> "Sweetie" smile
> p.s. Blousee
> Besure NoT Mess up
> Take huggyein
> BASomT.

But on the majority of Wednesdays and Fridays, I came home, made myself a snack, and stuck to Blouse like glue. I would join her in the part of our basement that was unfinished, next to the garage, with my snack and something for her, too. The radio would be blaring KMOX and she would be ironing and interrupting herself to maneuver clothes in and out of the laundry machines. I didn't lift a finger and didn't stop running my mouth. What did a twelve-year-old Jewish kid and a thirty-nine-year-old African American cleaning woman talk about for hours on end!? A lot. But mainly:

1. Soaps. (She was a CBS devotee, so it was a stretch for both of us to meet in the middle, but we made do.)
2. Diana Ross. (She wasn't a fan and I was—so it was a debate. She was on Team Gladys.)
3. The family. (She worked for my aunt and uncle, too, and told me every damn thing that went on at my cousins' houseful of chaos and dogs and cats and a real ice cream parlor, all gossip that I would report to my family at dinner.)
4. The mailman. (What on earth could we have said about Mr. Collins? No clue, but I know he was a major subject.)

From the basement, I would follow her upstairs, room by room, as she put my family's clothes away. Occasionally I would carry the laundry basket up the stairs for her. I did try to keep her entertained, so that was something.

Though I rarely lifted a finger to help Blouse with her housework, I wasn't a totally spoiled kid. Every summer, my parents sent us to work at the family company, Allen Foods. While Emily and my cousin Jodi thrived and later went on to work there, I was terrible at every task I was given, from driving a forklift to, in my schlemiel, schlemazel moment, working on the assembly line screwing bottle tops. One summer I made deliveries and most notably delivered cheese to a hospital and forgot the cheese. Still, it was fun being around my whole family, all of whom paged each other over the loudspeaker incessantly. My dad was always a relief to the eyes, strolling around the manufacturing plant making gentle conversation with ungentle forklift ladies—Large Marge types—looking to me like a model in a Ralph Lauren ad. No matter what the job, we always went to lunch at Steak 'n Shake with my uncle and Grandpa, who would completely tear the waiters apart. For about twenty-five years straight, Gramp ordered a small salad in a large bowl at Steak 'n Shake. As soon as it came, Evelyn's father would bark, "YOU CALL THIS A SALAD!?" He was out the door and back at his desk in thirty minutes, ever more respectful of being on the clock than I. The family business was always a tremendous source of pride, but what I did there never felt like a real job because I knew that I couldn't get fired and that I wasn't going to spend my life in the food industry.

☺

To be clear, I've been gay since the day I was born, but even though I knew it somewhere in my head, I didn't want to face the facts of what that meant. Biltmore Drive wasn't exactly Christopher Street, and I didn't know anyone who was gay, unless you count the waiters at a few St. Louis restaurants. My mom always doted on such men—she called them "cheerful." But I didn't have any faith that her love of cheerful waiters would translate to her son if I ever admitted that I, too, was . . . cheerful.

Things weren't much better on TV. This was pre–*Real World* and *Will and Grace* and Bravo, so basically you had Paul Lynde being a mean queen in the center square and Charles Nelson Reilly kibitzing with Brett Somers on *Match Game*—hardly role models for a kid. So, like many a young gayling, I gravitated toward strong, outsized female personalities—on-screen and off.

As I got older, more and more of my close friends were women. I got involved in their friendship falling-outs and stirred up plenty of shit between them. Jackie Greenberg and Jeanne Messing were pre-Housewives boot camp for me. They were my training wheels, "Li'l Housewives" if you will—lots of entertainment and flash and

At the prom with the Li'l Housewives, Jeanne and Jackie

turmoil packed into training bras and junior high botherations, and I was happiest hanging out with—and in the middle of—them. I was constantly putting my foot in it, telling one something that the other said about her, getting involved where I shouldn't in plans and invitations and parties, and then, when I tried to keep secrets, I'd be punished for favoring one over the other.

In the junior high school social landscape, I was Switzerland, pleasantly popular, and had a self-preservative skill of deflecting attention away from myself by getting involved in other people's conflicts instead. No one, upon no one, knew that I had my own intense drama roiling just under the surface of my skin. At least that's what I assumed.

One Sunday in eighth grade, I went over to Jackie's to play Atari with her. Her mom gave me a ride to Glaser's Pharmacy and I was standing on the corner waiting to cross the street as she and Jackie sat in the car at a red light. I was leaning on the lamppost in an apparently unmasculine way.

Jackie looked at me and turned to her mother and said something. They laughed. Sensing that I knew exactly what they were chuckling about, I walked over to the car and asked what was funny. Jackie didn't want to answer at first but then hesitantly responded, "I think that when you grow up, you are going to be a homosexual."

The light turned, they drove off, and I just stood there in traffic. I realized that my friend had only said something I already knew was true. I also realized that from that minute on, nothing would ever be the same for me. Because now, ready or not, I actually was what I was afraid I was. I was overcome with anger that I had to deal with this truth. That my life was now destined to be clandestine and covert. I didn't blame Jackie. Being gay was a secret I had kept from everyone, including myself, like a lock without a key. Jackie had merely shown up with a set of verbal bolt-cutters. It's ironic, of course: All that trouble my motor-mouth caused me, all the annoyance it caused others, and the biggest disturbance of all was caused by what I wasn't saying. In those days, and at that age, it was not freeing to know that I was gay. It was tragic. Even at that age, I had an inkling of the tough road that might lie ahead for someone like me. At that point in our culture, there were black heroes, women heroes, Latino heroes, but there were no homosexual heroes. Even Paul Lynde was in the closet. (Of course, we hadn't seen anything yet; AIDS was still around the corner.) I walked home, sobbing my heart out the whole way.

After that, I barely allowed myself to think of "it" during the day. Late at night, though, I would lie awake thinking about my future, the inevitability of my sexuality, and the improbability that anyone would accept me once they knew. I really believed my life would be over once I came out and that this happy kingdom in which I lived would fall to pieces. Or that I would.

TALKATIVE Andy Cohen tells all to CREATIVE Jeanne Messing.

CHAINS OF LOVE

y the time I was a senior in high school, I'd established myself to Jeanne, Jackie, and everybody else as—for lack of a better phrase—one of the girls. Boy-girl non-romantic best-friendships were unusual for that time, at least in my circles; nonetheless I was always surrounded by women, a circumstance that prepared me well for my life today. I had guy friends, too, and was popular—president of the student body and voted (big shocker) Most Talkative and (irritatingly, but not exactly shockingly) Biggest Gossip in my senior class. (I was pissed I didn't get Best Dressed, but that's another story.) Looking at me, you'd have thought I had it all together. But, without getting too After-school Special about it, underneath the gregarious exterior was a whole other story.

Late in high school, Jackie's parents went on vacation and asked me to stay with her, to look after her and their house. My mom was mystified. A boy staying alone with a girl? What kind of parents would allow such a thing? "Why would you trust your DAUGHTER with my SON?" she asked Jackie's mother, Jan. After a pause that was way more pregnant than I would ever get Jackie, even alone together for a week, Jan said to my mom, "Andy's . . . safe."

She was right: I was "safe," in that way. Of course, I didn't feel very safe. I felt like if anyone found out my secret, I was done for. But for now, no one knew I was gay, and I played right along with the normal high school shenanigans, such as deciding to take magic mushrooms with some friends and go see Eddie Murphy live in concert.

Like everybody, I had loved Eddie Murphy on *Saturday Night Live*. Unfortunately, his live routine differed from his television shtick; namely in that it mostly consisted of ridiculing gay people. Every other word out of his mouth was "faggot." And with each and every gay joke, the crowd went wild. They loved it. My friends loved it. I was surrounded by thousands of people in hysterics, and they were all laughing at "faggots." And ipso facto, laughing at me. Unfortunately, the drugs I was on didn't act as any sort of emotional buffer, but instead like a magnifying glass intensifying the huge beam of hate and mocking cackles trained on me. I ran out of the arena and into the bathroom, where I spent most of the concert in a stall, rocking back and forth wishing and praying that I could somehow unzip my skin and throw it away. I wanted to walk out of that bathroom a completely different person, and yet I knew I couldn't.

When my legs finally stopped shaking enough for me to stand and leave the stall, an alarmed stranger looked at me: "Are you okay? You look like you don't feel right." I saw my reflection in the mirror. My pink Polo button-down shirt was drenched with sweat. I splashed cold water on my face and rejoined my friends while Eddie Murphy continued to merrily spew his best faggot material.

(Though I would never be able to laugh at Eddie Murphy's comedy after that night, rest assured I was highly entertained years later in 1997 when police pulled him over with a transvestite prostitute in West Hollywood.) Watching my friends cheer Murphy on that night reinforced my secret fear that homophobic bigotry was perfectly acceptable. It also reinforced that I should never do mushrooms again, and I haven't. I do love me a mushroom pizza, though.

☺

When it came time to go to college, I chose Boston University because of everything it wasn't. Its social fabric wasn't dependent on a fraternity system. It wasn't built around a campus. It wasn't the only thing going in a small town. It wasn't anything like St. Louis. It was urban, with a good communications school and, I'd found out on the sly, a semblance of a gay community. Not that I was rushing out of the closet yet, but I needed to know that if I came out (or was pushed out), there'd be a safety net there to catch me. My two girlfriends Jackie and Kari decided to go, too, and so off we went from St. Louis to Boston in the fall of 1986.

Over orientation weekend I was randomly assigned a dorm room with a guy who would become, thank God, my best friend, like a brother, and—some would say—the straight version of me: Dave Ansel. Dave had arrived in the room first and dropped off his duffel bag. When I got there and saw his bag, I did what any self-respecting freshman would do: I opened it up and snooped around. I found the same pair of Vuarnet sunglasses as I had and the same kind of paisley boxers I wore. When I returned to the room later, Dave was there.

"Hello, Louis," he said. Not only had he read my luggage tags (with my dad's name on them), but he soon confessed that he, too, had snooped in my bag. We bonded over our lack of boundaries immediately, and as suburban Jewish boys whose families were both in the food business, we had even more in common. From that day on, we were together 24/7. It was a new kind of friendship for me. He was the first guy to tell me he loved me; it was a platonic, brotherly love and we were deep in it. He told me everything and I listened. The one hitch was that during our hours-long late night talks, Dave offhandedly peppered the conversation with a catalog of gay slurs. Which meant that while I was getting to know every detail about him, he didn't really know who I was at all. It was a kind of torture, feeling that close to someone but not being ready to tell him the truth. And as the months passed, I often wondered: Would he ever be ready to hear it? And would I ever be ready to tell?

For most college kids, the point of going to Europe for a semester is either to experience a foreign culture or maybe to figure out what you want to do with the rest of your life. I saw it as an opportunity to convince my nearest and dearest that I was a raging heterosexual. But fate was against me.

Before I began BU's London Programme (that's how they spelled it, and it bugs me to this very day), I traveled through Europe for a month with Jackie. Apparently, her mother's conviction that I was "safe" still applied, because Jackie and I had already had one amazing trip together, escaping Boston freshman year to jet off to Manhattan. It was my first trip to New York, and every direction I turned, I ran into a place I'd seen in a movie or on TV, bigger and better than I ever imagined. The first time we left Jackie's parents' pied-à-terre, we had only walked just a couple blocks, and who came toward us but Andy Warhol. We screamed when he walked by. To this day I can't believe that I saw Andy Warhol on my first ever day in New York City; it seemed to portend something about my future and what New York had in store for me. (If he were alive today, I'd like to think Warhol would be painting the Housewives.)

The summer before my London semester, Jackie and I Eurailed our way through France, Spain, and Italy. Then she had to go back to St. Louis. For the first time in my life, I was completely alone somewhere far away, which made me feel scared and liberated all at once. I spent a couple of weeks doing whatever I wanted. Everyone back home surely assumed that I was hiking and seeing the sights, but what I was really doing was visiting a bunch of gay bars in Florence and Rome. It wasn't my first time in a gay bar—I'd been to a few in Boston and once or twice in St. Louis—but in Europe I wasn't terrified that someone was going to see me and turn me in to the authorities, or (worse) tell my parents. The freedom felt great. In retrospect, when I think of myself in those bars, I realize that I was a twenty-year-old freshly plucked chicken just out of the cage, and it's a miracle I got out of there alive. But that's giving me all sorts of credit, when I deserve none. The truth is, I had absolutely no game. First of all, and no small matter: my hair. I'd spent the earlier part of that summer following the Grateful Dead around and was now growing my hair out so I could put it in a ponytail. Have you ever seen a pony with kinky hair? No. My attempt was just a curly, fro-y mess. Making matters worse, I was draped in tie-dye, and my personal hygiene was questionable, even by European standards.

My fortunes changed in Paris. (Isn't that always the way?) I had a two-day romance with a dude named Jean-Marie; he didn't speak English and I didn't speak French, so we conversed in bad, broken Spanish. We had not a thing in common, but it was the most romantic two days of my life. He would point to things and say, in Spanish, "This is a very typical French building." Or "Summers in France are very warm." Scintillating! I bet I wouldn't last an hour with him today without having a narcoleptic seizure, but at the time I thought he was a poet. His apartment was the size of a Tic Tac, and despite its being a complete hotbox, I don't recall hot water actually being readily available; in fact I have a faint recollection of something (nonsexual) having to do with a teakettle. I thought it was *totalmente* quaint. He was handsome and sweet and had a big Parisian nose. But more importantly, he liked me. We held hands under the dinner table. The whole thing felt like a fantasy. In my heart, there was no turning back.

When summer ended, though, and I reported to London for a semester of serious study, I was back to reality, which meant pretending to be someone I wasn't. Some friends from BU were in my "programme." (I'll drop the quotation marks from now on, but is there anything that bugs you about this word, or is it just me?) Everyone was anxious to share tales of their amazing summers, while I couldn't conceive of telling anyone about what I'd just experienced. Which, I realized, was going to be an ongoing challenge. Because from the moment I got there, everywhere I looked and listened was gay, gay, gay.

You couldn't walk one foot in London that year without hearing Erasure's super-gay pop song "Chains of Love." Oh, and my flat was in the gayest part of town, Earl's Court. How the hell was I supposed to stay in the closet when living in a neighborhood where everybody looked like a Village Person? I certainly wasn't complaining, but it just seemed ironic.

I was committed to my secret, though, because I truly did not believe I had an alternative. I was terrified of being ostracized by my friends and family. I've always said that gay people and fat people are two of the last minority groups that it's acceptable to make fun of across America. That's finally starting to change now, but gay-bashing was still de rigueur in the eighties—and Eddie Murphy was hardly the lone offender.

On the trip from Paris I'd concocted a fairly elaborate story about my summer, and the minute I got to London, I began relaying it to friends back at BU and in St. Louis. I told them—through letters and phone calls and eventually just word of mouth—that I had taken a train from Switzerland to Paris (true), where I'd met a German girl (true) with hair under her arms (true) who asked me to get drunk with her (true) and that I did (false) and she attacked me (false) with her hot body (eew, false) and hairy underarms (again, true, but I didn't touch them). We spent a mad, passionate night together fucking and fucking and fucking some more on the rails and had a very dramatic good-bye in Paris (false, gross, false, gross, and no).

The Tale of the Fräulein Who Took Me on the Night Rails made an immediate impact on my friends, to whom I must've always seemed like a Ken doll (sans the stunning Aryan looks) with no genitalia and just smooth flatness "down there." They swallowed the Tale of the Fräulein like a fresh Slurpee, simultaneously happy for me and relieved that whatever questions they'd had about my— at best—asexuality were unfounded. And if it made any of their brains painfully freeze up for a moment, well, that was just from drinking it all in so fast.

Within one day of being in London I met two women who would become my best friends for the rest of my life. Amanda Baten was a petite, blond, earthy stunner with an infectious laugh and appetite for fun and drama; she was on the road to her eventual career as a psychologist and was already figuring out all our problems. Graciela Braslavsky was Brigitte Bardot on steroids, a New York City girl with an anything-goes vibe and a razor-sharp wit who was also enrolled at BU. That I'd never been somehow magnetically drawn to her on campus back in Boston seemed unfathomable. I connected with both women deeply and immediately. The image I portrayed to them was of a hetero hippie, and when I shared the Tale of the Fräulein Who Took Me on the Night Rails, they had no reason to question it.

The programme itself consisted of a couple of (fairly bogus) courses and an internship at United Press International Radio, which sucked. My hoped-for internship at the ABC News London Bureau never materialized, so I was stuck in this dead-end job in the Docklands, which was essentially the middle of nowhere. At this point I'd had several amazing internships already. I started young, as the "littlest volunteer" for Senator Tom Eagleton's re-election campaign (I was twelve and felt strangely at home among adults wearing corduroy sport coats). At sixteen, I was the youngest

Graciela, Amanda, and me. No, that is not a pot pipe in my hand.

intern at the CBS affiliate in St. Louis. Then came the internships at the CBS radio station in St. Louis and a classic rock radio station in Boston (where I worked the switchboard and felt like Jennifer Marlowe on *WKRP in Cincinnati*, except that I was nowhere near as hot as Loni Anderson and way more efficient), so maybe I was spoiled with regard to internships. And maybe spoiled in general. I had decided already that there was absolutely no way I'd ever work in radio. My plan was to graduate, move to a small market, and become a reporter and local anchor. So it all seemed pointless and for naught.

My life in London became a balancing act. I spent most of my time hanging out with Amanda and Graciela, doing stupid things around London like smoking buckets of hash and going to all-you-can-eat pasta nights at Fatsos in Soho. One night Graciela dared me to slide down the median of what was probably a four-story escalator in the middle of a packed tube station; I did it and cut my hands to bits. I was in massive pain, but to us it was hilarious and proof that I was completely under Graciela's spell. I was—

and am still—powerless to resist her dares. Decades later, when she was sitting in the audience of *Watch What Happens Live*, Jimmy Fallon was the guest, and during the commercial break she dared me to do a large shot of Maker's Mark. Jimmy looked at me like I was a madman to be considering this dare, but with the clock ticking down the seconds until we were back live on the air, I had to comply. She's like a Siren!

When I wasn't acting like a fool with my girlfriends, I was checking out gay spots around town on the DL. I had an affair with an aspiring pop star. In my rearview mirror he appears absolutely ridiculous, but at the time, he was spectacular—Mr. Barrel Chested Gay UK 1988. He'd recorded a truly pathetic techno cover of the Petula Clark classic "Downtown," but his total lack of talent did not dissuade me from loving his angular A-Ha look and enormous chest. Concurrently, I feigned interest in Rebecca, a red-haired beauty (I liked Gingeys even then) in our program, who had a crush on my roommate. Thus, she was safe. (And there's that word again.)

I was also quietly empowered by some of my openly gay classmates. I remember running into one of them one morning on the street. He told me he was just coming home from his night and that it was "wild." He winked and walked away. I couldn't imagine being open and cavalier like he was. Later he invited me to his flat with a bunch of his friends, and we all watched *Sudden Fear* together. At the time, sitting with a group of gays watching a Joan Crawford movie seemed downright revolutionary. Now it sounds like a Sunday afternoon.

The dark side of my initial forays into the gay world was that I was absolutely terrified that I was going to get—or had already gotten—AIDS. I questioned every scab, cough, bruise, cut, and cold sore as though it were the beginning of the end for me. It was 1988, and the AIDS crisis was generating massive paranoia and uncertainty. Being gay seemed to go hand in hand with AIDS, like an inevitable one-two punch.

☺

As I went on with my double life, letters kept arriving from home:

September 1988

Dear Andy,

Well, by now you are quite the experienced traveler. I saw Jackie and she sounded as up about the trip as you. Can you take a Shakespeare course rather than a politics or some kind of English art course at least?? Are there any Jewish kids there? I can't believe that your damn coats and your polo towels and that damn white sweater are lost. Furthermore, it was not insured—can you believe it? Hopefully the tracer will find it. You better find a flea market and buy yourself a coat or you'll freeze. We have tickets to "Les Miserables" on the 15th, which is the evening we get to London. If you could get tickets to Phantom on Nov 16th, that would be fabulous. I do not wish to pay scalpers prices. The play we must see is *Lettice and Lovage*. Will you see about tickets to that and MasterCard them too? It's a comedy with Maggie Smith. I am so damn mad. I forgot to set the recorder in my room and didn't change the clock on the recorder in the basement back from daylight savings. So today I have 2 recorders and no soap! Palmer really set up Natalie and Jeremy to make them look guilty as hell. Nina had a baby boy. Erica's on a long trip. Nothing else major is happening. . . . Well, I hear the garage door opening and it is your dad. We love and miss you and look forward to hearing about all of your experiences. Don't forget to keep the journal. Have the time of your life.

LOVE MOM

A letter like this, brimming with the wonderfully mundane details of my former existence as a closeted mama's boy, now filled me with dread. The longer I was in London the more I knew that I was living a lie and that there could be no going back to my old life.

My anxiety intensified with each day. I honestly believed that if I chose to be open about my sexuality, I would be shunned by everyone I loved. It sounds so melodramatic now, but at the time, the decision of who to tell and when loomed like a life-or-death question.

To make matters more complicated, there was an added and potentially uncomfortable energy around my relationship with Graciela. We were in the midst of a love affair that happened to be absolutely devoid of any physicality. I hungered to be around her. She made me laugh, surprised me, stimulated me, and I wanted to tell her everything. She had a boyfriend back home, so I figured she thought that was why I wasn't making a move. Still, I did some deflecting. And I now know that she did a lot of wondering.

On October 19 (yes, I remember the date), I took Amanda to Pizza Hut (no comment) to tell her the news. Amanda seemed like the best place to start, like a loving sister with psych credentials. I explained that I had something urgent to tell her, something incredibly personal.

"I know exactly what you're going to tell me," she said. I was so relieved: She knew!

I said, "What?"

"You're in love with Graciela."

"I am," I said. "But I'm also gay."

Amanda's reaction was one that I didn't expect: utter joy and complete acceptance. "I think that is so natural and beautiful, and I'm so proud of you!" she said. "This is great news!" What I thought was going to be a tearful pity party, or bitter recriminations about betrayal, evolved into a celebration. I told her about Jean-Marie. I told her that the Tale of the Fräulein Who Took Me . . . was a lie. She asked me what I was going to do about Graciela.

I wanted to be truthful with Graciela, but the fact that we'd be going back to BU together when the semester was over complicated things. I wasn't ready yet for the information to return with me to Boston. So I didn't tell Graciela, or anyone other than Amanda and her accepting boyfriend, Paul. The closet door was finally open—just a crack.

But on the plane home from London something in me shifted unexpectedly. I felt like I was hurtling not only through the sky, but toward a new phase of my life, and a chance to have a new beginning. This new identity I'd revealed to Amanda was shimmering just underneath my dirtbag Deadhead costume, and I needed to devise a plan of action for revealing it. I wanted to be precise about how I told people. I wanted to answer every question that could possibly come to mind, clearly and in one sitting. I wanted to put their fears about me—or the "new" me—to rest.

On the long flight back to the US, I wrote a journal entry that I wound up reading directly to each friend after I told them my secret. It was a pages-long, very intense, and super-earnest explanation of who I was and a plea for acceptance. Some snippets:

> I've known I was gay for as long as I've had a sexual identity. Around the time that I started getting horny, I realized that my affection for men was not widely accepted, and was widely considered abnormal.
>
> I knew I was not abnormal, but that I had to make a choice as to whether I craved acceptance or full individuality. I chose acceptance out of basic social needs. I decided to try to suppress my feelings for other men in hopes that, by thinking heterosexual, I would just sort of become one. It obviously didn't happen, and no one can begin to imagine the pain and hurt that lurked deep within me when I would hear all of my friends—people that I loved and respected—deriding gay people. This happened daily. I lived two lives. My outer, gregarious,

happy self, and my inner self, which thought a lot about sex. The inner self often overrode me, and I became overcome with depression, fear, and self-hatred.

I was born a homosexual. I did not choose to be gay. I did not have a choice. I wondered how I was ever going to live with myself and this sinister need to have sex with men. I was convinced that no one would accept me, and I wouldn't get anywhere in the world if everyone knew that I was gay. And what would I do otherwise? The other choice, of course, would probably be worse—suppressing my feelings altogether, in hopes of leading a "normal" life. A wife and kids would give me a key to the world, but would also bring me further into hiding, and I would do things completely out of my control. When you have this feeling that you don't think you can act upon, it is crushing.

I don't understand why I feel this way. I can't say the amount of tears I cried just because I didn't know what to do. I fooled around with people but it was damn hard being hetero and a hidden homo all at once. When I got really down, I would just tell myself that I was strong because I had gotten this far and I was OK and well liked.

London made me confident in myself and my sexuality. I'm not ready to go tell the world. And I know that even my closest friends may have qualms, but this is who I am, and I can't bear to lie to them any longer about something so deeply a part of me.

☺

I'd been back from London a few days when Dave flew to St. Louis as a "welcome back to the US" surprise. He immediately sensed that something was drastically different about me.

"Andy left his soul in London," he told my mom one day while I was napping. When I woke up, my mother—naturally—reported back to me what he had said. It was the opening I'd been looking for, but I couldn't do it, not yet. That night I assured Dave that he was being distracted by my fancy new fashion—sport coats with big shoulder pads and Italian pants—and that I was still the same guy.

A few days after Dave left, on an unseasonably warm day, I picked up Jackie. "We're going to Shaw Park," I told her. "I need to talk to you." I was usually the one getting pulled away for a side-bar about someone else's drama, so this whole notion of taking her somewhere to talk felt very un-me. My palms were sweaty in the car and I couldn't concentrate on Magic 108 FM. I didn't expect any kind of bad reaction from her, but I couldn't be sure. When I was parking the car, I hit a lamppost, denting my mom's Honda. Awesome.

"What is going on with you?" Jackie implored. At this point she was amused. It was indeed funny, until we sat on top of a picnic table in an empty part of the park and I read her the journal entry that I'd written on the plane home.

My voice shook, and she cried as I read.

"I feel awful," she sobbed. "I feel like I hurt you when we were growing up." In the journal, I had mentioned her haunting prophecy, but I reassured her that I didn't blame her for anything she said. "What about AIDS? How are you going to protect yourself?" She was really worried, and said that was part of the reason she was crying.

"I'm worried, too," I told her. "But I'll always be safe. I won't get it." I wished I believed it. I didn't. I thought for sure, one hundred percent, without a doubt I was going to get it, but I didn't want to let on just how scared I was. I made her promise not to tell anybody. I wanted to be the one who delivered this news, and I was fiercely proprietary about how that happened. She hugged me and gave me every reassurance of support.

A couple days later I typed a letter to Amanda's boyfriend, Paul, who was still in England, and carelessly left it on the couch in the den. Or was it careless? I knew full well that my mom watched the *CBS Evening News* every night with a scotch, without fail, at 5:30, on the couch in the den. She read the letter, which detailed my confession, Jackie's response, and, for good measure, my all-consuming horniness.

"You might want to remove your LETTER from the DEN," she said as nonchalantly (but still loudly) as she could before dinner. I panicked about what the next few hours would bring, but everything was subdued and sedate—very *The Ice Storm*.

Dad came home and we sat down to dinner as usual. I pushed my tuna casserole around my plate like a little kid trying make it look like he's eating something, then I excused myself and went directly to my room to sit on my bed and wait for something, anything, to happen. Then, my parents did something they had never done before: They went to their room, closed the door, and spoke in hushed voices. Hushed voices were as rare as crucifixes at 7710 West Biltmore Drive. We were Jews who shouted across the dinner table. We didn't whisper behind closed doors. This was serious.

My father left to play tennis (it was Wednesday, his tennis night—the show must go on), and I called Jackie from my bedroom to tell her that big stuff was about to go down.

Then I sat on my bed and waited some more.

Finally, my mother came in and sat on the rocking chair across from me. The whole situation was so loaded and obvious; we could have been a Semitic version of Tad and Ruth Martin from *All My Children*. "I'm ready to talk if you're ready for that to happen," she said.

I looked at her and said that I wasn't sure she wanted to hear what I had to say. My voice cracked. She quietly stared at me and said, "Say what you need to say. Say the words out loud."

I sat there staring at her. Finally, "I'm gay."

She began crying. We both did. We discussed how long I had known, and if I was sure about it. She moved over to my bed, and we hugged and cried. She had been suspecting for several years, she admitted. Well, she had suspected a tiny bit when I was a little boy who liked to go to neighbors' houses to sweep their floors. As for the pink *I Love Lucy* book? "I wasn't so much worried that you were GAY, but that you were an AIRHEAD," she told me. But then she really suspected when she found a *Honcho* magazine under my bed. (Apparently she told her shrink when this happened, and her shrink told her to stay out of my room forever—going under my bed would be like an alcoholic going to a bar.)

We talked about AIDS. We talked about telling other people, about telling Dave. We agreed he wasn't ready to hear. We talked about how Dad would react, and she told me that even though she'd been saying to him for years: "What are you going do when our son comes home and tells us he's gay?" and even though they talked about today being that day before he'd left to play tennis, we knew he would still probably somehow repress it.

"I probably would have hated your wife anyway," she announced. And then we were laughing. Tension broken.

"How will you study when you get back to school?" she implored.

"What do you mean?" I said.

She said, "How will you STUDY, knowing this?"

I said, "I've known it all my life and studied in the past." Well, sometimes.

We talked for two hours. Then we heard the garage door opening. My dad was home. By the time Dad walked into the room, we were slaphappy.

"Sit down," I said.

"I was going to go eat an orange," he said.

"Go ahead," I said. "We'll be right here."

"SEE?!?" my mom mock-whispered, in full voice. "I TOLD YOU he'd repress it."

He returned, and I told him to sit down. He said he'd rather stand.

"I'm gay," I said.

He sat down. And took a deep breath. He muttered "shit" and "Jesus."

I told him it was no fault of his. He said he knew that. He asked me how long I'd known, who else knew, and if there was one particular guy I was seeing. The conversation then turned—I am not kidding—to a list of hypothetical scenarios in which girlfriends of mine entered the room naked, and whether I would get turned on by them.

"If Jeanne came in naked, would you get turned on by her?"

"Um, well, no," I said. "But if she rubbed herself all over me, and I closed my eyes, I probably would."

We both got up, and he walked over to me and said that whatever I decided was fine with him, that he would always be my father, and that he loved me. I told him I loved him, and we hugged, and then Mom and I hugged, and then I went to Jackie's.

The next day my dad took me to Steak 'n Shake to talk to me about AIDS and condoms. It was as awkward as any conversation about AIDS at Steak 'n Shake could possibly be, but it only made me love him more than I ever thought I could before, and it more than made up for the time he couldn't get me reinstated on the water polo team.

When I got back to BU, I told a couple more friends. After the hurdle of telling my parents, I wanted to pick off a few easy targets before marshaling my strength to come out to my nearest and dearest. Eight weeks after I'd returned from London, I let myself into Dave's room, lined up five shot glasses, and filled them all from a brown-bagged bottle of Jack Daniel's I'd brought. It was February 14.

"What's this?" he said as he walked in the door wearing a scarlet BU jersey. He didn't have a girlfriend, nor did he buy into the idea of a Hallmark-made holiday, so the fact that it was Valentine's Day was thankfully not on his radar. I will go to my grave believing it was a coincidence that I told him on that day of all days, but you are welcome to insert your own Freudian theories right here.

Me and Dave. Do I look straight or what?

"I gotta talk to you," I said. "Have a shot, or two." He took a shot. I could tell he thought I was priming him for a typical night of fun and drinking. It took me a few minutes to get up the courage, and I did a shot before launching in.

"I need you to read this." My hands shook as I handed him an envelope with a letter I'd written to him, which was a more personalized version of what I'd put in my journal.

We were sitting on the edge of the bed as he read the letter. It began with me reminding him how open he was and stating my hope that he could handle something that I needed him to know. I could hear my heart beating as his eyes moved down the page reading the part where I told him that I was exactly the same person he'd known and assured him that I was not physically attracted to him and that our relationship didn't have to change. He finished the letter and turned to me.

When his eyes met mine, I flinched. I pulled back. I can't believe it now, but at that moment what I expected was for him to hit me, to beat me up. He looked at my eyes and saw fear. But I just sat there as he came toward me and crushed me with a strong embrace.

"I love you," Dave said. "I would never hurt you." The bear hug did kind of hurt, but in the best way possible. Dave was shaken, but supportive. He quickly did two more shots. (I patted myself on the back for having the foresight to bring Jack Daniel's.) He asked how long I'd known—and, most importantly, why I hadn't told him sooner. Apparently, his parents had been on him since freshman year about whether I was gay and he'd been denying it to them all along. The longer we talked, the more he began to feel that I'd betrayed him by keeping something so big from him for so long. He wasn't that upset that I was gay. He was upset that I'd lied. I decided to wait awhile before admitting that, additionally, I didn't really care as much about Led Zeppelin as I'd led him to believe, either.

I spent the next few months breaking out my journal, reading my coming-out passage to various friends. Overall, the support was overwhelming, although two friends later confessed to barfing hours after our conversations. I'm going to choose to blame that one on processed foods, whether it's true or not. Dave had a bumpier road to full acceptance, which came to require weekly phone conversations with Evelyn Cohen. I don't know who helped whom more, but I was grateful they had each other. Even if it is incredibly weird to have your best friend calling your mom to rap about your sexual orientation.

But as for me, the road ahead, for once, seemed open and smooth. I finally felt free.

The Jewfro, brushed out to full effect,
always got a laugh.

I DON'T TRANSCRIBE

n the summer of 1989 the terror I had felt about coming out—about ever fitting in—was forgotten the instant I stepped into the massive brick monstrosity on a decidedly ungentrified block of Hell's Kitchen, a building anyone might have assumed was a rehab center or insurance headquarters if not for the simple and chic little black dress of an awning over the front entrance that read CBS BROADCAST CENTER.

I can remember sitting in the den in St. Louis as a thirteen-year-old with my mom and our neighbor, Mrs. Arkin, while they drank their scotch and watched Walter Cronkite hand the *CBS Evening News* over to Dan Rather in 1981. Even as a 'tween, I knew what a huge deal this was. It was an era when anchormen were anchormen—trusted, unbiased, larger-than-life authorities on the news. They were real journalists who mattered.

So when it came time to apply for summer internships in college, I had my heart set on working for the *CBS Evening News*. Did I want to be an anchor, delivering the news to a trusting, dinner-eating viewership, or did I want to be a producer, hustling behind the scenes to make it all happen? Seriously, I'm asking. Because I didn't know at the time. I just knew I wanted to Be There.

I wrote another impassioned letter—I was a pro at this point, having nabbed that Susan Lucci interview my sophomore year. As a backup, I'd also applied to the local NBC affiliate in St. Louis. KSDK was actually a powerhouse station with a competitive internship program, a place any college kid would be lucky to work at. But when the internship director there told me, "If you choose CBS over KSDK, you'll be making the biggest mistake of your career," I thought, What career? I didn't have one yet. Who needed that kind of advice? When an acceptance came from CBS, I didn't hesitate to accept right back.

All the helium instantly whooshed out of my elation balloon when I received a letter telling me I was being assigned not to the *CBS Evening News,* but to *CBS . . . , This Morning.* What?? I had never even heard of or watched that dud-as-a-doornail, dud-on-arrival dud. I was a know-it-all even then, and one of the things I knew was that CBS had never been a contender in the morning. This was like landing a White House internship only to discover I'd be painting the gate. Was that KSDK lady's taunt coming true so soon? Disgruntled, but having already burned my backup bridge, I packed my attitude and set off for Manhattan.

The sound track of that summer was Madonna's "Express Yourself," and I fully intended to. The first time I saw the video, I was at a gay bar called Private Eyes, watching it on a wall of TV screens—at that time, the height of cosmopolitan high tech. But it was the video itself that almost made my eyes fall out of my head. Of course, you recall the intricate plotline: Madonna has a harem of muscly wet men in chains crawling around on the floor. And there's a cat with the same eyes as Madonna. Madonna is in charge; she is the ruler and she is sexy and she is the boss. It was no wonder I was so transfixed: This was exactly the image I had of myself taking New York by storm. I would not go for second best, Baby. I was about to become a CBS News intern with all of the power and conviction Madonna embodied in that video, minus the lapping up of milk from a bowl (but only because I was lactose intolerant—meaning I don't really like milk).

This was long before Craigslist existed, and if a serial killer wanted to lure you into a trap, at least he had to put some real effort into it by taking out a classified ad. I prayed that this wouldn't be my fate as I perused the *Village Voice* and contacted random strangers looking for roommates. Soon enough, subsidized by my parents, I wound up sharing a fourth-floor walkup on East Twenty-first Street with a seemingly non-murderous gay guy who worked for TWA and traveled a lot. My very first day in the apartment, while snooping (duh), I discovered my roommate's extensive pornography archive thoughtfully displayed in his bedroom. Wow, do gay people keep all their . . . media . . . out in the open on shelves like this? I wondered. Life in the St. Louis suburbs provided exactly zero guidance when it came to filling in all those niggling details of gay life such as where to store your spank mags. I figured as long as I was trespassing, I might as well educate myself by taking one of my roomie's tapes off the shelf and popping it into his VCR. Which promptly broke. Mid-scene. I was mortified. I was going to be evicted my first night. What a tragic waste of youthful promise. This was not what Madonna, or my mother, would have wanted.

When my roommate came home, he shrugged off the broken videotape and laughed at my angst. I loved New York.

From my tiny room on East Twenty-first Street, I had to take two buses to get uptown and west to CBS, which at that time was home not only to the morning show but also to *The CBS Evening News with Dan Rather, West 57th, 48 Hours, As the World Turns, The Joan Rivers Show*, and WCBS-TV. Walking into the building that first day I felt a glimmer of hope that maybe this morning show gig wouldn't be so lame.

I joined the other interns waiting in the lobby and sussed each of them out. I didn't see anything big in the way of competition. I suppose that has to be the day that I met Julie. She and I were in the same internship "class," but I barely took notice of her, other than when I caught her rolling her eyes at me for trying to be the brown-nosiest teacher's pet while she couldn't wait to hit the curb at five o'clock, where her boyfriend would pick her up. If you had asked me that day if this Julie and I would ever become friends, I would have said, "Um, no." And if you had asked me if I could ever see big things happening for this Julie in the future, I would have said, "Um, no!" Foresight has never been a strength. (BUT FIRST: spoiler alert.) Julie Chen went on not only to anchor the very show on which we were interning, but also to rule the *Big Brother* house and marry the head of CBS. And I'm crazy about her.

While I was busy underestimating my future friend the Chen-bot, we were greeted by an all-business, very New York woman with hair so frizzy, I instantly assumed we'd connect. She had a pencil skirt, skyscraper high heels, and a list of names that she unceremoniously checked, announcing, "Cohen, you're in con-sumer. Go find Erin Moriarty." I was flabbergasted. I'd been assigned to the *consumer* unit? Some of these turnips were going to be work-ing for the entertainment unit and I was in consumer? Who watched consumer news in the morning, on that show? It just seemed dread-ful; it was as if I could hear my recently formed tiny bubble of hope bursting.

"I don't think I want to work in that unit," I declared. "Where's Jerrianne?" I was already trying to go over this person's head, looking for the bosslady in charge of the internship program.

"She's not in today," Pencil Skirt said matter-of-factly. "Consumer's your unit. Give it a shot. If you don't like it, then we'll have a discussion." Even in my agitated, unreasonable state, I recognized the tone of menace in that sentence. Pencil Skirt's big strong hand hadn't lifted me to a higher ground; it had smacked me down, hard.

It took all of an hour for me to decide that the other interns at *CBS This Morning* were utter dumbshits, and as time went on they did nothing to disabuse me of this notion. I remember walking into the newsroom on that first day and hearing a girl from Westchester ask our supervisor what three channels the TVs were on. That line killed me, and it also pissed me off. Why hadn't *that* dummy been assigned to the freaking consumer unit? My superior attitude was a result, no doubt, of the experience I had in my many previous internships. I viewed my CBS internship as something of a graduate course—but I was the only one who saw it that way. To this day, when I look at a crop of interns, I always try to pinpoint which ones are desperate to be there and which ones are just collecting a college credit, and proceed accordingly.

My disgruntlement over not being immediately recognized as the heir apparent to Dan Rather dissipated when I realized that an internship at a network, even in the worst unit on the worst-rated morning show, beat all hell out of a summer internship at KSDK in St. Louis. Turns out we booked names as big as anybody. Henry Kissinger came on to do the weather that year! And even better, Erin Moriarty, the reporter I'd been assigned to work with, was a real journalist, not a Barbie doll with a teleprompter. She researched stories herself, spent hours on the phone chasing down leads, and was a lawyer. Plus, she had this gravelly voice and wore sexy skirts and, I would find out soon enough, did not suffer fools or cocky interns gladly.

My 'fro was gone at this point, and instead I was working my ponytail hard. My internship look also included a shirt and tie with clip-on suspenders. Occasionally, when feeling especially bold, I wore Bermuda shorts with a tie. It was my idea of dressing like a dandy, when what I probably looked like was a Dexy, or one of his Midnight Runners, or a douchebag. Oh, and I was Andrew. That's what I wrote on my application, even though everyone had always called me Andy. (Be careful what you write on your internship application. My name became Andrew for twelve years and I almost had to go to court to change it back. My name in the credits of our shows still reads Andrew, which I guess still feels grown-up to me.)

Another advantage of working on a national show was the abundance of free food, which to a starving student (and a Jewish person) was an incredibly big deal. I think it was when I was

Bring your college roommate to your internship day!

stuffing my face with gratis carbs at the welcome lunch for interns that I began to view the actual staff—not the other interns—as my colleagues. They all seemed to be living the life that I wanted: urban, well traveled, well dressed, and well compensated. I took note of a few gayish guys on staff, only to find out later that they were in the closet. Being freshly out myself, I understood why someone might make that choice, but at the same time, I couldn't imagine being in the closet in my thirties. I was surprised there even were closeted people in New York in 1989, and deeply relieved I wasn't going to be one of them. I had no plans to advertise my sexuality in the workplace, but if anyone asked, I'd promised myself I'd simply tell the truth. That decision proved to be one that would guide my entire life: I've never hidden who I am, and being gay doesn't define me. It is one of the things I happen to be. I'm also a Gemini, an asthmatic, and a lover of disco balls. And long walks on the beach. Call me!

☺

Of the two producers I worked for in the consumer unit, I was quickly electrified by, and quite possibly obsessed with, Lynn Redmond, a gorgeous black woman with style and a magnetic personality. I constantly stopped by her cubicle, asking her to tell me about the celebrity profiles she'd produced at Essence TV. Lynn had met everyone from Gladys Knight to Oprah, and I couldn't get enough of her stories. (Example: Lynn had produced the Janet Jackson interview in which she revealed her secret marriage to El DeBarge, the singer of "Who's Johnny?" from the movie *Short Circuit*, and a vocal dead ringer for one Michael Joseph Jackson. Which I just put together now, writing this. Ew.) One day, Lynn and I chemically bonded like atoms over a mutual love of Whitney Houston, but, as was typical when she thought she'd given me enough of her time, she said, "Okay, kid, get back to work." I lingered in the door of her cubicle and waited a few beats.

"Can we be friends?" I asked. Subtlety was not my strong suit, and I was nervous. I wanted to be her friend so badly I could taste it.

"Friends!?!" I can still hear her incredulous, high-pitched response, as though I were asking for her pancreas. She was older and married and living in Connecticut, and here was this gay college kid knocking at her cubicle door with a promise ring in his hand. She didn't even pretend to let me down gently.

"You're an intern," she said point-blank. "I don't see the common ground. You're twenty!"

I was twenty-one. And we had Whitney Houston in common! What more did we need? I'd dated a guy in Paris who didn't even speak my freakin' language, so how could this woman tell me we didn't have enough in common? And you know what? Despite how annoying I must have been as I repeated to her all summer long "We ARE going to be friends," she eventually relented in a major way and remains one of my best friends today.

Imploring Lynn to be my friend

Newsrooms are a crazy mixed cocktail of contradictions—
fervor and indifference, devotion and irreverence, curiosity and
cockiness—but I knocked it back in a single giddy shot and bellied
up for more. I had found somewhere that I belonged. Instantly
and irrevocably.

Unlike Five O'Clock Julie, I couldn't get enough of the place. I
would have happily lived out of a sleeping bag in the mailroom.
Sometimes I'd ditch my job and just walk around; there was no
door that I wasn't bold enough to enter. I could have come upon a
door with a sign reading MORLEY SAFER PEDICURE SUITE, PROCE-
DURE IN SESSION, and I still would have barged right in. I would
waltz into the *As the World Turns* studio and just stand there, or slip
into the control room and watch how the soap sausage was made.
(As discussed, I hated CBS soap operas, but it was still extremely
cool. All the actors were much thinner and better-looking in person, and whenever any of them passed in the hallways, I always
said hi, because even though I wasn't a fan of their show, I was a
fan of saying hello to celebrities and having them say hello back!)

One day, I sauntered down to the (closed) *CBS Evening News*
set at airtime. I knew they'd pan the newsroom during the bumps
to commercial breaks, and I wanted to be on TV. The show was in
progress and the room was eerily quiet with the exception of Dan
Rather's comforting voice. I plopped my narrow ass down right
behind him at a desk that didn't belong to me and started reading
someone else's newspaper. Then I picked up that person's desk
phone and dialed my mom to tell her to watch the show closely.
Everything seemed to be going fine until a tall redheaded bully
came up to me and asked me who I was. I sheepishly told him I was
an intern at the *Morning News*.

"You don't belong here," he snarled. "Get off the set."

He kicked me off the set! At least he did it during a commercial break. I wanted my mom to see me on TV, but not being forci-
bly ejected.

It was utterly humiliating. What was I thinking, walking

around the place like I owned it? Maybe Madonna had steered me wrong? What if they told Lynn? Needless to say, I never returned to the *Evening News*, and being bounced only added to the inferiority complex I had already with the *Evening News* interns, of whom I had not been chosen to be a member, and who all wore suits and looked like they were better at standardized tests than me. I was scared those Ivy League interns would find out what I did. Scared of what, I'm not exactly sure, since intern beat-downs weren't exactly prevalent in the halls at CBS. (Incidentally, the big ginger-haired bully who kicked me off that set was Bill Owens, who later, probably despite his better judgment, became a great friend and the executive producer of *60 Minutes*.)

I should've let that little set-crash be lesson enough, but I soon got another mini-can of Whoopass shaken up and opened in my face. It happened a few days later, when a *Morning News* producer pulled me into the conference room for a "little talk." At first, I was excited. Little talks are my favorite! And this one started out like gangbusters with him saying I was bright, and aggressive, in a good way, and well liked. He said I had a lot of potential, and that I reminded him a lot of himself, which on one hand was really cool, because he was only twenty-four and already a producer, but on the other hand was puzzling, since he was Asian and a little chubby. Did he mean that he thought I acted like him or looked like him? Did he see himself looking like me? By this point my ponytail was in full effect and I was working a coordinated suspender/tie combo almost every day. I did not see a physical connection between us.

When my wandering mind stumbled back on track, he was telling me that I could really go far this summer and make a big impression, but . . . And are compliments followed by "buts" ever good? No. He said that I was a bit "rough around the edges" and needed to work on some things. He said there were important people in the newsroom and that I needed to "tone it down."

"Do I need to talk softer?" This was not the first time in my life that I'd been told to tone it down, thanks to a volume modulation problem I'd inherited from my mother.

"No," he said. "Remember, Andrew, this is CBS News."

I'm sure that what my older Asian twin regarded as being gentle, I mistook for vague. I asked him for a specific description of what to do. He said I needed to be more "introspective." *Introspective, adj.: the act or process of a reflective looking inward to one's own thoughts and feelings.* Oh, kind of like the complete opposite of expressing yourself? Dammit, Madonna! He concluded by saying the only reason he had given me this talk was because someone had given him the very same talk.

That night I went to Uncle Charlie's, which that summer became my favorite (gay) bar of all time. There was something comforting and familiar about Uncle Charlie's brass and wood and TV screens. (Don't look for it now; it's been closed for years. Of course, like the dozens of Original Ray's Pizza Parlors in NYC, there's another Uncle Charlie's that also happens to be a gay bar, but that's not it. My Uncle Charlie's, much like most real elderly uncles, is no longer with us.)

As I sat thinking over a few beers, I decided that it was possibly possible that I was acting a teeny bit too familiar with certain people. Like, the one day I was introduced to the newsblock producer and I said, facetiously, "I think I read about you in *The Undoing of CBS News.*"

And another day, when I was answering phones and someone called us from an affiliate in Spokane, Washington, I asked them if they were number one in ratings. When they said they were, I said—loudly—"We don't know how that feels here!"

Then there was the time Erin Moriarty gave me some tapes to transcribe, and I, summer intern to this seasoned news reporter, replied, "I don't transcribe." And that seasoned news reporter looked like she wanted to shove the tapes down my throat and use my nose as the "play" button. She was pissed, and it was the first time I'd ever been yelled at by a superior.

"Are you kidding me? You do now." And I did.

Oy. I'd easily thought of three examples right off the top of my head while drunk at Uncle Charlie's! I vowed at that moment that I must remember that this was CBS News, and I was only an intern, there to learn, but not a true member of the team. Not yet, and maybe not ever if I continued to put the "punk" in "spunk."

Since we'd kind of shared a moment, and we maybe looked alike, I'd hoped that that producer would notice my new self-reflective streak. Maybe I'd earn his respect. And then maybe he'd stop asking me to hold the elevator for him. Literally, he'd make me run down the hall two minutes before he went to the elevator. Was he that important? And, by the way, can I point out in the light of 2012 that there's got to be some kind of teachable moment in that elevator story for him? I've never made any intern fetch an elevator for me, no matter how introspective he or she wasn't.

Later that summer I pulled Green Room duty for a whole week. That meant a Town Car pickup at five-thirty in the morning, which was a privilege surpassing even free food. I didn't care that I had to wake up in predawn darkness; the idea that I got to take a black car through empty Manhattan streets to a live network TV show where there was unlimited coffee and people getting ready to appear on-camera was so glamorous that I could barely handle it. When I got there, I headed to Studio 47—"the fish bowl"—and checked guest pickup times while Charles Osgood anchored the morning news. Then I greeted those guests in the Green Room and escorted them to the studio. In that week, I met the Karate Kid (Ralph Macchio); a hair expert; the writer of a book about only children; a Vietnamese author; Jack Scalia, who had been a regular on *Dallas*; some actor from *Batman*; Martin Luther King III; and Kerry Kennedy. Although I was only an intern, and it wasn't televised, or probably very much fun for any of them, for me working the Green Room was like hosting a cocktail party. Actually, a weird cocktail party with a group of incongruous attendees that took place way too early in the morning. To this day, putting oddball combinations of people in one room is one of my favorite party devices, and a hallmark of *Watch What Happens Live*. When I was in that Green Room, I felt like I was in the center of something very, very good.

On the day that gay rights activist Vito Russo appeared to talk about AIDS, I felt as if I was in the center of something great. Russo was one of the storytellers in *Common Threads*, a documentary that had just been released about the first decade of the AIDS crisis, told through profiles of thousands of victims memorialized by the AIDS Quilt Project. Russo had contributed a quilt panel honoring his companion, Jeffrey Sevcik. As Russo spoke about contracting the disease himself, I was proud that he was on our show—that a gay activist and a gay issue were considered important enough to merit the thoughtful interview Harry Smith was conducting that morning. As I watched his appearance from the control room, though, a few staff members started laughing and cracking dirty homophobic jokes while Russo recounted the death of his lover. Despite my vow to be true to who I was, at that point in my life, there was no way I was going to speak up and say something to these people, who were my superiors. It was a crushing moment. But internships are a time to learn, and some lessons are way harder than how to collate scripts. Vito Russo died the following year.

Despite my initial doubts, I immersed myself in the consumer gig, and the more I got into the groove, the more responsibilities were entrusted to me. One afternoon, I was doing research on a tattoo-eyeliner scam and another story about contaminated orange juice, when at 5 p.m. someone yelled "Plane crash!" The whole room froze, and Charles Kuralt came on with a Special Report. A United Airlines DC-10 carrying 296 people from Denver to Chicago had crashed in Sioux City, Iowa. Miraculously, there were reports of survivors in the smoking debris.

The newsroom went into a frenzy. People were screaming, "Call, call, call! Book everyone in Sioux City!" "We need families of victims!" "Get rescue workers!" I picked up the phone and, working on instinct, was able to book an interview with the Sioux City fire chief. Then, out of nowhere, some magical elves laid out a huge buffet for dinner, and everyone buckled down to work through the night. Most of the other interns had left, but I couldn't fathom going home when actual news was breaking. The adrenaline, smarts, and intricate choreography that came together to feed a story as it unfolded live on-air was incredible. The whole night was controlled chaos and, terrible tragedy aside, wildly energizing.

When I finally stumbled out of the newsroom at eleven o'clock, I went straight to Uncle Charlie's. My mind was about to explode. I couldn't believe I'd booked someone for the show, that I'd been part of something that was kind of important. I started to have second thoughts about my plan to go to a small town and be a reporter after graduation the following year. What if I just moved straight to New York to try to get a job at CBS? Even if I didn't get on the air right away, wouldn't working behind the scenes at a network in New York City be worth it?

As my internship drew to a close, I managed to finagle a lunch with one of the senior producers of the show, who had been nice to me all summer. I wanted to pick his brain about what he thought my next move should be. He said he admired my people skills and how I was always so happy. He impressed upon me that it was crucial not to let your job run your life, because there were no paybacks in this business, and nobody would congratulate you for not taking a vacation. He mentioned that it was good that I didn't seem to let important people affect me.

At the end of the lunch, I just blurted out the question I really wanted an answer to. I asked what he thought of me going on the air.

"Your face is good," he allowed. "But . . ." And are compliments followed by "buts" ever good? The answer is still no! "Your overall look needs some work," he said. My overall look. What the hell did THAT mean? My ponytail? I'd cut it off. Done! Then he went for it.

"Your wandering eye might keep you from any on-air career entirely."

My wandering eye? What the fuck was he talking about? I'd had these eyes my whole life and this was the first I'd ever heard of either of them wandering and he's talking about my entire career goal and everything I'd decided was my reason for living!

"Wha—what do you mean, wandering eye?" I stammered. Great, now I had a speech impediment, too.

"Oh. Every so often your left eye goes off course," he replied a little too nonchalantly and a little too authoritatively for my taste, using his index finger to point down and to the right in front of his face. I started thinking maybe he was trying to make me feel bad, or maybe he was jealous of my unbridled youth. Had he said the same thing three years before to my faux twin, the Asian producer?

I went back to the office and called my mom.

"That's just BULL, Andy!" she over-modulated into the receiver. "What the hell is he talking about, wandering EYE? I've never SEEN IT. You do NOT have a wandering EYE. Get OVER IT."

And that was pretty much it. I believed her. For twenty years, I pursued a career behind the scenes, but because that's what I ulti-mately decided I wanted, and not because I was thinking about some nonexistent lazy eye. And then someone actually let me be on TV, and boy, did I hear about it. Every blogger and tweeter and commenter that encountered me on-air had something to say about my wonky eyes. And of course, now when I look at a picture of myself it is all I see. Come to think of it, it's kind of miraculous that I can see anything at all, when you consider how horribly crossed my eyes are.

I was on the bus heading to my final day of work when I glanced over at the magazine the man sitting next to me was reading. It was called *Blade Trade*, all about the knife industry. I'd been in New York long enough to stop assuming that every unfamiliar man was a serial killer, so I all but dismissed the notion that he was placing a murder weapon order before writing another fake room-mate ad. A slightly more likely explanation was that he was just a fella who worked in the knife biz and was catching up on the lat-est knife knewz. That concept floored me. Had he always wanted to be a knife guy, or had he just bopped around going from job to job until he fell into the knife lifestyle? This odd voyeuristic moment on the bus made me so grateful to have figured out what I wanted to do in my life, something glamorous, exciting, and important. I was going to work doing something in TV, somewhere. Not only that, I had learned about modulating the level and tone at which I expressed myself, and maintaining some kind of deco-rum. In the office.

I spent my last week in New York unemployed, running around, being gay, and lying out in the Sheep's Meadow. I called the morn-ing show one last time to try to connect with the senior producer who had informed me about my eye. A newsclerk named Cornelia told me he wasn't there.

"We kept your mailbox up," she said. At the beginning of the summer, each of the interns was given a mailbox. I was flushed with excitement. "We all know you're coming back here."

I knew, too.

Sunrise with Tammy Faye Bakker

TUPPINS

fter my internship, I went back to college having identified two critical things that some people take a lifetime to figure out—who I was and what I wanted to be. Now I had to figure out how to deliver on the latter. The monkey was off my back and I was out and free, but I had turned a corner smack into a new, chilling reality—AIDS.

Along with every other gay man in 1988, I was convinced I would become infected. I filled the empty bin in the back of my head that used to house all my coming-out fears with my updated paranoia, and I equated every ailment with the one I feared the most. I stared at all my bruises, sores, and blemishes, convincing myself that I was going to die. I was too scared to get tested because I thought it simply meant finding out that I had the disease. I didn't talk to anybody about AIDS; my friends were just coming to terms with the new me and I wanted to project an image of calm, of health.

Watching Oprah and *All My Children* every day after class provided refuge from my fears. Even when I thought I didn't care about Oprah's topic, she had a way of making the show great. Nobody else could do that. And my hair was huge, almost as big as Oprah's.

Just before senior year, I finally told Graciela that I was gay. I'd saved her for last for some reason. I guess I felt like if I was going to be with a woman, it would've been her, and to eliminate this possibility by admitting I was gay meant I was breaking both our hearts. One day at Amanda's parents' house, while looking at her painted toenails, she asked me if I liked girls with painted toenails. Amanda and I gave each other a long look.

"I'm gay."

"Oh, okay," Grac said matter-of-factly. "I have to make a phone call." She disappeared inside the house. Amanda and I sat in disbelief, thinking she was in serious denial. Grac said later that she'd been worried how she appeared in front of us, and, like Dave, felt left out of my circle of trust. We barely spoke of it all day, and that night we saw *Do the Right Thing*. The next day we talked for hours and went deep, agreeing that if I were straight we probably would've wound up together. It was all very melancholy.

We recovered by reframing our friendship, becoming even closer. We were partners in crime and on the dance floor, where we always came together. We went to several B-52s concerts that year and danced our butts off. That year Grac had the best college job of all time: She was a moderator on a "Big & Beautiful" chat line, for people who are big and the people who love them. Sometimes the conversation got really dirty, and she had to jump in and tell them to clean it up. But mostly she just let them talk dirty, because she believed that fat people had a right to enjoy themselves. I agreed.

My job through college was running a pushcart at Faneuil

Hall—the prototype for renovated urban outdoor malls—in downtown Boston. I sold Deadhead gear, Mexican blankets, Baja pullovers, and little woven bracelets. I was always broke in college—I have no clue what I spent my money on but I had none—so I took a lot of shifts and would just sit in my high director's chair and listen to Tracy Chapman and the Dead and read *No One Here Gets Out Alive* and hypothesize about whether Jim Morrison was really dead. My best day was when Lisa Whelchel ("Blair" from *Facts of Life*) showed up in the mall and I ditched the pushcart for about an hour to follow her around at a respectful distance. Essentially my job consisted of watching idiots walking into each other all day (spend a day watching tourists and you'll see that they really do become herdlike and walk right into each other) and endlessly answering two questions:

"Where's the bathroom?"

"How do I get to Cheers?"

Occasionally I would make sure that people knew that when

they went to Cheers—by the way it's not even called that, it's called the Bull and Finch Pub, and it doesn't look a thing like the set of the damn show—they would *not* be seeing Sam and Diane. The irony is that I would've been one of those people if I was visiting Boston for a weekend. But I wasn't, was I?

My other job during college was as a waiter at a restaurant on Boylston Street. The job of waiter may have been created especially for me. I loved talking to strangers and getting them drunk and then getting tipped for it. Sadly, I got fired—for the one and only time in my life—for accepting a "shift drink" after closing time. Every waiter was entitled to one free drink, but the glitch was that I was not twenty-one years old. Maybe that's why I drink on my show now.

☺

All my obsessing over my imminent death led me to finally go get an AIDS test at the end of my senior year. After many sleepless nights, with a backdrop of intense buildup and drama, Jackie came with me to get the news. And I was negative. I felt like I could do anything. Finally, I felt I had the opportunity to live a full life. Now I knew I had to strive to enjoy life, take opportunities, follow my dreams, showcase my worth.

That meant moving to New York after graduation and getting a job as a waiter until something opened up at CBS. I didn't even have to get the waitering job—CBS hired me as a newsclerk on *CBS This Morning* before I had a chance to unpack my bags.

☺

Newsclerk—I hated the sound of it. The "clerk" part was what bugged me. But then again, look what I was doing: I answered phones, ripped scripts, collated packets for the anchors, and did irritating grunt work for producers, some of whom seemed to me like Michelangelos of the mediocre. I was a ball-and-chain to the ringing phones and absolutely stank at ripping scripts, but my

Me as a newsclerk at CBS. This is what we used to call a computer.

respite was how I began each morning, running the Green Room, which was always a parade of insanity—a coffee-based cocktail party featuring an always unusual guest list. One morning, Tip O'Neill asked Sammy Davis's widow, Altovise, if she was "here to sing." She said, "No, but my late husband was the greatest singer of all time." Why do white people always assume black people are going to sing?!? Every morning saw some type of weird interaction, and I lived for those moments.

Even though it sometimes took years to get promoted, and the show always seemed to be a hair away from cancellation, after about six months I was convinced I'd outgrown my role as a news-clerk. They'd been letting me produce live segments, and when Connie Chung filled in for Paula Zahn, I produced a whole series for her about soap stars (I'm pretty sure it was award-worthy). I was also sent to West Palm Beach to help book a juror in the William Kennedy Smith trial. We got juror Lea Haller, and every-one said it was a coup. Years later, she would marry the prosecuting attorney, Roy Black, and years after that, she became a Real Housewife of Miami. (Small, freaky world.)

My new best friend Lynn let me conduct my first interview ever (I was off camera). It was with Robin Williams, renowned for his manic energy during interviews. I stuck to my questions, didn't listen to his answers, and essentially killed all of his shtick. Later, we watched the tape together and she critiqued my performance. Lynn gave me a C- (equivalent to credit for getting through it).

Maybe because I was openly gay, or maybe because my boss was giving me a shot, I was sent to LA—for my first time—to try to book somebody associated with Magic Johnson, who'd just revealed he was HIV-positive. Even though by that point I'd tested negative a couple times, I was still racked with fear, and the news of Magic's diagnosis was huge, symbolic of this being more than a gay disease. I booked a Laker, and it felt important, being part of a story that was to be a watershed moment in the history of AIDS.

On the plane ride home from LA, flying MGM Air (where every seat was first class!), I was sitting behind these two guys who seemed to be talking about CBS. Since I never met a discussion I didn't like to bust in on, I leaned right over their seats, poked my head in between them, and said, "Hey! Do you guys work for CBS?" I was humiliated when one turned to me and I immediately recognized Jeff Sagansky, then president of the network. I quickly told him I worked for *CBS This Morning* and to please not cancel it, then made my head pop away to a place where he couldn't see it again.

When I got back to New York I was promoted to assistant producer. Free from the ringing phones and Xerox machine, I was exactly where I wanted to be. At that broadcast, I went on to become associate producer, producer, and senior producer and always made it a point not to give the newsclerks my grunt work. I knew one day I'd be working alongside—and for—them.

☺

After I'd been working at CBS for a few years it dawned on me that as I traveled the country, I wasn't merely parachuting into stories: I was parachuting into lives. I would land smack-dab in the middle of someone else's drama, before disappearing forever. I became a highly trained professional voyeur. I had a walk-on role in everyone else's soap opera.

I had produced a slew of feature-y live shots, and they all amounted to pretty fun little vacationettes, but not always scintillating television. It sounded great in New York when I pitched going to Boulder, Colorado, and having the cute editors of a rollerblading magazine demonstrate the latest craze to Harry and Connie Chung in New York. If you're lucky, you missed that actual segment, though, because it boiled down to Harry and Connie wondering on live TV what they were doing watching two people doing lame rollerblading tricks in a half-dark parking lot at dawn. As bad as that one sucked, it was miles ahead of the "National Family Learn to Bowl Week," remote from a bowling alley in San Francisco. The piece I produced featured the darling bowling Higa twins, who could neither bowl nor were very darling. And have you ever seen a bowling alley at 5:15 a.m. PST? You're not supposed to, is the thing. I called my mom after the segment. "That was so BORING!" she said, supportively. "Is that NEWS?!?! It's no wonder your show is in the PITS." When I got back to New York, I kept saying, "It wasn't my idea!" to anyone who would listen. That's the thing about morning shows: You have to fill a *lot* of time.

I wasn't always assigned to the nobodies. For instance, I spent the morning with Mary Jo and Joey Buttafuoco at exactly the time all three networks aired movies based on the insane story of Joey's teenaged lover walking up to their front door and shooting Mary Jo in the face. The saga of the Buttafuocos and Amy Fisher, the "Long Island Lolita," was the biggest story going that year, and I was in their living room after courting Mary Jo on the phone for a week.

It was a satellite remote, and that morning, Mary Jo told me

Seven a.m. in the Buttafuocos' living room

that she wanted to show Paula Zahn the X-ray of her head live on the air. I thought this was a bad idea and called the control room to ask what they thought. "Sure, let's do it," they said. Okay, maybe it was more like, "What kind of fucking idiot are you, Cohen? Where's your news judgment? Show the X-ray, you moron, and then maybe go get YOUR head X-rayed!" That's the kind of nurturing, mentoring talk I could always count on from the control room, but of course they were right: Boy, was it ever a memorable moment when Mary Jo whipped out that huge transparent film showing the contents of her skull and then waved it at the camera, yelling about the bullet Amy *Fish*-ah lodged in there. The segment got picked up all over the place.

At the time, I didn't totally understand the complexities of TV as theater. I thought the introduction of a prop like Mary Jo's X-ray would complicate things and screw up the interview. Of course, it only made it more dramatic. Nowadays, I almost never say no to a prop. When Danielle Staub wanted to bring a dummy head to the *RHNJ* Season 2 reunion so she could demonstrate how hard her hair was pulled by Jacqueline's nineteen-year-old daughter, I said, "Please do!"

One of my favorite remotes was when I was sent to Las Vegas—my very first time in that city. CBS sent me with the sole purpose of making sure Buddy Hackett showed up for a live early-morning interview.

When I checked in to the Desert Inn, I watched an awesome and informative video on the in-house TV about Suzanne Somers learning to gamble, then I called Mr. Hackett's room and left him a message telling him I had arrived and would like to buy him a drink before the interview, and that I would be by his room early the next morning, thinking that buying him a drink would be a good way to make sure he actually went to the interview.

When I showed up at his room at 3 a.m., he smelled of lotion. And though his skin was presumably soft, he was not, and he proceeded to tear me a new asshole. "YOU'RE gonna buy ME a drink? A KID is gonna buy me a drink???" he screamed. "I BUILT this town. I OWN this hotel! Who do you think you ARE, kid?"

Unsure of how to respond, I laughed, and thank God, so did he. He drove us to the location in his banana-yellow 1970 Buick convertible, which happened to be exactly the car I drove in high school. I wanted to find out what else Buddy Hackett and I could possibly have in common, but all too soon, it was time for his live spot. When the interview was done, I expected to send Mr. Hackett off and to find my own way back to the hotel, but when he asked, "You gettin' in or what?" I did not hesitate for a millisecond. Instead of taking me straight back to my hotel, he gave me an unforgettable sunrise tour of Vegas, telling me firsthand stories of Bugsy Siegel and the Rat Pack.

"Hey, kid, ever seen a million dollars in cash?" he asked. Of course I hadn't. We were in what used to be downtown Las Vegas, off the strip. "Run inside that casino. They have a million bucks under glass in the lobby. Go look!" he commanded, pulling the Buick to a stop right at the casino's front door. I felt like a boy with his grandpa—or like I might be Buddy's little buddy! I ran inside and saw the million dollars and got back in the car. "Isn't that something, kid?" It was.

Next, Buddy started giving me unsolicited life advice. He told me never to accept offers from people I didn't trust. He urged me to hold on to my memories. And perhaps by way of illustration, he got a dreamy look in his eyes and reminisced about some of his own misty, watercolor memories. "Every one of these streets reminds me of a different girl I fucked."

I really liked him. I actually liked the Buttafuocos, too. Many times I would find myself back at my desk in New York months after a remote, longingly fingering the cards in my Rolodex, fighting the urge to call these people up to say hello and that I'd been thinking about them. Did they miss me, too? Probably not. Let's not be naïve. These people were accustomed to having someone drop into town, see them as they wanted to be seen, and then get out of their hair. And while I may have only ever met one Buddy Hackett or one Mary Jo Buttafuoco in my travels, they'd probably met hundreds of me.

One remote pressed every voyeuristic button I've got, and it was so memorable that I kept a souvenir from the encounter for almost a decade. In 1994, I went to Palm Springs to produce the first joint interview Tammy Faye Bakker had agreed to since marrying her new husband, Roe Messner, a business partner of Jim Bakker's, who'd designed Heritage USA, the 2,300-acre Christian theme park and residential complex, before everything went to hell in a multi-million-dollar handbasket. Roe, as you may or may not remember, had reportedly handled payoffs to Bakker's mistress, Jessica Hahn. Jim ended up spending some time behind bars, but not before Tammy divorced him and married Roe. It was all very 1980s, back when big shoulder pads and thieving adulter-ous televangelists were the rage. When the scandal broke, Tammy Faye cried through her unfathomably heavy mascara (think taran-tulas mating) and managed to emerge from the whole mess a slightly streaky pop-culture icon. You had to love her for the way she stood her ground even as she was being mocked by every drag queen and comedian (Jan Hooks was my fave) in America. I did, anyway. I tried booking her for a few years. When I got her, I convinced everyone in New York that landing Tammy and her new man was kind of a big deal. Because, by the way, it kind of was.

I was stoked to spend time with Tammy Faye and see her spi-dery eye makeup up close and, better yet, see the habitat in which she lived. But there was another kind of insane aspect to my Palm Springs jaunt; I'd done something I bet not too many people would think of if they came to town to interview the former cohost of *The PTL Club*: I booked myself into an all-male clothing-optional "resort." The resort was simultaneously kind of disgusting and kind of awesome. Of course, no one on West Fifty-seventh Street knew where I was staying—the place wasn't exactly on the "Approved Hotels" list provided by the network's travel department. But then again, it was certainly not my problem that they hadn't thought to provide a "Disapproved" list as well. Still, I allowed myself to feel a tiny bit righteous because it was cheaper—in every sense of the word—than anywhere CBS would've put me. I was a company man; I was being fiscally responsible! Fine, that wasn't the only reason. There were waterfalls and grottoes and—well, the whole place looked like a low-rent version of the Playboy mansion. For me, it felt like the perfect opportunity to make up for lost time. My friends had all been to strip bars and every trashy place under the sun, and, by comparison, I was a mere babe in the woods—or des-ert. I had some serious catching up to do. At that time, though, my sense of adventure was still pretty Midwestern, and I could never have imagined checking in to this place under any usual circum-stance—as a vacation destination, or with a friend—but as long as

I was in the neighborhood on assignment to produce a story on a figure from the religious right, it seemed like a perfectly genius idea.

My first morning in Palm Springs, I cruised over to Tammy Faye's house so we could get to know each other and discuss the interview. I love seeing the inside of strangers' houses. It's usually the little things that excite me the most, like seeing what magazines they have in the bathroom. Tammy's home was in a gated community, and she had her very own fake lake in her backyard. As soon as she opened the door, I was greeted by a full frontal assault on my nose. Flowery perfume, scented candles, potpourri in every flavor, gusts of Glade, and I have no clue what else, all combined in a sweet and savory fight to the death. I'm a sensitive Jewish boy with delicate sinuses and contact lenses who is more than mildly obsessed with the smells of people's homes—every house has a special stink, and this one was un-mildly unique. My eyes started watering instantly, but through my veil of tears I could see that Tammy Faye had many, many, many figurines, miniatures, mirrors, collectibles, photos (of herself), and framed gold records adorning every nook and cranny of the house. There was a copy of *Lears* magazine in the bathroom, in case you need to know. And to complete the effect, a yippety yappety dog called Tuppins, who flew around our knees in hysterics.

Tammy was dressed exactly as I'd envisioned her: in head-to-toe winter whites. (Jews don't really do winter whites, and Palm Springs doesn't really do winter, but stay with me.) Tammy was kind of a miniature of her photographed self but loud and fun and full of life and love. At the same time, she seemed really fragile. She gave me a tour of her home and introduced me to Roe, who, I quickly learned, was half deaf. Tammy prattled on about how most of her furniture had been on TV before, from the set of *The PTL Club* and *Tammy's House Party*. How could that be? Shouldn't it have been in some government warehouse with other seized loveseats and disgraced ottomans?

The plan was to film Tammy live from her living room, with Harry Smith interviewing her from our New York studio. Tammy was still licking her wounds from that tough interview—also by satellite—that Ted Koppel had done with her a few years earlier, and it was part of my job to reassure her that Harry planned to proceed with a much lighter touch. We fell in love with each other in no time (well, I fell in love with her, and I think she was fond-ish of me), and I was able to reassure her of my intentions, which really were pure—I wanted her to have a fair shot at telling her story. I gave her a hug and told her I'd be back the next day for the site survey with the crew, and then we'd go live in thirty-six hours. Which, by my calculations, would give me a few hours of quality resort time.

Back at the hotel, I was surprised to find a camera crew shooting a naked aerobics video in the common area outside my window. Surprised, but not necessarily delighted. I sat in my room (fully clothed) watching something that I might've considered hot at one point, but up close was ultimately pretty gross. I began to wonder if it really even was an aerobics video, given the poor slim-nastics skills of the dancing twinks in front of me, or if this was just the poorly written exposition of a scene that was about to turn hard-core at any moment. The boys were unsynchronized and un–my type, so I crossed my fingers, hoping that things were not heading in that direction. That's when my deep thoughts were interrupted by the dreaded noise:

"BEEP. BEEP. BEEP. BEEP."

On a LONG list of pet peeves and "hates," my beeper was at the top (others included know-it-all cabbies, waiting in line, and carrots). It was one square plastic pain in the ass and essentially my ball-and-chain for most of the nineties, beeping furiously with bad news at every turn. To this day, I'm sure that its seemingly innocuous beeping was actually Morse code for "GET OFF YOUR ASS RIGHT NOW AND PREPARE FOR YOUR DAY TO BE RUINED." Without fail, the second I relaxed and forgot it was there, it would come to life, bidding me to call the office right away where someone at the assignment desk was ready to shout me out of my peaceful state, which was often a deep sleep. The orders were always urgent. "Sinatra died, get in here!" or "You're booked on the last flight out to New Orleans—we need you to be there when Hurricane Andrew hits tonight!"

My response was usually some form of incredulous disbelief. "Wait—you want me to fly INTO the hurricane?" (They did! I did. I got very wet, it sucked, but I got to see Dan Rather hanging on to a pole during gale-force winds.) When that beeper went off, it was never to let me know something fantastic had happened. I started to form a negative mental association between that sound and tragedy—like one of Pavlov's dogs if it suffered from PTSD. I'd take a breath and wait a couple minutes before calling back, hoping the breaking news would somehow un-break in the interim. I also didn't want to seem too available. I'M BUSY! I've got like eighteen balls in the air!

In Palm Springs, I finally called the CBS newsdesk and was put through to Jim Murphy, senior broadcast producer on the show. "Dude, there's a massive storm near Petaluma, California," he informed me. "Millions of dollars in damage and flooding. You gotta go there and get us some guests for the top of the show."

"I can't!" I pleaded. "You have to find someone else!" I mean, I was in a paradise of my own making and there was no way I was leaving. They were not taking me away from the weird, naked aerobicizers, whose weird, naked aerobics had taken on a mesmerizing quality, like something out of a David Lynch film. And, more importantly, they certainly weren't taking me away from my new best friend, Tammy Faye.

Back and forth we went, with me arguing vehemently that this Tammy Faye Messner exclusive was HUGE, and she would go right to *Good Morning America* if we didn't proceed with the interview as planned. I guess I was convincing. Jim said he would call me back.

I spent the next half hour sulking in my room. Couldn't someone from the stupid LA bureau cover the stupid rainstorm in stupid Northern California? (I know I sound hateful and crass, but that is how jaded you become in the news business. It's not that I didn't care about a devastating storm; I just wanted to do *my* story.)

Jim called back. "We're sending someone from LA, but we pushed Tammy Faye up to tomorrow's show, and you may have to go up north when the interview's done." I was still pissed, but grateful for the twenty-four-hour reprieve. I could go back to having fun, which immediately set my demented mind off on a new (but related) tangent. The voice of my friend Graciela was in my ear, she was my inner prankster, and she was encouraging me to hatch a wicked plot. Maybe I would swipe one of the filthy movies lying around my hotel and hide it under one of Tammy Faye's settees that might or might not be fugitives of the IRS. How hilarious would that be? Maybe not super-professional. Or adult. Careerwise, this was shaping up to be a really tough decision. This joke might be funny to play on your mom, but as much as you'd love it, Tammy is *not* your mom, I chided myself; you can't play such an awful joke on her. So, in the end, Tammy Faye was spared a potentially brilliant prank by a twinge of conscience over the havoc I would no doubt have wreaked. I made a note to stash a porno in my luggage in order to hide it somewhere fun on my next trip to St. Louis.

It was two o'clock in the morning when I drove to Tammy's house to meet a satellite truck the day of our interview. By then, it had become normal for me to start my workday in pitch darkness while the rest of the world slept. The farther west I went, the more painful the morning would be, because the setup stuff that had to happen before we got on the air took hours. It was all about establishing the shot, lighting it, getting the satellite truck fired up and in a position where it has a clear signal facing the right direction (don't ask me—I still don't get it twenty years later). Once you've "uplinked to the bird" you begin the pleasurable back-and-forth with the Michelangelos in the control room in New York who would like a plant shifted four inches, the camera turned in another direction, and some snow in the background. "Um, it didn't snow here," you tell the disappointed person who thinks since your interview subject is resplendent in winter white, there should be snow.

We were going live at 5:30 a.m. PST. When the door opened, Roe was standing there, and I kid you not that he was smelling intensely of lotion, though it was impossible to say whether it was Buddy's brand. Was the desert so devastatingly drying to older people that they had to lube up before they could even bend their limbs in the morning?

Tammy appeared in a stonewashed denim jumpsuit. To some, she might've looked like a drag Eva Gabor on her way to a *Hee Haw* audition, but to me she looked perfect. Waiting nervously for her segment, she listened to Harry interview Liam Neeson about *Schindler's List* and narrated what she was hearing in a very loud TammyVoice to her half-deaf husband, who was sitting there with the same monitor in his ear. "Oh, how depressing!" she shouted cheerfully. "Auschwitz! The Jews!" She shook her head. I worried that following such a sad story might affect her energy negatively, but, ever the pro, she snapped out of her Holocaust funk within seconds to open up the half hour singing our theme song, "Oh, What a Beautiful Morning," with Tuppins on her lap.

Remember that old showbiz truism, "Never work with kids or animals"? I was so glad Tammy Faye had never heard that. She sat holding Tuppins so tightly that the poor thing started yelping more than usual. On TV, this loving act of strangulation actually read as if Tuppins were howling in misery over Tammy Faye's singing. It was a crazy, fantastic moment. The interview was a classic.

When we said good-bye, Tammy and I went outside in the rising sun to take a picture by the fake lake—which became my Christmas card that year—before she presented me with a batch of fudge that she'd made me the night before. It was a priceless piece of pop culture memorabilia, and I took it home without sampling a bite so I could preserve it in my freezer for years to come. That fudge went with me through two apartment moves, until I finally summoned the willpower to pitch it, sometime after the turn of the century.

As you know, Tamara Faye LaValley Bakker Messner fought a long battle with cancer that took her from us in 2007. She was a good person who opened her home to me and treated me like a friend. And, because I'm sure you're wondering, I was indeed sent up to Petaluma. But I still don't know if a video (adult or otherwise) ever resulted from that naked aerobics session at the resort. If it did, I hope there isn't a shot of a young guy in the background with unruly hair and an expression of horrified glee. But if there is, and you have it, please send me a copy. I want to hide it under my mother's couch.

ΕΛΛΑΔΑ - GREECE - GRECE - GRIECHENLAND

Hi Mom & Dad, I'm having a
long, peaceful vacation. I'm reading,
sleeping and tanning a lot. Haven't
met anyone of any interest but that
is fine due to my constant pleasure
with MYSELF. 😊 I got hurt on my
motorbike yesterday and my feet are
all cut up. But I'm dealing and I
returned the bike. Greek people cut
in line; my hotel is great; and I
cut off all my hair. Now which of
the above statements do you think is
false?

Br. & Lou Cohen
7710 W. Biltmore Dr.
St. Louis, MO
63105
USA

Andy

ADAM EDITIONS ® ADAM EDITIONS 275 MESOGION AVE. 152 31 ATHENS
TEL: (01) 6721801-3, 6470072 TLX: 214223 ADAM GR., FAX: (01) 6725015

CRY INDIAN

I wasn't kidding about hiding that porno under my mom's couch. There was a long period of time where I absolutely loved pranks. Let me be more specific: I loved playing pranks on my parents. So indulge me in kind of a long (but worth it) ramble down Memory Lane for a story that's become something of an urban legend among my friends, and will either make you think I'm a brilliantly creative fool, or just a fool.

Though I have lived away from them for more time than under the same roof, my family is in constant touch. One of the ways this manifested itself in the early nineties was in the form of a weekly phone call that started the same ridiculous way every Sunday.

When I was "ready" to speak to my parents, I'd call them collect—usually using a pseudonym. (It was always one of the male characters from *All My Children*.) The phone would ring at my parents' house. The operator would announce, "I have Adam Chandler calling collect," as we all struggled to keep our composure. The parentals would reject the call, I'd act dejected for the operator, and then my phone would ring a minute later.

"Hello, Adam Chandler," my mom would say. "It's Brooke. BROOKE ENGLISH!"

And . . . scene! The conversation could go down in flames thirty-five seconds later, but the call always started with a big laugh. This system of scheduled family calls was devised by Evelyn Cohen during my freshman year at Boston University. The reasoning behind it was twofold. See if you can follow this line of thinking:

First, my collect call would be a signal that I was available to talk so they wouldn't have to "disturb" me by calling me first. This, of course, was bullshit, because I got phone calls from them all week long with no regard to my mental state. I guess since Sunday was the "Lord's day" it was sacred? Even though we weren't Christian?

Second, Evelyn's careful consumer research had told her this was somehow cheaper and smarter than actually accepting the collect charge or one of us dialing up an unprompted direct call. Looking back now, I do wonder if this elaborate ruse—two phone calls and a fake name just to have an actual family conversation—didn't somehow influence a thing I'll refer to as "the Shawnee Incident." But first, some background.

The further I was from my parents, the closer I got to Graciela. Our senses of humor fused into one demented organism, and we were constantly laughing about the doings of my parents in St. Louis. She'd fallen in love with them when they visited me in London, but she had a funny way of showing it. Grac, sensing immediately that my mother was gullible and fun to prank, took the possibly imprudent tactic of winning my mother over by torment. Her first misstep was telling my mom I had a crush on a gawky, mannish girl in college. By the time we graduated, the stage was set for a prank, masterminded by Graciela, that was wildly funny at the time but, in hindsight, might've gone too far.

The hijinks started small.

It was the dawn of the cordless phone—very early nineties. Graciela and I were each living and working in New York—I in midtown at CBS, and Graciela for future Bravolebrity Kelly Cutrone's downtown boutique public relations agency repping, among others, an unknown young Tyra Banks. One afternoon, I was lying on my bed chatting like a schoolgirl to my mom while my Agent Zero, Graciela, listened in on the living room extension. I told my mother that I was sorting and folding my laundry—not such a crazy thing, except that I wasn't doing that at all. My only task at that moment was playing a joke on my mom. So we talked about the latest in St. Louis and who my dad had run into while he was out jogging, and occasionally I'd make reference to a fave T-shirt I was "folding" or throw in a *Metropolitan Diary*esque yarn about my laundry room experience . . . all made up, of course. Then I slowly grew . . . "agitated."

"Gross! What is this?" I cried.

"What? What?" said Evelyn. "What is WHAT?!?!" She was half pleading, half castigating. You should know that my mother has a hair trigger that allows her to go from calm and cheerful to things-falling-from-the-sky shrieking in the space of a breath.

"Oh, nothing, I guess. I thought something was in the laundry."

And then we got back to the story of what her friend Harriette did. And again I'd interrupt.

"Gross—what is this stuff? It's everywhere!" I yelled.

"What is it? What STUFF?!"

"It's like—squishy and mushy a little, and all over my clothes! Gross!" I amped up the drama. "In the pockets of these pants! Damn! All in this shirt!"

"I don't understand what that could be! Is that from the laundry detergent?!"

"No—I can't . . . I have no idea. GROSS! Wait—it's like, it's like a banana."

"A BANANA!?" she screamed. Now I had her. Full bedlam. It was time for the turn.

"OH! I know what this is from . . . Oh, gross!" My voice loosened as I began laughing. "Oh, I know."

"What?! What could that possibly be from?" I'd hooked her. She wanted in.

I sighed. "Oh . . . I was just at a party the other night and Grac convinced me to put a banana in my pants. So of course I did and I guess when I took the pants off, the banana got into the laundry."

"GOT into the laundry? Andy? Graciela made you do that?"

"She didn't MAKE me, Mom . . . She just—it was funny. Don't worry about it. Wait 'til I tell her what happened. Oh shit, I'm gonna have to do all this laundry again . . ."

There was a long pause. And then: "Andy?"

"What?"

"Be your own man," my mother said.

"What? What are you saying?"

"I'm saying 'BE YOUR OWN MAN!' I'm serious!" And she was.

"Okay, but it was funny, Mom! I mean, you should've seen it."

"Yeah. I bet."

The laughter in my apartment started the second I hung up the phone. "Be your own man, Andy!" Grac squealed. "Be your own man!"

My mom thought Grac was pulling my strings like a marionette and that on my own I would act with some level of common sense, or even (gasp) judgment. But wait: My whole life, when I was being my own man, or my own boy before that, I was one hundred percent clown. I've always loved playing meaningless pranks on my parents, specifically my mom. I don't even know if "prank" is even the right word. Maybe fibbing? Long-drawn-out elaborate lies?

Once, as a kid, I went to the dinner table and told my parents

Grac, looking like the cat that ate the canary, with my parents

that Richard Nixon was dead. According to my *TV Guide* memory, *Hart to Hart* was on in those days, so Nixon was long out of office, but it still came as a big shock to my parents. "When? How?" they sputtered.

"This afternoon. I just saw on the news." I let it go on a few minutes and then told them I was kidding.

"Kidding? I don't get it," my mother said. "Is that funny? Do you find that funny?"

"Sort of." I chuckled.

"How? How is it funny if Richard Nixon died?" She turned to my father. "LOU—do you UNDERSTAND this? Lou?"

I knew it then but I didn't say. It wasn't Richard Nixon dying that was funny, it was the notion that I could march in, make up a bold-faced lie, and get a genuine, sometimes horrified, but always true, reaction out of my parents.

When I met Graciela, though, she helped me take it to another level. After all, what kind of fun is being "your own man" when you can conspire with a like-minded accomplice to achieve a higher plane of stupidity?

"Tell them we had sex," Grac said once. We were smoking pot and trying to think of new ways to disquiet my parents.

"That's just mean." Even the gays know which lines aren't crossed. "It'll get my dad's hopes up too much. And you're already on thin ice with my mom. Too risky."

"You want another hit?" Grac knew the herb would get us thinking.

"Okay. I know. I'll tell them I sprained—or broke?—my arm because I was dancing in a tub full of corn oil. And that you told me to do it."

"Too much of me telling you to do stuff," reasoned Grac. "I need to be involved but not totally responsible. Especially since you've been warned—"

"To be my own man. Okay."

☺

When your life and job are a little twisted, it's easy for plots to just appear. "Okay, so I told you that Queerdonna was a no-show at Bank last night," Grac said on the sixteenth minute of our fourth conversation of the morning. Even though we both had busy jobs, it was amazing how much time we were still able to spend on the phone with each other.

"Yeah, so who'd you get to replace her?" Queerdonna was the three-hundred-pound hairy Madonna impersonator who was just one of the colorful characters in Grac's life working for Kelly Cutrone.

"Lady Bunny did two numbers. Anyway, Queerdonna came by the office today and thought tonight was the night. And still wanted to get paid even though she missed it, the fat fuck!" And,

without missing a beat, Graciela said: "Hey. Tell your parents you're an Indian."

"Excuse me?"

"Tell them that you're convinced you're, like, an Indian."

I can guarantee that at that time we weren't the only two jack-asses who still didn't know you were supposed to say "Native American."

"Okay . . . What kind?"

"A Shawnee?"

A scheme was hatched. An ill-advised, politically incorrect scheme. "I'm gonna tell my mom that you introduced me to some guy at a club who looks just like me, and that he's an Indian. An actual Indian, a Shawnee." My mind was spinning. "And that, wow, do we really look alike. That's all I'll say, but I'll mention him in a week or so and keep bringing him in and that's maybe how I'll eventually be convinced . . ."

"That you're a Shawnee, too," said Graciela.

We put our work aside for much of that day, calling each other back and forth about eighteen times. Who could work? Besides, CBS should have been funding my creativity so I could run wild with an idea like this. Maybe it would translate to some out-of-the-box winner of an idea that would revolutionize morning television! Probably not, but we'd never know if we didn't follow through. The plan became more elaborate as the day continued, and so did our commitment to it.

At week's end, I had the ears of both my parents for our regularly scheduled phone call.

"Tad Martin calling collect," the operator said in classic monotone operatorspeak.

"I do NOT ACCEPT charges," Evelyn barked. She always felt she needed to act out her rejection of the call, as though the operator were going to call bullshit on our weekly charade and report us. Sometimes I actually took her rejection personally.

A minute later the phone rang. "Well, hello, Tad!" she chirped.

"Hey, Tad," said my dad. He loved it, too.

Step one of the plan was uneventful. I told them about Grac's friend the Indian who looked like me. I told them he was Shawnee. They took it as typical commentary from a night out in Madhattan and we moved along.

The next week, I told them I'd run into my Shawnee look-alike again . . . and that we'd spent hours discussing his heritage and that it was interesting—even inspiring—to me.

"What's so inspiring?" my mom asked.

"Well, his tribe had a lot of land taken away," I stumbled. "And he just has a lot of passion about his heritage. You should really see him, Mom. I mean, we could be twins."

"Well, maybe you're Indian." She chuckled. My father was silent. Probably watching TV with the phone eight inches away to reduce the impact of hearing Evelyn in quadraphonic surround-sound from the next room.

"Well, maybe I am," I said matter-of-factly. "He's bringing me some Shawnee books next week."

A week later I went for the kill. "These books are fascinating."

"What BOOKS, Andy?"

"These Shawnee books I got from Grac's friend. I look like these guys. I'm not kidding. The bone structure, the whole thing. REALLY interesting."

"Yeah, I bet you look like them," my mother snickered.

"No, I mean their hair, their eyes are just like mine."

"Uh-huh—and do they look Jewish, the Indians? JEWISH INDIANS?" She was feeling it. Her son was being a boob.

"I don't know, Mom." Time to turn up the volume. "I wonder sometimes . . ."

Pause. "You wonder WHAT?"

"Just, like, who I really am."

"Who you really ARE? Who are you? Who do you THINK you are?"

"Well, you know . . . these Shawnees had reservations in Southern Illinois. And I just wonder if somehow I could have Shawnee blood or be part Shawnee."

"What do you mean? You're JEWISH! You're RUSSIAN and POLISH! How do you think that happened? Do you think your grandfather had an AFFAIR with an INDIAN??"

"I don't know. You never know. What about YOUR grandfather?"

"WHAT?!?!?! LOU!? Are you hearing this?"

My father rejoined the land of the living. "I hear it. I don't really understand it, but I'm listening. Andy, do you think you could be an Indian, really?"

"I don't know. I'm just thinking about it. Is that really crazy? I mean, first this guy that looks like me and now this book."

My mother broke in. Obviously, my dad was doing no good by reasoning with me.

"The GUY who LOOKS like you has nothing to do with anything," she said. "I don't think there were Shawnees in Southern Illinois. I think they're something else."

"But you don't KNOW, Mom. I don't know either. I'm just thinking about it."

"Okay," she relented. "You're an Indian. What do I know? Your grandfather Allen had an affair and you're one-fourth Indian." She chuckled as though she was going to humor me, but I knew the truth: Inside, she was in knots of fury.

Grac and I were in rotten-kid heaven. I had slowly, deliberately gotten under my parents' skin with the most ridiculous notion since someone gave Pia Zadora a contract.

A few days later I lobbed this:

"You know what I realized? And it's ironic, actually. You can accept me completely for being gay but not for being Shawnee."

"WHAT?!" She screamed loud enough to rattle the ASK ME ABOUT MY GAY SON button on her lapel. "Oh my god, that is RIDICULOUS."

"Well, it may be true."

Brilliant. Mean, but brilliant.

This silliness had gone on for months when one day a new bolt of inspiration hit me during our afternoon uptown-downtown kill-time-at-work chat.

"We have to do something that gets to them in their home," I said. "To bring the whole thing to Biltmore Drive."

"Okay, here's something," Grac mused. "We should send them a letter or something from a fake, shady Shawnee organization thanking you for all the money you've given them. That'll get them going: Money that you've spent. Wasted money, Andy. YOUR wasted money."

My parents' biggest fear in life has always been my sister and me "throwing money away."

Another spoiled egg of a plan was hatched: Out of fervor for my hidden ancestry, I'd bid on a pair of Navajo Raindance boots at an auction benefiting some Displaced Navajo cause. Because now, one of my pet causes was inter-tribe unity, and I was a representative of goodwill from the Shawnee. The twist was that the boots had been mailed to my parents' house in St. Louis because the woman who took my check wrote down the address on my driver's license, which still had the Missouri address. The explanation was VERY iffy, but it wouldn't get much of a second thought.

Graciela's packaging was genius. She mocked up some letterhead using Wite-Out, scissors, and a Xerox machine and soon was "Lauren" writing from "Cause-Effective," a nonprofit who-knows-what of which I was a "booster." Between the words "Cause" and "Effective" was an arrow. Nice touch. The typed letter thanked me for my generous bid toward the boots and my endless enthusiasm for the organization. She handwrote and signed a PS: "All our books on Shawnee are being reordered—I will contact you when they arrive—Lauren." The boots Grac found in her closet were perfect; leftovers from a junior high school trip to Tucson—suede and cheap and full of fringe. She attached a lot number on a Minnie Pearl tag and marked it $300. Within a week the bundle of carefully crafted crap was headed straight for suburban terror.

My mother called the moment they arrived. "CBS," I said.

"Do you know what I just opened?" She sounded part amused, part amazed, and part pissed off.

"No, what?"

"The UGLIEST pair of SHOES that YOU supposedly BOUGHT at some auction."

"What? What shoes? Wait. How did those get THERE? You got my Navajo Raindance boots?"

"Oh, yeah, WE GOT 'EM!" She howled. "And WHO is LAUREN?"

"Who?"

"LAUREN. She wrote you a little note. There's a LETTER here, too, you know."

"Oh, LAUREN! I love her. What does it say?" My nonchalance was killing her.

"Your BOOKS that you ordered will be in soon. Andy, how much money are you THROWING AWAY on this? You spent THREE HUNDRED DOLLARS on these KIDS' COWBOY BOOTS?"

I was silent.

"This is RIDICULOUS! Do you realize that? YOU HAVE GOT TO GET OFF THIS! YOU ARE NOT AN INDIAN! WHAT IS IT GOING TO TAKE?"

She actually got to me. I was rattled and remorseful for the first time since we conceived of the whole thing. My mom genuinely thought I was crazy; she was worried. So was my dad, and when he called baffled about the boots, I felt like I'd gone too far, which often happens when you carelessly hatch a silly plan. Graciela agreed. "We have to end it," she said.

I had been a Shawnee for months, and now the game was up. I was scheduled to go home a few weeks later, and I'd be there over April Fools' Day. When better to break the news?

"That is too perfect," said Graciela. "This is going to be the April Fools classic of our time. I need to be there." And she was right, it would be something. But I had to do it alone.

Before I could make it home, the tide turned.

"Well, you're never going to believe what happened today." It was my mom on the phone. This was a common opening line, and I braced myself to hear who she'd outed me to from my childhood. Would it be Nardie Stein, my camp director? A former babysitter of mine, perhaps? My mom LOVED to out me to people.

"Does Andy have a girlfriend?" someone would ask her unassumingly.

"A BOYfriend?" she'd say. "No, he hasn't met the right GUY. He's GAY!"

"I was at a tea at Helen Kornblum's house," she said this time. Right down the street, the Kornblum home was a veritable hub of the great liberal minds of the Midwest. She continued, "She has the best photography collection. You really should go by there when you're home. Just to see it."

"So you keep telling me," I groaned. "What? What happened?"

"Well, you know Helen has a house in Santa Fe and collects quite a bit of art in addition to photography, and Andy, I'm NOT KIDDING: I want you to go see this photography when you're home. IT'S REALLY SOMETHING!"

"The more you tell me to go, the more I'm *not going to*. What happened?" I was the one irritated this time.

"Okay! Jesus, you are a PILL, you know that? Anyway I met this woman who Helen knows from Santa Fe and I told her about those Navajo boots and—"

"Wait, you did what?" I interrupted.

"I told her you bought those boots at an auction and you know what she said?" Mom was gleeful now. "She said you probably got a good deal for them for three hundred dollars and that that stuff is really hot right now. Everything like that is going for big money down there!"

I was floored. She was actually EXCITED about my boots now and thought that I was on to something. She continued.

"But you know, she's not the first person who told me that. I was telling Cheli about the whole Shawnee thing the other day." Cheli, mom's manicurist, knew more about me than most of my relatives did. "She said that Indian stuff is all over the place right now. And she said she knew someone who was Shawnee . . ."

As my mom continued, my heart was wrenched.

Acceptance. The last thing I ever expected from this whole

mishegas stupid joke. My mom was beginning to accept, or at least adapt to, the lie I had been hammering into her head for months, and furthermore, she was working so hard to be okay with it that she was starting to TELL people about it. She had begun outing me as an Indian! She had accepted my being gay and now, in her way, was accepting my being an INDIAN—or at least THINKING I was one.

Do I have the best parents in the world? And do I deserve them?

On April Fools' Day, I brought the fraudulent Navajo Rain-dance boots into the kitchen and set them on the counter. My parents were settling into their ritual 6 p.m. glass of J&B on the rocks when I asked them what they thought of the boots.

"Well, I STILL think they're pretty ugly. But what do I know?" Mom said. "I mean, Helen's friend did say you probably got a great deal on them. I guess it's an investment?"

"Dad?" I implored.

"Well, I just don't know what you're gonna do with them. You say you're putting them out for display, but then what? I just don't see any use for them is all." That's my dad: reasonable to a fault.

I broke it all with a big breath. "It was a joke," I said.

"What?" my mother asked. "What was a joke?"

"Everything. The Shawnee thing. I don't really think I'm a Shawnee." I was not feeling good about myself. It seemed too big—or stupid—to explain.

"What do you MEAN it was a joke??" my mom asked. "Which part? The shoes are a joke? You're telling me that these SHOES are a JOKE?"

"Not the shoes. Well, yes, the shoes. Everything, really. I mean, Grac and—"

"GRAC and you," she interrupted.

"Yes, we came up with this kind of ridiculous thing about me being a Shawnee and just really kept going with it. And, I mean, it was funny. Because I love to wind you up, you know that. But the shoes—these are Grac's from forever ago and she wrote the letter from the charity." I was spitting it all out as fast as I could.

I'll never forget the way my parents looked on that April Fools' Day. Standing in the kitchen of our colonial home, drinks in hand, faces calm, both completely blank and uncomfortably puzzled.

"How long?" My mom finally spoke. "How long has this been going on?"

"I don't know. A while. Six months, maybe." I was speaking softly now. The fun was long over.

"Six months you've been doing this. Why?" My mom was as still as a painting.

I did not have an answer.

"I mean, why? Was it funny? Why did you do this?" She seemed on the verge of being genuinely upset.

"I think originally just, well, you know how I play tricks on you sometimes. I mean, I thought it was funny and you have to admit—those shoes—I mean, that letter . . . it's pretty funny." I could hear my own voice and it sounded like I was trying to convince myself. I was such a jerk.

Then my mom's face turned. One thing about my mom: She appreciates a good joke. And I had gotten her. And now she knew it. She laughed. Thank God. "This is unbelievable. I mean, what a joke." She was taking it well. I was relieved. Then my father left the room without saying a word.

"Lou? LOU?! Where are you going? Come in here."

"I'm going in the other room to watch TV," he said. He had better things to do.

On that day, the art of the prank more or less died for me. I had gotten such pleasure from the whole thing, but my father's quiet disappointment erased it all. I don't blame him for not knowing how to react. Now that it's in the rearview mirror, I hardly know what it was about, either. An armchair psychologist could maybe surmise that I'd spent so many years hiding my true self from them—my gay self—that once I was out and they knew who I was, there was a hole left where the lies and pretending had been. But then I remember that I'd told them Richard Nixon was dead when I was still in the closet, and I realize maybe I was just being a dick.

Did they get over it? Yes. Did I? Not really. I never played another joke on them again. I guess you could say I became my own man. Though, in truth, Graciela probably paid the greatest price. My mom hasn't believed a word out of her mouth since.

Ross Perot and me in a rare moment when both of our mouths were shut

BREAKING NEWS

You might be thinking that my emotional maturity was stunted at age thirteen—and if so you may have a point. But when I wasn't goofing off, my job at CBS had become intense, and often really serious. I was in the thick of a few bona fide disasters—and I don't mean when we added a live audience. While I loved covering entertainment stories and spectacular events such as the Olympics, I'm most proud of my work in breaking news situations. I was actually on the scene for hurricanes, floods, fires, plane crashes, and the aftermath of a bombing.

The first major disaster I covered for CBS was way bigger than those floods in Petaluma and, ironically enough, in my home state of Missouri. The Mississippi and Missouri Rivers had overflowed simultaneously, covering a massive swath of land. This flood ended up lasting seven months, from April to October, and would become, until Katrina, the most costly and devastating flood in American history.

CBS sent me to Southern Illinois for what was supposed to be just a day, to produce a live shot. I grabbed a rescue worker named Rick Shlepper (in case you didn't know, in Yiddish that means someone who's awkward or dumb—I love a name with a double meaning). By the time we went off the air, I was told that I was staying indefinitely and that Harry Smith was coming down to broadcast from a different water-gutted town every day. I spent the next week shooting during the day, writing a script and editing the piece at night, then driving to a new spot and doing it all over again.

My next stop was St. Louis but in a part of town I'd never even seen, and I felt far from home. I was in a neighborhood of low-lying land and tract houses when I met an older man named Rufus White, living on his own. He showed us around his soaked living room—all of his belongings were ruined, the place stank like hell, and the floor was a big muddy puddle. As we surveyed the damage, shoes soggy and noisy, he tried to salvage scraps of keepsakes and knickknacks. I watched him go through his damaged photographs—the record of his life erased by water. When I asked him about his plans for the future, he tried to be optimistic but his voice cracked. At that moment, I realized that I had started to cry.

A few days later, I arrived in Rocheport, Missouri, before my colleagues. It looked like it had once been a beautiful town. My assignment was to book flood victims for the next day's show. I met a group of wonderful people who were filling sandbags for anybody who needed them in the parking lot of the firehouse. The simple things people were doing for each other felt very Midwestern, and that's when I finally felt I was indeed back home. I joined them, shoveling sand for several hours and feeling good about helping, rather than just taping and watching. Eventually I hit a wall, probably built on a combination of sleep deprivation, hunger, and pre-heatstroke. I'd been up for a couple days, I stank, and I could feel myself on the precipice of turning nasty, so I wandered away from the folks I was helping to be alone. Kind of like David Banner would right before he turned into the Incredible Hulk— though no such transformation awaited me.

A couple hours later I was sitting on the curb in the middle of town talking on what was probably a brick-sized cell phone (that's how we rolled in '93), and I looked up to see Harry, normally one of the sunniest and most decent people in the business, towering over me. I got off the phone to discover that he was in a mood as bad as mine. He said he didn't like the guests I had booked for the next day's show and told me to un-book them. He paused and glowered at me. "You're putting out really bad energy. It's all wrong, sitting down on the ground on your phone while other people are going through this mess and working all around you." He turned and walked away.

I was sleepless and dirty and pissy, and at that moment I thought I might cry. Or maybe I would just leave. What the hell was I doing there, anyway? Was this what I'd signed up for? I flashed back to my lunch five years before with Susan Lucci. Should I have tried to work in soaps? Before I could answer my own question, a woman came over and thanked me for helping to fill sandbags and for being a considerate reporter.

"See that man over there?" I pointed to Harry. "Will you tell him that?" And she did. Probably not the most altruistic request, but I felt somewhat vindicated.

The next morning's mission was right up my alley. We got word that Ross Perot was coming to Rocheport to survey the flood damage. We booked him to talk to Harry live. Perot had taken the country by storm the year before as a fast-talking, shoot-from-the-hip Texas billionaire who'd made an unlikely, but quite serious, run for the presidency. Perot didn't win, but his "maverick" campaign style—candid, anti-insider, folksy—set the stage for your George W. Bushes and Sarah Palins in the decades to come. Perot was like a one-man band, traveling with no handlers or hype. I was put on Perot duty and he was sent a message to meet a kid with a ponytail (I swear, that hairstyle will haunt me forever) in the lobby of our Best Western hotel at 5 a.m.

Morning dew covered my filthy rental-car windshield as I rolled out of the parking lot with the most recent object of America's obsession as my passenger. He exuded eccentricity and a heavy scent of lotion. (No surprise there.)

"Say, boy, got any SHPRAA!?!" he shouted. I couldn't understand him. "SHPRAA!" he repeated, unhelpfully. "Got any?"

What the hell was this pint-sized politician yelling at me about at 5 a.m.? I told him I still didn't understand. "The wipers! You need SHPRAA! Clean 'em, kid! Use your SHPRAA!"

He wanted me to clean the damn windows with the wiper spray. I did, and he visibly calmed. Then the ride turned into the Ross Perot Show. I barely had to ask him a question before his conversational autopilot kicked in and then there was no shutting him up. He told me he'd run into Michael Jackson in the Bahamas. Jackson apparently said, "You wouldn't remember me, but we met a few years ago." Perot thought that was hilarious. "HOW am I gonna FORGIT Michael Jackson?! Now, later that day, I took him motorboating with that kid he's always with—the *Home Alone* kid. Nice kid!" (Okay, so Ross Perot, Michael Jackson, and Macaulay Culkin are motorboating in the Bahamas. Is that not the beginning of a joke? Or the end?)

Perot was proud of the fact that he traveled sans entourage and he wore it like a badge, but his boast became my burden when we pulled into Rocheport. Everyone in town wanted a piece of Perot. Suddenly, I was clearing a path for him like a security dude, answering reporters' questions about whether they could interview him, taking pictures of him with fans, and all the time attempting to move him closer to Harry and the live shot we had set up. It was, as they say in the news biz, a clusterfuck, and I was at the center of the cluster.

My day as Ross Perot's personal escort wore on. The longer we were together, the more I realized that Mr. Perot never, ever shut up, blabbing away without caring who he was talking to or whether anyone was even listening. I had finally met my match! Years later, sitting in the middle of the Season 4 *Real Housewives of New York* reunion show, I was overcome with a feeling of déjà vu when I realized that my PTSD (Perot Talking Stress Disorder) had been aggravated by the ladies.

After I dropped Grandpappy Perot back at the hotel, I was scheduled to go up in a helicopter to shoot a piece with a team of search and rescue guys. I had done a similar piece with the Coast Guard on a search-and-rescue mission over the Louisiana bayous in the days after Hurricane Andrew, and I couldn't wait to go again. First, there was the chance that we'd be able to help someone and get some dramatic footage. Second, Ross Perot wasn't coming. Finally, there's just something about being up in a whirlybird with burly rescue guys in jumpsuits that's a brilliant palate cleanser to a sleepless week. Everything went well, I gathered some aerial shots of the flood, and we landed without incident. I got my seventh wind and was happily editing my footage in a remote truck that we were working out of somewhere near Jefferson City when, around midnight, the door of the truck opened and Harry grabbed me.

"I have a big favor to ask you," he said.

I bristled. I was still smarting from the other day when he'd chastised me for giving off bad energy. "I beg you to get me a toothbrush," Harry said. "Can you? I have to go to sleep and I don't know where to look for one, and I don't have anyone else to ask. I will be forever indebted."

A *toothbrush*? I drove around like a maniac—cursing at the top of my lungs—looking for an open gas station. I finally found one and drove back to where The Anchor was waiting, and I bit my tongue as I handed off his toiletries.

The next day was Friday. Everyone was in a great mood. Harry was going home to New York for the weekend and he and I drove to St. Louis together. High from a week of grueling work and a light at the end of the tunnel, I forgot my anger as he told me stories of his early days.

We pulled up at the airport. Harry gathered his things, then shocked me by turning to me and acknowledging the elephant in the car. "I'm sorry I yelled at you at the fire station in Rocheport," he said. "I was a putz."

Harry was, and is, a truly good guy, and working with him reminded me of why I loved this business. In a galaxy of journalists who pretend to be "folksy" and of the people, he is the real deal.

It was also while covering breaking news that I got my first taste of Orange County. Prior to my visit as a news producer, the only thing I knew about the OC was that it was home to Disneyland and rich right-wingers. One day in New York, I was sitting at my desk, whining to a coworker that I had nothing to do that week. As if summoned by the very words, my senior producer appeared to tell me that wildfires were raging in Laguna Beach and I had to go. I went from thinking of leaving work early to hustling home to pack and catch a 6 p.m. flight to Los Angeles for who knew how long.

Any kind of location shoot is dependent on luck. A location shoot for a disaster? Luck sends her ugly stepsister, Pandemonium. On the way to Laguna Beach to get this live shot of the wildfires, it was unclear whether there'd even be a satellite truck to *do* the live shot. After hours of phone calls and confusion and maybe a few threats on people's lives, I was ultimately told there would be a KCBS truck waiting for us. When I arrived, there was a truck, and suddenly it was 2:45 a.m.—fifteen minutes before our first hit, when the *CBS This Morning* was to go live on the East Coast. At this point I was driving up a mountain looking for a site where we could both get a transmission signal *and* see a fire in the background. (Tip from a Pro: You cannot do a live shot from a fire without a fire or smoke in the background.) It was getting so late and we were cutting it so close that I ultimately made the call to just stop in the middle of Newport Coast Road and crank up the satellite right where we were.

A crusty CBS News veteran, who I'd been instructed would be meeting me at the location to do the live report, arrived in a cab. When he got out, he took one look at our setup, charged over to me, and barked, "Have you ever done anything like this before?"

In truth, I hadn't done much at this point—a plane crash, a hurricane, and the Great Flood—but I didn't tell him that. As far as I was concerned, the fire wasn't the only tragedy happening in Laguna, because we had been in full Keystone Kops mode all morning, losing trucks and changing locations over and over. We hadn't had time to regroup before *CBS This Morning* started at 4 a.m. The bureau had sent some backup to help me book guests, but, unfortunately, that help came in the form of an entertainment producer who booked some old men who were on the scene to wash out the firemen's sooty eyes. Is hearing from the eye-cleaners interesting to anyone, or is it a TLC show in the making? When the crusty newsman saw these guests, he flipped out—at me. "Go book some actual firemen, why don't you?!" he screamed. While I didn't disagree with him about the news value of the eye-washers, I already had an idea what the answer was going to be when I left the site to request an interview with some firemen. It turns out that no firemen were available to be on the show as they were otherwise engaged, *PUTTING OUT FIRES*!

I did, however, meet a home owner who had just lost his house. Bull's-eye. I convinced him to come with me to the satellite truck, explaining that his story would help bring attention to what was going on in his area. Then, on my way back to the truck, devastated home owner in my possession, I got lost. When we finally arrived back at the spot where I was certain I had left the truck, a local crewmember came over to tell me that it had been moved because the smoke was inhibiting their ability to get a clean shot. The poor home owner lost his shit. He began screaming at me, saying I was leading him on a wild-goose chase. It was actually a wild *truck* chase, but for once I kept my mouth shut.

I did wind up getting the poor home owner to the new location, where he was interviewed, but he remained furious with me. Who could blame him? As if that man hadn't been through enough.

After sucking up smoke all night, I was informed by the newsdesk that I'd be spending the day doing something far worse and possibly more damaging to my health: shooting a piece with the crusty newsman who'd screamed at me. I almost had my *own* meltdown, and I cursed and screamed the whole way back to meet Mr. Mean. By the time I got to the truck, the guy had fled—I think he was as excited to shoot with me as I with him—and I got a message from New York that instead, I was to meet the very kind CBS News reporter John Blackstone back in town. John and I spent the day driving around neighborhoods formerly made up of brand-new gorgeous mini-palazzos. Now the homes were gutted. We met home owners who had lost everything but inspired us with their gratitude and calm. These victims were different from the people I'd met covering the Great Flood. They were fortunate, and had the resources to rebuild, and though I didn't know it at the time, in just a few years, and through a series of then unimaginable circumstances, I'd come to know those even newer mansions like my own while making the maiden show in the Real Housewives franchise. That day, we shot until three in the afternoon, and though I was again without sleep, I nearly levitated when I found out that Blackstone had arranged for us to beat the traffic back to CBS Television City (at least a two- or three-hour drive) by taking a helicopter. Landing on the roof of that historic building, once the home of *Carol Burnett* and *Sonny and Cher*, made up for the fact that I was wheezing from smoke and smelled like a blast furnace. When I got out, tapes in hand, I skipped across the roof, loudly singing, "Gypsies, Tramps and Thieves."

But the truth was, the job was really starting to get to me. Or *I* was starting to get to me. My emotional disconnect from the stories

I was covering was nothing new, but the realization that I was getting better at the disconnect was disturbing. It wasn't that I didn't feel *anything*, it was that I was growing more and more able to put aside the human faces of my stories for the stories themselves. Flying in, helicoptering out as fast as I could—I didn't know how long I could sustain it.

AHA MOMENTS WITH
OPRAH

This is a perfect time in our little story to pause and pay devotion to Miss Oprah Winfrey. Over the course of 4,561 episodes, I logged at least 3,192.7 hours of my life watching Oprah. That's equivalent to the course hours necessary to earn ten master's degrees, but Oprah was my academia. And in the course of my studies, I noticed the show's progression over the years: how she used to hug and touch everybody and run around among them, and then how they just put the mic in the audience and people stepped up to it and Oprah stayed on the stage, at a distance. Finally, the audience members stopped being allowed to talk at all and just fainted and cheered like people who'd been healed by the Reverend Ernest Angley. Despite these shifts, and through all the theme songs (especially the one Oprah recorded herself, and the one with Miss Patti LaBelle), the different set decor and hairdos and weights, *Oprah* remained one of the best-produced shows on television.

As a TV producer, I was fascinated to see how Oprah's show evolved from fairly exploitative standard talk show fare to celebrity-driven and public-service programming with the book club and courses in miracles and the Angel Network and a school in Africa. For all of the crap that folks throw around about the idol worship of Oprah and her deified persona, she's done so much good that the haters should consider just shutting their faces. Oprah's genius was such that she could make important, newsy topics entertaining and set an agenda no matter what the subject.

I sat glued to every episode of her final season and thought she went out on top. No matter what the issue, no matter whether the audience was expected to be quiet, no matter if she was standing by a Radio Flyer wagon full of fat, Oprah's personality kept me watching. She is someone whom everybody wants as her or his best friend, myself more than included. But I'm here to tell you, I've struck out three times with Lady O. My professional karma with Oprah stinks. And that is something I have to live with every day. And no matter how hard I've tried to live *The Secret*, I've had to keep this terrible secret. Until now.

Since the day I started working at *CBS This Morning* in 1990 I tried to get an "in" with Oprah and somehow get her on our air. I badgered her publicist, Colleen, for *years* and finally booked a date for O.W. to come into the studio for a taped interview with Paula Zahn, whom Oprah had known for quite some time. She was coming in advance of the Daytime Emmys, for a regular ol' interview. (Some would say it was a "profile-raising" interview, but since we had none and she didn't need that, I'd call it a "sympathy interview.") Simultaneously, I was producing a weeklong series featuring the big talk show hosts of the day—Geraldo, Joan Rivers, Sally Jessy Raphael—in which I had requested that Oprah take part, in addition to her interview with Paula, but which Oprah, via her publicist Colleen, had declined. Looking back, I don't blame her. Oprah was already in a different league, and she didn't need to be a part of our series. But I was feeling spunky and decided not to take no for an answer. Oprah's interview was to be taped after we'd gone off the air for the morning, and we'd timed her arrival so the studio was fired up with Paula in her chair ready to go as soon as Team Winfrey swept in. She arrived wearing a tenty bright green outfit that was, from the vantage point of 2012, Garanimalsesque. She was Outsized Oprah: together, in-command, super-nice, all-pleasing, touchy-feely—and surrounded by handlers including an assistant publicist (not that naysayer Colleen, to my initial delight).

But I had set up a con job. Oprah, my idol, was the unwitting victim in a scheme that I can only look back on now with horror. I'd casually told Paula and my executive producer that Oprah hadn't yet *totally* agreed to be a part of my talk show series, but that when the (agreed-upon) interview #1 had concluded, the control room should simply keep the cameras rolling, Paula should keep Oprah in the chair, and it would actually be fine for her to begin a separate (not-agreed-upon) interview for my (stupid) talk show series. I was vague with Paula. I told her to in turn be very vague with Oprah about our intended use for this separate (not-agreed-upon) interview. Dear reader, *I was not living my best life.* I recall this now with a mix of total shame and maybe the tiniest speck of admiration for my ballsiness. What the hell was I thinking? What a little liar I was! This weasely shit doesn't fly, and I can't imagine doing something like this today with anyone, never mind a star of Oprah's prominence. It would put the show in jeopardy, it would put the anchor in a bad position, and if things were to go really sour it would be a fire-able offense. It just never should have happened.

As we began (unauthorized) interview #2, Oprah's assistant publicist (still not Colleen, but also not a total idiot, apparently) was in the Green Room, watching and wondering what this second interview was and why she hadn't been told a single thing about it. I feigned ignorance. Then, like any professional who is good at her job, she slowly pieced together what was happening and told me that we could not air it under any circumstances.

Like the lying weasel-coward that I was, I hung the blame on Paula, saying they were just "talking." I explained to her (dishonestly) how important the series was to Paula and that I didn't actually intend to air it. (I totally intended to air it.) I was still delusionally determined to legitimize my (stupid) series by having Oprah as a part of it. As Team Winfrey left the studio, I made myself scarce, knowing that I'd be hearing from Colleen in Chicago but kinda feeling like I'd somehow won the day. I was under the impression that my con had ultimately worked because we had Oprah on tape. That was all that mattered. The worst was over.

The phone rang at my desk.

"Andrew . . . it's Oprah."

She was calling from her limo. Keep in mind, this was the early nineties, years before everyone had a cell phone. Calling from a car was most impressive. Calling from a car and being Oprah was THE most impressive. And she was calling *me*! I lost all professionalism, and also full sight of the fact that she probably hadn't phoned to chat or congratulate me for anything. I began hyperventilating like a crazed fan receiving an out-of-the-blue Oprah call on *Oprah*. I was a blithering idiot, not believing my *luck* that Oprah was calling *me*. I sputtered and screamed. Had I won a trip!?

"Calm down, Andrew," Oprah said. "Calm *down*." And I did. I guess she was used to calming down hysterical people. "I am very upset about what happened," she said. "I need to talk with Paula."

Oh. My. Lord. Oprah was "upset." Because of me. Because I'd

lied to Oprah. I felt sick. I was in Big, Big, Big Trouble. Big TrOuble. On the outs with Oprah. Whom I loved. I'd hurt the one I loved. And whom I'd wanted to love me. This did not feel good. And—worst of all—she was about to take out her anger on Paula, my boss in this world of television I'd waited all my life to be a part of. Because I'd blamed all of my misdeeds on her.

I was shaking. Years later, in 2006, I would watch James Frey sweating and squirming under Oprah's gaze and think: *I've been there, brother. I've so been there.*

I called the control room and had them pull Paula from the studio to get on the phone with Oprah. I ran to the other end of the CBS Broadcast Center. The building is an old milk factory the length of an entire city block and I was just able to breathlessly intercept Paula right as she hung up. Paula looked at me and said, "What just happened?" She was confused and not completely pleased, but she wasn't angry. We were on the same team, and she trusted me. She trusted me!

Somewhere between leaving our studio and getting into her car, the assistant publicist had clued Oprah in on what had gone down. On the phone, she told Paula that she was displeased with how unprofessionally we'd handled this situation after her publicist had made it clear that they could not accommodate our request for two interviews. *However,* Oprah continued, the second interview had gone so well that she had decided to allow us to use it. Don't forget: This was Forgiving, Pleasing-Others, Early-Nineties Oprah. Who knows what would have happened in another Oprah era. I breathed a huge, shuddering sigh of relief.

Amazingly, I had not only conned this icon whom I loved with all of my greasy little heart, I had also allowed Paula to be implicated in my sordid scheme by withholding the entire plot from her, which she now made me explain in detail. It had worked—surely the singular reason I wasn't fired—but it had been shoddily executed and had put Paula in a terrible, terrible spot.

Paula sent Oprah flowers and a heartfelt note. I called Colleen in Chicago and apologized as profusely as was humanly possible. She was rightly furious and never forgave me. We aired the two-part interview as part of the (stupid) series, which made little impact on our ratings. I figured that I had seen the last of Oprah.

My Oprah Angel Network Book Club Aha Moment regarding this experience was learning always to tell the truth, to be up-front, and not to lie on behalf of, or to, your anchorwoman. If you do it the truthful way, sometimes you will get what you want and other times you will not, but your reputation and your word will always be good.

Oh, but that was only Strike One.

A couple of years later, I somehow booked another interview with Oprah and planned to fly to Chicago for the day with Ms. Zahn to shoot it at Harpo Productions. Was Oprah so highly busy that she'd completely forgotten the bad blood between us? Or was she so highly evolved that she'd absolved me of my sins? Either way, the thrill of having a second chance with Oprah could only be matched by my enthusiasm for another newsworthy event occurring at the same time. Newsworthy to me, anyway. After growing my hair out from a buzz cut to a Jewfro to an early nineties ponytail, I was finally ready to cut it off, and my executive producer had greenlit a "producer makeover segment" featuring me and a colleague, Judy Hole.

I deemed my haircut to be as important, or of more importance, than any live segment I'd ever produced. Thankfully my coworkers also viewed my ponytail with similar gravity. And so it was Beverly Hills hairstylist Christophe, who had just given President Bill Clinton that notorious two-hundred-dollar, runway-closing, air-traffic-jamming scandal of a haircut on the tarmac at LAX, who would be my barber.

Thoughts of the upcoming haircut consumed me in the same way I'd later obsess over preparing for my stint onstage with the

B-52s, meaning I completely overhyped this as an epic event to anyone who'd listen. If you think I'm a li'l bit of a windbag now, imagine me talking about my hair 24/7. I don't know how anyone tolerated me. Around that time I ran into photographer Spencer Tunick at a party. Tunick is now known around the world for taking large-scale nude photographs in public places (say, 5,200 naked people in front of the Sydney Opera House). In those days, he was taking solo nude shots in public places, and he encouraged me to document my lustrous long curls before they were shorn. I agreed—it was important (for the arts) to memorialize my tresses hanging on my naked shoulders somewhere in Manhattan.

Days before the haircut, I met Tunick at 6 a.m. (he always shot in the wee hours to minimize chances of arrest or complaints by passersby) in front of the New York Public Library. I was, as instructed, wearing sweatpants so I wouldn't have any lines on my waist from underwear. (The *thought* that goes into every work of art is just something, isn't it?) He had me climb up onto one of the two lions guarding the library; I'm not sure whether it was the lion named Patience or the lion named Fortitude, but it seems pretty obvious that he was trying to draw an artistic parallel between the permanence of the lion's mane and the impending slaughter of mine. Or he just wanted to take some skin shots of a dumb kid on a statue. He instructed me to quickly strip off my sweats and lean my bare ass against the stone. Sorry, Patience or Fortitude. The photographer then directed me to assume various poses at the base of the lion, while I tried to convey any feeling other than "I'm freezing" with only gooseflesh as a prop and not a fluffer in sight. Then, like most other nude adventures, we were done in about four minutes.

The night before the big makeover, I barely slept. The next morning I went to the studio to get my "before" photo taken (with my clothes on this time), and my physical condition would've been diagnosed by any doctor as "barfy." Throughout this entire tribulating trial, I spent every spare non-hair moment scrambling to set up the final details for Paula Zahn's interview with Oprah Winfrey in her study at Harpo. I was determined not to screw things up this time. Yet the interview would take place on the same afternoon as my own live reveal, and believe it or not, the haircut loomed larger and more nerve-racking than seeing Oprah again.

I stumbled into the L'Oréal salon for my appointment, and when they offered me coffee or tea, I requested Valium. Christophe studied my face and gave me three options:

1. A Sting crew cut.
2. Short on the sides, curly on top.
3. Straighten it "and see what happens."

He had mentioned straightening the day before and I'd wigged out, but two friends in the know separately reassured me that this was the way to go. So without listening closely to the "and see what happens," I chose door number three, and he cut that tail right off. It *felt* good, so I relaxed a bit as he quickly shaped some kind of flip look on my head, and I noticed a hairdo emerging that seemed like it could be a winner. Then came the straightening, which was very painful.

I'd taken Christophe's advice to "see what happens," and in the end, the master had developed a look for me that I felt would have been at home on the pages of *GQ*. A look that I could style with or without a pompadour, *my option*. If it's hard for you to understand my gaiety at the very notion of having a hair option, you are a person who has never had Jewish hair. I freaked out again, this time in a good way. I met six friends at Coffee Shop in Union Square for an unveiling and got rave reviews. I felt so hot that I laughed at my foolish self for every second that I'd wasted worrying.

The next morning, I was picked up at 5:45 for my live reveal and interview, and Christophe was waiting in the makeup room to do my do for the "after" shots. Everyone at work was ogling the new hair.

My on-camera appearances prior to that point had been rich but limited. When I was eight, I'd done an interview on the local news in St. Louis regarding my love of Pop Rocks. At twelve, I showed up on local TV coverage of election night as Senator Eagleton's "Littlest Volunteer." Stoned in college one day, I called in to *Donahue* and asked President Reagan's press secretary a question. Probably four years later, from my parents' den, I phoned *Larry King Live* and yelled at Marilyn Quayle with great passion as Evelyn and Lou looked on in shock and awe. (Of those early TV "appearances," yelling at the Second Lady was by far the most satisfying.)

Despite my impressive on-air résumé, this was to be my *network* debut. I had read—and probably written, for that matter—the questions Paula was about to ask me, and I wanted her to stick to them. No hardballs! I was trying to act as her producer, and my own, all while the segment was live on the air. This is something I've grown used to doing now, and probably one of the reasons that transitioning to a host's chair on live television years later didn't scare the crap out of me. But this first time? At least one brick was shat.

For me, the haircut was as close to looking like Donny Osmond as I'd ever get, and running my fingers through my cowlick on TV made me feel badass and chic. Like Ponyboy from *The Outsiders*. It felt natural and fun being on-camera, but it was my home turf—our set, with our crew, and with Paula. It was a great little segment, as I remember it. I had set up an extensive phone tree of friends and family beforehand, and the reviews were through the roof. As Paula and I hustled to Newark Airport immediately after, I felt like my feet weren't touching the ground. We celebrated with a 10 a.m. hot dog and she generously used her frequent flier miles to upgrade my seat to first class. One of our flight attendants had seen the segment and recognized me by my new swingy style. That's the funny thing about TV that you often forget when you're working in it—people everywhere watch. Even the lowest-rated stuff. If you make something and put it on TV, somebody somewhere is almost certainly watching.

When the plane was finally in the air, Paula and I reclined in our luxurious seats and went deep with each other. I felt important: still a producer, but now, in a way, not so far from an anchor. We gossiped about which producers were good and what we should do with the show; I pussyfooted around my opinions of the other on-air people and the whole conversation culminated in my leading a delicious trip down Joan-Diane-and-Katie Lane, which was always my favorite topic to bring up with her.

We got to Harpo Studios, and it was, hold on to your socks . . . amazing! Vaulted ceilings, wood beams, a café, and the enormous and beautiful palace that was the *Oprah* studio. As we were walking in, out came Oprah's personal chef, Rosie Daley. I felt like I was at a character lunch at Oprahland. She was so down-to-earth and welcoming, I wanted to eat her up. Everything was so warm and inviting, it was like floating in the amniotic fluid of Oprah's womb. But then we were led to Oprah's study, and it was somehow like being in her womb *and* suckling sweet cream from her bosom all at once. (Okay, that was gross, but I think you get my spirit.) The study was homey yet stately, professional yet personal: pure Oprah. We were told she was running very late, and we happily changed our return flights, then sat and soaked it all in.

I don't know what had me the most fired up: my on-air make-over (!), my new look (!!), Paula bumping me up to first class with her (!!!), the flight attendant having seen my makeover on TV and loving it (!!!!), or showing off my new look to Oprah under the roof of Harpo (!!!!!). Not to mention that I was about to get another chance with my Queen.

Oprah entered. Thin, Superstar, Mid-Nineties Oprah. She was very matter-of-fact. All business, this Oprah. She sat down, and as the interview began she fluidly transitioned into TV Oprah. A glowy golden aura radiated from her. Paula asked her how it could be possible that she was "every woman"—as her theme song suggested—while simultaneously being a now svelte multigazil-lionaire, perhaps growing apart from her viewers. Oprah turned it on, telling us a story about an hour she'd just taped on the topic of anorexia and the women who'd touched her. She cried! She became . . . "Oprah"! She went from cool to warm to hot damn. THAT'S how she's every woman, I thought, she sees and FEELS and is just IN IT. She goes there. I went there, too.

The interview over, I was dying to have my own personal "favorite things" moment by snapping a photo with Oprah, *my* longtime favorite thing, with my most recent favorite thing, my new GQ/NKOTB haircut. I moved toward her, camera in hand, for the pic—and was restrained (gently) by her assistant.

"No photos with Oprah," she said briskly. Time stopped for me. I felt so uncomfortable, two feet tall and very dumb. I'd forgot-ten: I wasn't there for a photo op with Oprah, I wasn't there as a fan. I was there to produce an interview, which had gone well and which was now over and it was time to take my new hairdo and my unprofessional self back to New York. I couldn't bear to look, but I'm sure my hair wilted three inches that day.

My Oprah Angel Network Book Club Aha Moment regarding this experience was not to ask for something personal, like a picture, during a professional situation. It is uncool and amateurish. (That being said, *I'll* take any picture with anyone at almost any given moment—not just because I know the feeling of wanting one, but also because I'm shocked that anybody wants my picture.) My other Aha Moment is that Jewish boys should NOT straighten their hair, which quickly went from fabulous to bad to worse. Christophe's "and see what happens" went from a gentle, encouraging suggestion to an ominous curse. *SEE WHAT HAPPENS?!* A haircut, after all, still has to contend with the *hair*, and my temporary Joey McIntyre special was no match for thousands of years of kink. On my own, I had no aptitude with a blow-dryer, and though Lynn bought me some black hair care products, which was a noble last gasp, my hair quickly became a losing proposition. The ease with which it was delivered and demonstrated could never be re-created by me, so I gave up on it and sadly cut off the kicky cowlick. But as my hair was being clipped into a decidedly less glamorous cap, I felt like I was transforming into something better. I instantly regretted all those years of having a ponytail in the first place. Everybody was right: I looked better without it. Good riddance to bad plumage.

Although my 'fro had shrunk, my self had grown, just as the Queen of Talk urged us to do through our TV screens every day. But since we're keeping score: That overreaching photo attempt was only Strike Two with the real-life Oprah.

A few years later, ever-resilient me was back in Chicago working on some story, and I set up a quick "hello" meeting with Oprah's new publicist, who was gloriously not Colleen, and who thoughtfully arranged for me to sit in on a taping of the *Oprah* show. I was ecstatic to be in the audience, as a fan. During a commercial break I got up the nerve to say hello. To *Oprah*. Again, I could not possibly overstate my level of respect, devotion, and esteem for this woman.

"Hi, Oprah, I'm Paula Zahn's producer!" I chirped.

Steeee-rike Thuh-*ree*!

Apparently Oprah had seen *CBS This Morning* just the day before. Now, the good news was that despite our rocky history, Oprah somehow caught a moment of *CBS This Morning*, which was a miracle in itself given that it was relatively unwatched. But the bad news was that she'd caught a snide comment that Mark McEwen—our weatherman, who *never ever* made snide comments—had made about her, Oprah, and her weight loss and something to the effect that if *he* had a chef and a trainer then *he'd* probably lose all that weight, too. Awesome.

She recounted the entire story to me. Into her microphone. As I sat there amid three hundred Oprah-adoring audience members all wearing red blazers and obvious expressions of sympathy. She proceeded to say how *hurtful* it was for someone to *assume* that a trainer and a chef were the only reasons she was able to lose all the weight. As the ladies all scowled at me, I felt like the living, breathing example of her hurt. She was displeased. Because of *me*. Again!

During the next commercial break, in which I planned to stare at the floor with my head down, I got the urgent beep (it was still beepers then) to call CBS News in New York. It was Bill Owens—the guy who'd kicked me off the *Evening News* set when I was an intern and was now a colleague—telling me there'd been a huge explosion in Oklahoma City and that I needed to get on the next plane headed there. I tried to beg off, and what I am about to recount to you is something that shames me far more than the time I tricked Oprah at the very beginning of this chapter.

"Bill, I am in the audience at *Oprah* right now. I can't possibly leave. Is this story really a big deal? Are you *sure* I have to go?" I pleaded. "I *really* think it's best for the show if I stay. Oprah's *really* mad at Mark, CBS, and our show. Can't we wait to see what develops in Oklahoma, because I don't even get what the story is . . ."

I did end up going to Oklahoma City, and it soon became all too clear what that story was. And if I'd ever felt silly and small because of a few dumb things I'd done in front of a TV idol, I felt absolutely humbled, chastened, and reduced by what was unfolding in front of me. For years afterward I watched *Oprah* with a twinge of guilt.

My Oprah Angel Network Book Club Aha Moment regarding this experience is something I still haven't really learned, and maybe never will . . . sometimes it's not about you. Not one little bit.

SIX MOMENTS I'D LIKE TO FORGET

I've had enough embarrassing moments to fill a book, but maybe it does matter that you think I'm cool, so I'm only going to mention six more.

★ On a remote in New Orleans for CBS, I said some unkind things about one of the anchors in New York City to our weatherman. Little did I know that his mic was on and it was open in the ears of both our anchors. When I got back to Manhattan I had some serious 'splainin' to do.

★ I got busted by open mics again years later on the set of *Top Chef* in Miami when I inadvertently regaled the entire control room with a detailed story of a sexploit between me and a woman. (I'm not saying anything more about that.) I thought I was privately telling Gail Simmons, Padma Lakshmi, and Tom Colicchio as they waited to begin taping, but they were wearing live mics. Will I ever learn?

★ While I was an intern at the CBS affiliate in St. Louis, Helen Slater came to promote her movie *Supergirl*. I assumed that the woman with her was her proud mother. Wrong! The woman informed me she was her publicist and that she and Helen were the same age. I then made the classic stupid male move of assuming the publicist was pregnant and asked her when she was due. Do I even have to finish this story?

★ I was hosting the Miss USA pageant when the director told me that we were running short, meaning we had time to kill. What he didn't tell me was that they'd added material to the teleprompter, including an introduction of Miss Universe, Ximena Navarrete. The degree to which I botched her name on live national television was fairly extreme: I read her first name as Eczema, like the skin condition.

I wish I could explain this outfit to you. This photo qualifies as an embarrassing moment, right?

Months after insulting the Venezuelan population, I further revealed my moronic teleprompter skills on *Watch What Happens Live*, when I read that someone from "La Calif" had a question, not realizing that I was meant to say LA, California. I made myself Jackhole of the Week for that one.

★ The first time I was ever overserved—I believe it was Tanqueray, and I know I was in high school—I awoke in the middle of the night and became immediately aware that I wouldn't make the ten steps to the bathroom without throwing up. Thinking fast, I took off my boxer shorts and threw up in them. I then tossed them out the window onto my front lawn, I suppose in an attempt to get rid of the evidence. As if Evelyn Cohen would miss that one.

★ At my job selling Deadhead gear out of a pushcart at Faneuil Hall, some guy came up and started talking to me about pot. He was getting a huge shipment later that day and told me he would sell me an ounce for the unimaginably low price of $450. I literally walked to the bank machine, emptied my account, handed him the money, and waited for two hours for him to deliver my pot at a bar across the street after work. I realized when he was five minutes late that he wasn't coming, and I have never felt like a bigger sucker. At least he wasn't a cop.

FEEL THE PAIN

Here's what . . . I'm sort of a wimp. I was the kid in glasses who couldn't even mow the lawn because of grass allergies. Being risk-averse doesn't lend itself well to the news business, and I got the same pit in my stomach every time I headed in what most sane people would consider the wrong direction—into, instead of away from, disaster. When I arrived in Oklahoma City on April 19, 1995, I rented a car and headed straight for the Alfred P. Murrah Federal Building. I quickly found myself in the midst of fiery rubble, with devastated families helplessly looking on as first responders performed triage. A truck bomb had exploded at 9:02 a.m., demolishing the building and making a huge chunk of downtown Oklahoma City look like a battlefield. A light rain was falling, which underscored the somber mood of the shaken city that from that day forward would be synonymous with America's worst act of homegrown terrorism.

I was far too hardened to mass tragedy for a twenty-seven-year-old, but like a lot of journalists, I needed that emotional armor just to do my job. By that point in my life I'd gotten pretty good at showing up on the scene—plane crash, wildfire, flood, hurricane— quickly establishing relationships with people in the midst of devastating trauma, and getting them to talk about it on-camera. It was like some sick kind of speed dating where my job was connecting to people in their most vulnerable moments, getting what I needed, and going. It's not that I didn't have empathy; there was just always another plane to catch. These were years where my life was divided into two-week increments that totally revolved around what stories I was covering or who I was producing live in the studio. The only variation that ever occurred was when news broke and I was pulled into the fray.

There's incredible adrenaline involved when you become a competitor in what amounts to the broadcast news edition of *The Amazing Race*. Teams are dispatched, planes are chartered, and the pressure is on to get to the story first, plant a stake, and own it before your rivals. The way you win is by getting the people with the most compelling stories to stand in front of your cameras and spill their guts.

Because I flew there from Chicago—on a flight packed with journalists and so turbulent that the reporter next to me crossed himself several times—I thought I'd gotten to OKC quicker than any of my New York counterparts, but I soon discovered that any self-congratulations were premature.

While there were plenty of people still en route from New York, the private charter flights had already landed, and a familiar but yet still surreal scene was taking shape on the perimeter of the disaster zone: Every major and minor media organization was camped out with tents, trucks, and lights, forming some kind of gruesome circus that, if not for its proximity to catastrophe, might otherwise seem kind of glamorous. I could tell just by the intensity of the frenzy that this was the biggest story I'd ever seen. While searching for my camera crew I saw every broadcast journalism star you could name, and I finally walked right into Connie

Chung smoking a cigarette. I greeted her probably too enthusiastically, given the morose scene around me, but I was caught up in the camaraderie and drama of the race.

I stayed awake for two days shooting with correspondent Jane Robelot, writing and producing stories about rescue efforts and volunteers to air during the morning newsblocks, those news segments on morning shows at the top of the hour. Camera crews were in short supply, and to give you an idea of our relative importance, the freelance crew assigned to us was from Topeka, Kansas, and included a sound woman who didn't know a microphone from a microwave but was a dead ringer for Shelly Duvall as Olive Oyl.

We worked out of an empty space in the back of Oklahoma City's CBS affiliate, and I was running on adrenaline and deadlines. It's no accident that in TV news, working this way is called "crashing" your piece. We shot, wrote, and cut three stories a day, which meant going into the field and talking to people on-camera, coming back and screening the tape, writing a script, then working with an editor to put it all together, advising on shots and sound. A good editor, by the way, is the heart and soul of any story, and editors are certainly the unsung heroes of the news business and reality TV as well. He or she can take what you and I would see as ordinary raw footage and hone it into something like a work of art, by lingering on shots of people's faces, or cutting at just the right moment to an emotional scene, or creating tension by juxtaposing a stark voiceover with jarring images.

Oklahoma City was the closest I'll ever get to being in a war zone. The people we met were heartbroken and in shock. Someone had come and blown up one of their most visible buildings, killing men, women, and children for a political statement. I knew that somewhere inside, a part of me was wailing and crying for the survivors, but my directive was to chronicle their pain, not to feel it with them. I silenced my own emotions and focused on getting my scripts done and crashing my pieces. And I understood: This was the job. But I also understood: This was not normal. Every time I left a victim at the site of the bombing, it wasn't two minutes before I was back among my team of coworkers in our little tent city, and that area—with its craft services tables stocked with snacks and hot coffee, and the makeshift makeup stations and the camaraderie—was controlled and predictable. My flirting with a pockmarked intern from the affiliate and partaking in the time-honored journalistic tradition of gallows humor, I now realize, were not so much callous acts as they were a feeble attempt to shield myself from the mess outside.

My last day in Oklahoma City, I finished my final piece at 6 a.m. and headed to my untouched motel room to take a quick shower before catching a plane home to New York. I turned on the TV and watched Harry Smith interview a woman whose baby had died, and the firefighter who'd had to carry that baby out to her. After days of being in the center of a tragedy, the reality of Oklahoma City finally had a chance to sink in. Alone in my motel room, I broke down and wept. I sobbed all the way to the airport, primally and uncontrollably, and while I was at it, I cried for most of the flight home. I didn't care. I was off the clock.

☺

When September 11 happened six years after Oklahoma City, I was a "civilian," having left CBS just the year before, after a decade in TV news. I stood on my fire escape first thing in the morning, watching dumbstruck as the Towers fell, and for much of the rest of the day I watched streams of people walk, like a dazed army, up the street from downtown. For days, I walked around the neighborhood, which was acrid with what every New Yorker would come to call simply The Smell—an awful, dread-inducing mix of electricity and jet fuel and ashes. And like nearly every New Yorker I saw during those days, I'd burst out crying in the middle of the street at any given moment, because everywhere you looked, bus stops and fences and streetlights were covered with thousands of hastily copied flyers, each with a picture of another person who had shown up for their job that gorgeous morning and was now missing, and, as we learned before much time had passed, was never going to be found. Here's why I'm telling you this now: If it was even remotely possible to feel grateful for one thing about 9/11, besides just being alive, it was that I didn't have to find the people who had hung those flyers and interview them about whether or not they still held out any hope. I didn't have to sit in an editing bay trying to make a piece *work*, looking for that certain something that would elevate it over everyone else's 9/11 pieces. This time, I was just another New Yorker. I was just another person. And while I had never felt worse before, at least I didn't have to try not to.

I WAS A JEWISH GO-GO DANCER

Can we please move on from *me* being a drama queen to a story about my fave drama queen? In my personal pantheon of stars, Diana Ross may be even bigger than Susan Lucci. I know what you're saying: How is this possible? How, Andy? Who could be bigger than Susan Lucci? I think it's because TV stars seem, in the end, more approachable than pop stars or movie stars. After all, they're in your home, sometimes every day. Miss Ross is the ultimate diva superhero: big hair, big sequins, big poses, big anthems, bigger than life. And you never have the idea, not for a second, that she'd ever set foot in *your* home.

Through my work, I began meeting people who'd been idols—and, just as memorably, the people behind those idols. All my co-workers had their own short list of celebrities they were personally obsessed with—usually baseball players or authors or politicians or random heartthrobs like Kevin Costner (boring!)—and they let their lists be known around the office; if someone on your list got booked on the show, it was expected that you'd wind up producing their segment.

Everyone at the morning show knew that I was first on the list to produce a Diana Ross interview, and I only had to wait three years to do it. In 1993, Miss Ross was holding a press conference at Planet Hollywood in New York to announce a new boxed set and other events surrounding her fortieth year in show business. My boss, Chris Fahey, assigned me the piece. Not that she really had any choice: Had she given it to someone else, I'd have quit. Or at least cried.

I was too overwhelmed to even try to get anything meaningful out of the experience. When we met in a small room upstairs at Planet Hollywood, I murmured to her that downstairs they were displaying one of her outfits from when she was in the Supremes. I knew this probably wasn't news to her; I just wanted to say the word "Supremes" to Diana Ross. Also, I hoped she would catch the undertones hidden in my seemingly innocuous statement: "I read Mary Wilson's book and she said you weren't nice to her— what's the real deal?" Diana Ross didn't address my telepathic question, but she did assure me that the dress downstairs, which she hadn't seen, was a fake.

"Those dresses are in storage and at Motown. They're not here," she declared. Let's pause a moment and gather ourselves together in the wake of this news that Planet Hollywood may not always be one hundred percent genuine in its star-studdedness.

I was quiet from that point on, just shrank into the background. Still smarting from my Oprah experience, I didn't even try to get a picture with her. I was too scared. But later that photo—or lack thereof—would haunt me. It would have been proof of our meeting, as much to myself as to anyone else. Without it, I'd be stuck just claiming I'd met her, then struggling to describe how she smelled as proof of our encounter (a bit cocoa-buttery with a top note of exotic flowers?).

The experience was terrifying, thrilling, and also a letdown. You meet someone you've spent an eternity thinking about and you expect it to be the culmination of something very significant, the celebration at the top of a mountain. Instead it is two people meeting in some relatively normal moment and situation. And it always happens that one of the people cares a lot more about what's going on than the other one does.

Next came Joan Collins. Which, let's be honest, may be the only way to follow Diana Ross. By this point I had already learned that, for the most part, people don't resemble the characters they play on TV. But I very badly wanted Joan Collins to *be* Alexis Morrell Carrington Colby Dexter Rowan. I wanted to be *abused* by her. Not in a creepy way. I just mean that I wanted to be emasculated and snapped at by one specific character/woman.

At 7:30 on the morning of the interview, I dutifully waited in front of the CBS Broadcast Center for Miss Collins's limo to arrive. I never, ever waited downstairs or in front of the building for my guests to arrive. That was work for a CBS page or intern, the latter of which I'd already been; producers waited in the Green Room. But I wanted to experience Alexis fully. I got what I wanted.

"Please don't come anywhere *near* me with that coffee," she snapped at me the moment she stepped out of the car. "Someone spilled red wine on me last night and you're making me very *nervous*." She wore a pinstripe suit, her face was fully made up with bright red lips, and she wore a wig that was Curly Alexis Perfection. What was not to love?

"The limo was *late*. And *hot* as a *sauna*! And the driver did *not* know where he was going! He thought we had some sort of *radio* interview. Do I *look* like I'm on my way to a *radio* interview?" She looked around, though I was right in front of her. "Who do I *follow*? Where are we *going*?"

Thank you, Ma'am, may I have some more! I was ecstatic. This was exactly what I'd wanted. For just a moment that morning, I was one of Alexis's slacks-wearing male assistants at ColbyCo.

"Follow me, please, Miss Collins," I happily whimpered. "We're going to the second floor."

"We are very *prompt* people," she lectured. "We are not *late*. Who is interviewing me? We're not showing the exercise video. I only want to discuss my *book*. Now, is there a wardrobe mistress? Where is she?"

Not to put too fine a point on it, but I might've had a boner by the time she said *wardrobe mistress*.

"I need a *safety pin*!" she barked. I found her one in the makeup room, thank the lord. Momentarily.

"*No!* That one is *far* too large. I need a small one for this blouse. If you'll find a *wardrobe mistress* I am *quite* sure she'll have the right one!" She turned to her publicist. "I thought *Live at Five* was *horrible* yesterday. This *'Matt'* was supposedly interviewing me, but the woman kept chiming in and interrupting and I was saying, 'Exactly *who* is doing this interview?'"

The interview was with Harry Smith, and it ended up fine. Collins was charming and chirpy, but nowhere near as entertaining as she'd been backstage. I went for it and got a quick photo with her on her way out, though I knew it wasn't going to be any good right after it was taken (sometimes you can just tell). I didn't dare risk suggesting we try it again. Years later I got to know Joan Collins socially and found her to be disarming and totally charming, with a great sense of humor about herself and the world.

I'll tell you about one other idol-meet, and this one went a little differently. For one thing, it was only tangentially work-related. For another, it was in front of several thousand people and was the cause of a major, summer-long odyssey fueled by ridiculous expectations.

I've always loved a stage. In 1996, Graciela and I learned that our favorite group, the B-52s, were allowing "friends of the band" to be go-go dancers onstage during their summer tour. We immediately took action. I'd met the band's manager a couple years before when they recorded the music for the *Flintstones* movie, and since then he had very sweetly set us up with concert tickets. In all, Grac and I had seen the B's probably twenty times.

The band's manager told us we could pick any date on the tour. We chose Graciela's thirtieth birthday, July 19, when they'd be playing outside Chicago. We told every single person we knew that we'd be dancing with the B-52s. In fact we didn't talk about anything else all summer.

That's not strictly true. For a few weeks I'd been nervously monitoring a massive reddish welt on my stomach, with something of a bull's-eye in the middle. It changed size and shape every week and was sensitive to the touch. Berated by my mother's constant nagging to "GET THAT DAMN BITE CHECKED OUT!" I finally showed it to the *CBS This Morning* doctor, a woman who gave medical advice on TV every day to a few million Americans.

"Spider bite!" she proclaimed. Relieved with the diagnosis, and maybe even hoping that the spider had somehow imbued me with super dancing powers, I went on with my summer and concentrated on the only thing that mattered to me. Graciela and I would meet anywhere and everywhere to practice our moves. We danced in Sag Harbor, we danced on sidewalks, and we turned her den into a stage. Graciela had incredible natural dancing talent; I, on the other hand, had only blind confidence and a love of what I was doing—a common theme with me.

When we had our dance moves down, we took the next most

important step and rented stage outfits at Odds Costume Rentals on West Twenty-ninth Street. Grac rented a yellow dress with billowy transparent sleeves and a matching yellow vest with fringe. I got myself a pair of blue sequined pants—which I'd always wanted—along with a green metallic shirt and silver sequined shoes. Those shoes, as you will see, would become forever tainted in my memory.

Meanwhile, my spider bite was not going away. Of course my mom was relentless in her quest for information concerning its size, and she was especially hysterical about its endlessly changing shape. She finally made me consult (in her words) "an ACTUAL doctor. A real medical PROFESSIONAL." I went to a doctor who asked me to raise my shirt, took half a look, and said, "Lyme disease. I'm a hundred percent sure of it." This doctor, despite never having been on television, was correct.

You may have noticed that TV doctors do about nine hundred segments a year about Lyme disease, about the telltale signs (the bull's-eye!) and symptoms. While *I* go to the bathroom during these segments, is it too much to think that the TV doc is paying attention to the words coming out of her own mouth? I was furious, but I had no one to blame but myself—who else but a man hopelessly devoted to television would receive a serious misdiagnosis from a TV doctor? The real-world medical professional prescribed an array of medication, including—hold your breath and cover your nose—suppositories.

"You want me to dance onstage with the B-52s with a suppository up my butt?" I asked. The mood of the summer quickly morphed from B-52-phoria to a *Hope over Heartbreak* movie-of-the-week dilemma. While I wasn't about to let a little case of Lyme disease get between me and the B's, I also had no intention of using those suppositories.

On the weekend of Graciela's thirtieth birthday, we flew to Chicago. The night before the gig, we danced around the Ritz-

Carlton like banshees, rehearsing moves we'd made up à la the Molly Ringwald (think *Breakfast Club*): the Stand-March-Jump, the Freeze, the Honeybun, the Right-Armed Lasso, the Strobe Light. We anticipated nothing less than the best time of our lives.

It wasn't easy, but we'd made arrangements with the Jumbotron people at the venue to give us the footage of the concert afterward, so we had to look great. Graciela spent several hours of her birthday afternoon getting her hair done, and the effort paid off. Her hair was blown out into a high Jackie Kennedy flip with bangs, and she put on big spidery Twiggy eye makeup, exaggerated for the stage, which I thought was an especially smart touch. As far as my look went, I was in crew-cut mode and happy to let Grac's hair be the main attraction.

When we arrived at the stadium, the parking lot was strangely empty. I don't mean the lot wasn't full, I mean there was *nobody* there. At all. We finally found a parking attendant who told us that we were the last people in Chicago to discover that the concert had been canceled. We were speechless. We were devastated. We would never have been able to articulate it at the time, but it was a measure of how blessed our lives had been to that point that this was the single worst thing that had ever happened to either of us.

Hysterical, we called our band contact, who told us that Cindy Wilson's father-in-law had died. Poor Cindy! Poor Cindy's father-in-law! And to an admittedly lesser extent, poor us. The band was doing a shorter set the next night—without Cindy—in Wisconsin. We pondered driving there, but in the end we went back to the hotel to look at the band's tour schedule and choose another date. We scrolled through a summer full of complications but at last found a date we could both make in Los Angeles at the Universal Amphitheater one month later. I was so excited—or relieved and/or possibly still discomposed from the letdown—that I got on the bed and jumped up and down like a six-year-old. The rented silver

Moments before I fell on my taint!

sequined shoes I was still wearing were so slippery that I fell off the bed, which would have been bad enough. But in the cramped hotel room, on a night that was already steeped in terrible luck, I fell violently and landed on the sharp corner of the bedside table. Taint first. I injured myself so badly that I could barely move for the rest of the evening, and poor Graciela spent the remainder of her milestone birthday fetching ice. For my taint. (For those of you who don't know what a taint is, it's the area between one's butt and one's balls. As in: " 'Tain't your balls and 'tain't your butt." Now you can say you learned something from this otherwise breezy tome.)

By the time the date for the LA B-52s concert rolled around, we were almost over the whole thing because we'd exhausted ourselves—and everyone we knew—obsessing over it all summer. We checked in to the Mondrian and dragged out our stage costumes, and Graciela reimagined her hair into a classic bouffant, a real B-52.

Meanwhile, I'd had another setback. My newest undoing came in the form of watching a video of myself practicing dancing in Chicago. Based on the footage, I'd deemed myself not only unfit for the stage but also possibly neurologically unsound. Did my body move like that because Lyme disease had affected my brain function?

Before the concert, diseased and newly insecure, I calmed my nerves backstage with Jack Daniel's and Pop Rocks (which, if you think about it, should be the official snack combo for the B-52s) when the Pretenders walked right past us to get onstage. And just like that, all my sorrows and self-pity were erased by a nod from Chrissie Hynde.

Before we went on, I was told that Kate (Pierson, the divine) would at some point be joining me on my pedestal and that whatever happened, I should just do my own dance and not imitate Kate's moves. I assured him that this would not be a problem for a versatile dancer like me. Apparently, I'd suffered acute temporary amnesia about the dreaded practice video.

Graciela and I hit the spotlight—we were on pedestals on either side of the stage—for the third song, "Dance This Mess Around." From behind the band, without a monitor in my ear, the music sounded like a mashup of nothing I could recognize, and I had a hard time finding the beat. To complicate matters, I'd done one too many shots of Jack Daniel's before the show to calm my nerves. The Jack had calmed them so effectively that I felt like I was swimming in a pool of molasses. I was also, within seconds of going onstage, sweating like a pig. My silky green shirt was not breathing with me. Was it the alcohol/candy combo—or was I totally Lyming out with fever?

I looked across the stage, and Graciela . . . was a beautiful gazelle. She looked so perfect, she could've been *in* the band. This did not help my flailing, drowning feeling.

To further rattle me, within a minute or two of our first song, I saw Kate approaching my ramp. "Do NOT imitate Kate," I repeated to myself like a mantra, as I attempted some kind of a lame, modified, Jewish-boy Swim. Sure enough, Kate was on my ramp and I was dancing with her in what felt like slow motion. Imagine my shock when she started doing MY lame, modified, Jewish-boy Swim! I was horrified! Also confused, upset, and drunk. I tried to come up with a new move on the spot, but to no avail. Kate left the ramp—wondering, I'm sure, how the hell I got onstage with them.

The rest of the show was a blur. I sweated like a whore in church through it all. I'm pretty sure we kicked ass during "Summer of Love," and I still feel good about my performance in "Strobe Light," despite losing my way a few times. Surely the "bang bang" during "Love Shack" was a highlight? And my aborted somersault during "Rock Lobster" might've, frankly, saved the show. But it was all over so *quickly*. And thus arriveth the lesson: No matter what happened that night, it could never have borne the hype we piled upon it. But I'm still glad I did it.

A few years later, Graciela was working at VH-1, and the show *Rock and Roll Fantasy* approached us about dancing with the B-52s again. We said yes. Duh. This time we were sober, and disease- and injury-free. Total pros. I had a number of moves prepped and ready should Kate Pierson subconsciously feel the need to bite my style again. And clearly, my dancing had improved, because the Go-Gos, who were on tour with the B's at the time, saw us and asked us to join *them* onstage during *their* set. They made Grac dance in a bra and me shirtless, because we had no change of costume. And while I'm sure that seeing myself doing a lame modified topless Pony to "Vacation" would be totally cringe-inducing, I'm kind of sad that there's no videotape of that performance, for it was my last one. After that, I hung up my blue sparkle pants and my sweaty silky green shirt and those slippery silver sequined shoes for the last time. But all this reminiscing has got me thinking—if you're in a band and you find yourself in need of a go-go dancer, I still know where I can rent them. Call me!

THE NINE COSTUMES THAT GUARANTEED I'D NEVER GET LAID ON HALLOWEEN

A Hobo/Bum—This was my go-to costume as a kid. In retrospect, dressing as a homeless person seems a bit crass. PC hadn't been invented then.

Greg Brady after raiding Carol's closet—I accomplished this by wearing a jumpsuit that Graciela found in her mom's closet and wearing my hair down (when it was long). The jumpsuit was passed between Graciela and me for a period of ten years.

Elroy Jetson after realizing he's gay—This was in the same family as the above Greg Brady costume, and it didn't dawn on me that high-concept costumes with long explanations didn't really work. Graciela found some sort of unitard with the Jetsons on it. I added a blue Speedo and became Elroy.

Foxy Brown—Used the Greg Brady jumpsuit for this one, with an Afro wig. It was as close to drag as I've ever come.

Elvis—While working at TRIO, my best pal Bruce Bozzi and I dressed as Elvis and appeared on behalf of the channel in the NYC Halloween parade. Once the parade started, we realized that people expected us to perform as Elvis, but we had no act. We sang the same refrain from "Viva Las Vegas" all night and were booed and gay-bashed all along the route. It was a miserable experience, but we made it onto the WCBS eleven o'clock newscast.

Austin Powers—I had a really cheap store-bought costume and wore it to a party full of hot gay dudes who were wearing next to nothing. Needless to say, I went home alone.

Yellow Sequined Tails—I've thrown this jacket over street clothes countless times when I'm costumeless, and the sheer strength of the sequins has made it a crowd favorite.

Baseball Player—I wore the Cardinals jersey I had from throwing out the first pitch (you'll hear that story later) and might have enjoyed wearing my tight baseball pants more than I was supposed to.

Giggy—I'll explain when I tell you about the Housewives.

Guess who's taking my picture?

WILL YOU BE MY DADDY?

sometimes wonder if Oklahoma City precipitated a shift in the nature of American news; as our world became more somber—and scary—the news got lighter. Fluffier. More vapid. Over time, Paris the city would become less newsworthy than Paris the Hilton. You probably think I, of all people, snorted up this change like a line of fine Colombian cocaine, but I hate cocaine, and this shift had a downside for me. As someone who covered—and loved—both entertainment and news, I felt caught in the middle.

I was approaching thirty and I felt like I'd grown up at *CBS This Morning.* I was light-years away from the ponytailed smart-ass intern I once was, but the work was still challenging and exciting.

At CBS, I had learned much of what I know now about producing live segments, getting the most out of only a few minutes of TV time, booking guests, writing scripts on a tight deadline, and the art of the interview. And yet the show itself had no energy. It wasn't very good. Ownership of CBS changed several times during that period, and we worked amid constant rumors of anchor shake-ups and staff changes. I remember one week when every single day at least one paper, sometimes two, featured calls for the cancellation of the show, ending on Friday with the *New York Post* saying we were "unnecessary and unwatchable."

So, what did we do while the world either laughed at us or ignored us? We had FUN! We were a merry band of lovable losers. One day I taught the entire morning editorial meeting the game where you figure out what your name would be if you were a porn star. In the version I knew, you take your middle name, you make it your first name, and for your porn last name you use the name of the street you grew up on. (Or the name of your street now. I gave everybody a choice to make it more fun and because the street that I grew up on was boring.) According to the modified formula, my porn name was Joey Horatio, which I enjoyed because it sounded like rough trade. As we were all cracking ourselves up figuring out our alter egos, Andy Rooney came in and said, "Is this a party? What in the world is going on in here?" And so we figured out Andy Rooney's porn-star name: Aitken Partridge. Not porny at all, may God rest his soul.

Paula Zahn came in next. "What is this?" she demanded. Turns out Paula's name would be Ann Jennifer. Which is one sadly sexless name for a porn star. Stick to the news, Ann Jennifer.

Come to think of it, that little game revealed a lot about our problems: We had no *heat*. There was never any energy surrounding anything we put on the air, guests didn't come to our show first, and America didn't fall in love with our anchor team. Mention *CBS This Morning* today and you won't initiate any trip down TV's Memory Lane. Mention the *Today* show with Katie Couric and Matt Lauer, or Jane Pauley and Bryant Gumbel, and it's all gushing and rhapsodizing.

One of the lowest points of *CBS This Morning*'s history came when we decided to zig when others zagged. We couldn't compete with Katie and her window looking out over her devoted fans on Rockefeller Plaza, so we added a studio audience. Which sounds not bad, until you realize this audience has to be there at 6:30 in the morning and watch boring stuff live. Nevertheless, I came down with Lucy Ricardo Syndrome, the symptoms of which include a sudden desperation to be a part of the show. I didn't care that I wouldn't be on-camera. I volunteered to do the audience warm-up every day, thinking that getting myself in front of a crowd would eventually pay off in some way. Plus nobody else wanted to do it.

I had no routine—only blind confidence, which had worked pretty well for me at times in the past but had also effed me royally on more than one occasion. So, I made "jokes" about how early it was, though there was nothing funny about how early it was to these people. I made "jokes" about Paula and Harry Smith, only there wasn't much that was funny to say about them. "They're nice, decent people who are good at their jobs! Thanks, folks, you've been great!" I can't even claim to have bombed, because those poor dazed souls either stared through me like I wasn't there or, worse, mustered that horrible frowny smile that kindhearted people reserve only for pitiable wretches.

Around that time I got a call from an exec at ABC Daytime who was developing a talk show about soaps and heard I might be the perfect producer. This seemed to me like potential kismet— Lucci and Cohen reunited at last. I knew I could produce that show, but that blind optimism told me I should try to take it to the next level. *Why don't I audition to host it?* I thought. *Who would be more perfect than me for this?* I put the blank stares of *CBS This Morning*'s audience out of my mind and rushed out to make a demo tape of myself interviewing *The Young and the Restless* stars (whom I had access to, working at CBS) and sent it along. When I was called in to meet with the ABC Daytime producer I knew something big was about to happen for me. And my instincts were right, in a way. But instead of kvelling over my natural hosting skills and gorgeous, barely noticeably crossed eyes, she ripped into me for more than three minutes. And I quote: "How *arrogant* are you to think you could go from producing to being *on-air* with no experience? I'm in the business of making stars and the camera doesn't lie and in your case it CERTAINLY didn't lie."

But did you like the tape!? I wondered.

Meanwhile, our new *CBS This Morning* format was such a dud that people just stopped showing up to sit in the audience. Within a couple weeks of our debut, there were days when we'd have just fifteen people in the studio. We made the interns come in early to fill the rows, and we'd seat whatever sad (and usually exhausted, bused-in) group (of senior citizens or sick people) we could find

With Paula and Harry on my last day at CBS This Morning

strategically, in a bunch, so Harry or Paula could stand in front of them and it would *look* to the home viewer like an actual crowd. Oh, by the way, you know what's not made to be seen live on a stage? A morning show newsblock reporting on the latest in the Middle East or the weather report or a segment about consumer fraud. Fortunately, my pitiable routine must have been so unremarkable that no one upstairs caught wind of it, because one afternoon I got a call from a CBS exec offering me a producing job at *48 Hours*. The show's original incarnation was as a fly-on-the-wall documentary spotlighting various characters associated with one story for forty-eight hours. They called me because they were looking to expand into some celebrity-based shows and thought I'd be able to help. Eager to tackle something new, but also feeling a teensy bit like a rat leaving a sinking ship, I took the job and said a bittersweet good-bye to Harry, Paula, and the remaining fifteen audience members.

In edit rooms and in the field at *48 Hours*, I learned much that would later inform how I now give notes to the producers on Bravo shows. For instance, lingering on little moments—a facial expression, a tic, a swallowed word—can actually be far more revealing of someone's character than the big moments. On *Housewives*, a wig-pulling episode is naturally provocative, but I'm just as intrigued by hearing what our subjects order at a meal. *Ashley got the steak—?!!* can become a vital thread in the overall tapestry. I worked on every kind of story at *48 Hours*, including a segment on the original Broadway cast and production team behind *Rent*, a profile of Shirley MacLaine, and a piece about Barry Manilow's relationship with his British fans, the Maniloonies. That last one was funny to everyone with the exception of Mr. Manilow and his fans. Our approach was: "Aww, look at these ladies of a certain age (and dimension) who call themselves Maniloonies, worshipping at the feet of Sir Barry." They'd participated in the shoot willingly, but when it aired, they felt we were making fun of them, and Barry's publicist was furious that we'd portrayed his audience as anything other than frenzied teenyboppers. The reaction didn't surprise me. At

Manilow's concert, the publicist had repeatedly said, "Look at all the *young* people!" I looked around and didn't see any, but I nodded anyway. We see what we want to see. Another story reunited me with my intern mama, Erin Moriarty, who'd long since left Morning Consumerville for a gig in prime time. At a booksellers' convention, I'd been handed a book that I read and loved, a ten-hanky weeper that appealed to every schmaltzy bone in my body. I pitched Erin a story following the book's author, Nicholas Sparks, and his publishing team in the period (which worked out to be more than forty-eight hours) leading up to publication of what I was convinced was going to be a smash bestseller, *The Notebook*. After Erin's interview, I stayed behind in North Carolina to shoot some B-roll (that's TV-speak for "more footage") of Sparks at home. We happened to be there, and rolling camera, when he received a phone call: His father had just passed away. It was a heartbreaking moment and very real. He begged me not to include the footage in his profile. It was just too personal and he couldn't bear the thought of it being shown on television. He appealed to my decency and I wanted to respect his privacy, so I gave him my word. I never told Erin about that footage. The book went on to sell millions of copies, and Nicholas Sparks has been a best-selling author ever since.

Years later, I had long forgotten this incident and was surprised to learn that Sparks had written of me in a nonfiction book about his life. In it, he thanked me for my compassion in not airing that footage. I was honored, but mortified. Looking back on it now, I wondered if I should've included it in the story. This may sound unfeeling or opportunistic, but we were a legitimate documentary show, and we were there to tell the truth about what was happening to this man in the days leading up to the biggest event in his life. One of the reasons that I think the *Housewives* resonates with viewers is that we show *everything* that happens during our production period—good, bad, or ugly, it's real.

Some might actually say I flouted the laws of journalism by cutting the phone call. At the time, obscuring a detail about a fiction author's life did not seem the same as withholding information about a world leader. Last year, Erin took me as her date to a party celebrating the fifteenth anniversary of *The Notebook*. In the car on the way over, I finally confessed that I'd withheld the footage of Sparks receiving that phone call. Her reaction surprised me and instantly eased any lingering doubts I had. She said that had it been a hard news story, it would've been our obligation to show that footage, but since it was a feature, she was okay with my judgment call. I walked into that celebration with a light heart and loved reuniting with Nick, who still credits that *48 Hours* piece with much of his first novel's initial success.

One of my favorite stories as a *48 Hours* producer was a profile of Don Imus that I produced with Dan Rather. The plan was for Dan and me to join Imus for (a little under) forty-eight hours in Monu-

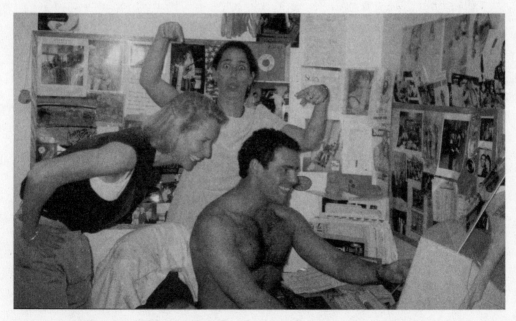

48 Hours. *"Shirtless Tuesdays" with colleagues Mary Noonan and Diane Ronnau—I was the only one who complied.*

ment Valley, Utah, as the famously abrasive radio personality took pictures for a new coffee table book celebrating one of his passions, photographing gorgeous Western scenery. (Who knew?)

I spent sleepless weeks before the shoot fretting about being entrusted with taking Dan Rather on location with no "adult" supervision. This was a very big deal, and, if I may say, a mark of my reputation at the time that I was even being allowed outside the building with Dan, whom I barely knew. Dan's legend preceded him: He had a heart of gold but could be tough and exacting and maybe a little on the edge of losing it sometimes. Oh, and he seemed to be a magnet for crazy.

Things *happened* to Dan Rather. This was the man who'd been punched at the '68 Democratic National Convention. This was the man who'd been taken for an endless taxi ride in Chicago by a possibly unstable cabbie trying to jack up the fare, resulting in Dan hanging out the window and shouting to people that he was being kidnapped. This was the man who'd been mugged on the street by a disturbed stranger who kept demanding, "Kenneth, what is the frequency?!" (which in turn inspired a hit song by R.E.M.). Even though Dan had gone some years without a bizarre incident, I didn't want any of that going down on my watch.

I was summoned to Mr. Rather's office overlooking the set of *The CBS Evening News*, the very setting of my humiliating ejection as an intern years earlier. I came prepared to brief him, in detail, on our plan. Dan's a tall guy, a massive anchorman with a very large head (all anchormen have exceptionally large skulls, by the way, with the exception of Matt Lauer). He smelled, of course, of lotion. Fully lubed for his broadcast and half-listening to me while knotting his tie, Dan was encouraging and kind, yet authoritative. He said he'd known Imus for years and this would be a breeze. "Sounds simple enough, Andrew," he said with a wink. He liked to wink and I like to be winked at, which I thought should work well. After that meeting, I couldn't reconcile the stories of Dan's nutbaggery with the steady, trustworthy anchorman who'd just put me at ease.

A few days later, I boarded Mr. Imus's Gulfstream jet, which was to carry us out west for our photography adventure. Dan hadn't shown up yet, but Imus had, and he seemed as geared up for Mr. Rather's arrival as I was. Imus and I had spoken already on the phone for a preinterview, and in the course of our conversation the shock jock had revealed himself to be nothing but a pussycat, tickled that Dan was coming on this journey. In person, he was a gracious host to me. "What kind of mood is Dan going to be in this weekend?" he joked. I told him Dan couldn't wait for the trip, which Dan hadn't actually said but seemed okay to convey in the interest of keeping our subject pumped up. Moments later, The Anchorman arrived, enthusiastically bounding up the stairway to the small plane and totally supporting my claim that he was stoked. I sat in awe, listening to the two broadcasting legends as they discussed the news that was dominating the morning's headlines: Frank Gifford getting busted with a woman in a hotel. Gossip! Of a celebrity nature—I was glad it wasn't politics they were discussing, and their tone was one of gentlemen who are quite pleased it was someone *else* getting busted in a situation like this. I didn't hear a ton of sympathy for Kathie Lee, either.

The whole weekend was basically a rugged denim fantasy. I was with a manly broadcasting legend and we were driving around a rocky American landscape shooting a grizzled radio legend while he took pictures. We are were in the middle of nowhere, under an orange ball of blazing autumn sun with just a nip in the air, surrounded by endless blue sky and natural mountainous sculpture. And we were all wearing the uniform of virility, two-piece denim suits. Dan and I were in a car following Imus, and when he stopped to snap a picture, we jumped out of the car and watched. But back in the car, it became a Dan Rather open mic, a super-personal one-on-one celebrity interview.

"Does Richard Nixon hate you? Do you ever see him?" I asked. He said they didn't see each other for twenty years and then ran into each other crossing a random street in New York City but didn't speak.

"What's the deal with Barbara Walters?" He said she was the most competitive person he'd known and had once high-heeled him in the foot running to interview someone.

"What's the most dangerous situation you've been in? Most embarrassing live TV moment? Why haven't you ever been on *Oprah*? What do you really think of Connie Chung? Tell me about the guy who mugged you." I was like a ravenous dog, and he answered every single query. "Oh, wait—Have you met Princess Di?" Yes, I was exactly this annoying. But this was a legend, and we were out in God's country, alone together, and I had to ask every damn thing I could think of while I had the chance. (Unfortunately, today I can't remember many of his answers. And that kills me, because I do remember an entire catalog of Captain and Tennille lyrics.)

With every passing moment, I became even more of a Dan Fan. He seemed like he was in the zone with me, too. "This is so beautiful. Why don't we stop the car and I'll take a picture of you, Andrew, that you can send to your mom to show her where you were?"

"Dan, will you be my daddy?" I asked. In my head, of course. We stopped the car and Dan carefully knelt on the dusty ground to get the best possible picture. Our cameraman took a picture of Dan taking a picture of me—a moment so meta and surreal you might not believe it if I didn't have the evidence.

At the end of the shoot, as we drove to our departure spot at a landing strip in the middle of nowhere, I felt like I'd climbed to the top of some sort of Broadcast Journalism Peak. *I'd worked with Dan Rather in the field.* As we'd been previously instructed to do, we parked our rental car on the edge of the landing strip, locked our keys inside, and boarded the private flight for home.

The plane turned to taxi, and I breathed a sigh of relief. Not only had I had the time of my life as a one-man captive audience to a TV news legend, we had also survived the shoot without incident.

No one had mugged Dan, I hadn't screwed up, Dan seemed relaxed and pleased, and I had the footage I needed for a great piece on Don Imus. I reclined my luxurious leather seat and had just popped the top on my first can of free limitless Diet Coke when suddenly the plane lurched under me and I noticed that we were tilting—sinking, actually—into the tarmac. The huge plane had hit a sinkhole in the asphalt of a runway ill equipped for aircraft this size.

I had rejoiced too soon, and now the earth was eating Dan Rather! It was sucking The Anchorman—and me—into the ground!

"Is the National Desk aware of what's happening?" Dan breathlessly inquired of me seconds later. "What's the plan from New York?"

"Um . . ." I stammered, when what I wanted to say was, "I am sitting here right next to you and haven't had time to alert the media that we have a sunken anchorman." I felt that I should have had a better answer, that I should have had a plan in place for dealing with a situation like this. But how can you plan ahead for the ground opening up underneath you?

I called my executive producer in New York and explained what had happened. The EP spoke with Dan, then wished me luck as the pilots scrambled to find another jet to take us back to New York. They found one a short drive away in Billings, Montana. Exiting the plane, I now saw that the earth hadn't exactly tried to swallow us but, more accurately, had taken a nice bite out of the plane. Dan and I grabbed the flight attendant, who grabbed her tray of veggies and dip, and we all headed back to the car we'd left on the edge of the runway.

The car! We'd dutifully locked our keys in the car an hour before, and now we had to break into it. Luckily, a newsman on the road always has a recently dry-cleaned garment on a crappy wire hanger, so a few intense rental-car-damaging moments of jamming and probing later, we got inside and raced out of there hoping to get to Billings on time. My fears that our not-so-near-death experience had ruined what was otherwise a grand weekend flew out the window as Dan, clearly in high spirits, sang in the car—songs like you'd hear at camp around the fire—and let it be known to all of us that he had Knicks tickets for that night and was confident that if we hustled, he'd still make the game. We were served nibbly bits by the flight attendant, and then the three of us kicked out a sing-along jam that lasted the whole way home from Billings. Best. Trip. Ever.

By the way, The Anchorman made it to Madison Square Garden in time for tip-off. But it was all downhill for me at CBS from there.

They say you can never go home again, but I sure as hell tried. I returned to the morning show in 1999 as a senior producer running their entertainment unit. My life became a resounding chorus of "NO" coming from every publicist in America. *"No, Julia Roberts can't come to the studio, she's on Regis that day. Tom Cruise? Yes, that would be NO!"* The last time I'd been at *CBS This Morning*, we'd consistently been number three. By this point, we were probably number nine: Competing with *Today* and *GMA* had been hard enough, but in the couple of years I'd been away, the competition for bookings had also started to include *Entertainment Tonight*, *Access*, *Regis*, *Rosie*, and a host of others. It was brutal.

I logged countless hours backstage at awards shows, which sounds fun but wasn't. I've spent a noticeable percentage of my life at the Oscars, the Grammys, and even the friggin' Country Music Awards, and it was tuxedo warfare. To make these evenings as punishing as possible, the awards producers made everyone backstage—including our poor camera operators and sound guys—wear black tie to impart an air of glamour to every hideous occasion. The morning after every sleepless award-show night, my bosses in New York expected an upbeat, flashy piece that featured Mark McEwen, yukking it up with all the big winners. Nobody knew the hell associated with delivering on that promise.

Backstage at the awards, each show has a little makeshift room constructed of what's called pipe-and-drape—which is exactly what it sounds like, curtains hanging from pipes, all lined up in this little velveteen shantytown. Every show creates a staging area

Backstage at an awards show with Mark McEwen

commensurate with the show's status. *Entertainment Tonight* and *Access* always did it up big. They'd haul in huge lighting rigs with portable spaceship set pieces, photo booths, comfy couches, and In-N-Out Burgers. Naturally, that's where every big star stopped first. Mary Hart and her tribe of blond producers always looked like they were having so much *FUN*, laughing and schmoozing with the stars. At that time in my life I probably hated Mary Hart more than that woman who suffered seizures triggered by hearing Mary Hart's voice. Today, of course, I look back on my hostility as wasted energy, but at the time, *ET* was everything we were not, with their big budget, and ratings, and power. And free-flowing burgers.

Over in Morning Show Alley, we'd be in the corner behind *Today* and *GMA*— shows that needed no other set dressing than their superstar anchors. Katie Couric adorably perched in a director's chair was like catnip that lured in frisky members of the glitterati. By contrast, our CBS area usually consisted of a blue curtain, a plant of the fern variety, a couple lights, and—in later years—

a bowl of loose LifeSavers. We were very proud of the candy jar because occasionally *the stars would take a piece*! That meant they *liked us*! "Candice Bergen ate a LifeSaver!" we would marvel. At the time, we never saw any irony in choosing that particular candy. And even though the stars straggling by our tent genuinely liked Mark McEwen, we were always last in the rotation, and that meant people were usually sick of giving interviews by the time they got to us. You know what makes for lousy television? One-word answers.

I would try to prebook celebs before award shows, calling publicists and saying that I *knew* their client was going to win and please don't forget to stop by backstage to show off the new hardware. We also started pursuing up-and-coming talents who had no real name recognition yet but had gotten some critical acclaim. The hope was that they'd do our show in New York when nobody else knew who they were, and later they'd feel some loyalty to us as they started becoming famous and winning awards. It seemed like a good idea, but it didn't really work. I remember one particular screaming match with Hilary Swank's publicist, who'd screwed us in some painful way after we'd gotten behind Hilary when no one else (the *Today* show) cared.

While everyone who was anyone in Hollywood was out celebrating their wins and trying to work through their losses with the help of recreational consumables, I'd be at CBS Television City writing and editing the piece. We'd always finish and walk out as the sun was rising and I'd complain to Mark that we looked too good to waste ourselves on the war we'd just fought.

To say that morale on that show was at an all-time low is really saying something, but it was true. One day I came in to work and the poster on my office door—for the film *Life Is Beautiful*—had been ripped down the middle. "Who the fuck ripped my uplifting Holocaust poster?" I yelled. "FYI everybody: I called security and they're pulling the camera footage from the hallway!" I had every intention of finding the culprit, and a day later one of the anchors came into my office and closed the door.

"I have a confession. I ripped your poster. It was five in the morning, no one was here, I was pissed about something stupid, and it was the first thing I saw. I'm so sorry."

Life was not beautiful at the bottom of the ratings, and nearing the end of 1999, the anchor was put out of misery with another relaunch of the show. This time CBS had lured Bryant Gumbel, an Emmy-winning former star of the *Today* show, back to morning television. In a series of decisions meant to reflect the hugeness of this development, execs changed the name of *CBS This Morning* to *The Early Show*, built an expensive, state-of-the-art studio adjacent to Central Park, and then, for some reason, fumbled the coanchor hire. She was quite lovely and cute and nice and I have nothing against her, but she had a mild personality and was no match for Bryant Gumbel, who could turn sitting presidents into penitent schoolboys. We all crossed our fingers and hoped for the best.

It was imperative that I bring out the big guns to salute Gumbel's return to morning television. I booked Mariah Carey to perform outside on our plaza, for her first-ever morning show concert. Mariah wanted it to be huge, and so did we. Within reason. I spent one month juggling her high hopes for the performance with our limited capabilities to meet them. Mariah suggested posing for the cover of *TV Guide* with Bryant, but CBS nixed it because they wanted to promote Bryant and his coanchor. Mariah took this in stride but upped the ante by demanding that the circle next to Central Park on Fifty-ninth Street be closed to traffic. I was sure that CBS could make this happen with the City and the Parks Department. Surely Mariah's concert was on a par with the Macy's Thanksgiving Day Parade? I kept telling Mariah's people not to sweat it.

But I was sweating the hell out of it. I felt more pressure associated with this booking than any before—or since. Mariah needed to launch her new album in a major way and CBS needed Mariah to launch this new show in a major way. But in the meantime, something else launched. This is as humiliating for me as it is gross for you: It was my first and only case of hemorrhoids. My bottom broke out in a mess of 'roids so terrible that I could barely walk, and it was all brought on by the stress surrounding the concert. ("Sit on one of those DONUTS," my mom implored in e-mails. "Take a SALT BATH!") The closer the date came, the more pressure I was getting from Mariah's camp to show them the street-closure paperwork and I didn't have it. The gears of municipal bureaucracy had chewed up our request but hadn't spit out any permits yet, and we were running out of time. We'd already announced the concert when Team Butterfly called to tell me they were pulling the segment, to appear instead on *Today*, if I didn't deliver the nonexistent paperwork. Mariah did cancel, and every newspaper in the country covered the "story." Even my beloved Oprah asked Mariah about canceling on CBS. Meanwhile, my ass was, literally and figuratively, in trouble.

On the morning of our launch, I stood in our control room watching the number one female recording artist of the nineties sing two songs on the *Today* show plaza, beneath a giant rainbow of balloons and surrounded by a sea of fans, as one lone clown from the Big Apple Circus did the saddest, most depressing "routine" on our plaza for probably the same fifteen people who'd made up our studio audience back when I'd worked on this show the first time. The show was a bomb, and even as my Mimi-induced hemorrhoids began to shrink, the chorus of *no*'s coming from every celebrity publicist on the planet grew to a cacophony.

I didn't know what to do. For all of the setbacks I'd been through in this career, I had never considered the possibility that it could all just end. And then what would I do? Go back to St. Louis and Allen Foods to resume my bottle-capping career? Luck intervened at exactly the right moment at exactly the right time, when I received an offer to run the programming department for a start-up cable channel, TRIO, helmed by the legendary Barry Diller. Cable was an entirely different world than network television, and I had no idea what the future would hold if I left it all behind to work for a channel that didn't even exist yet. On the other hand, I had a good idea what the future might hold if I stayed where I was. So, after spending ten years with a front row seat (albeit the least desirable one) to every major event of the nineties—Clinton's nominating convention, the Kerrigan-Harding Olympics in Lillehammer, the first *Vanity Fair* Oscar party, every award show, and Dan Rather almost biting it in Don Imus's airplane—my career at CBS News was over.

TRIO was to focus on popular culture and the arts with lots of original documentaries and live entertainment events, two things I loved. When I got there, I knew a good deal about how to produce programming but had no clue about marketing, promotion, ad sales, budgets, contracts, scheduling, distribution, and all the other intricacies that were part of the gig at a small newborn network. Crash course time!

I went from haggling with publicists to meetings with Barry Diller. Remembering the advice I'd been given as a CBS intern, I tried to listen more than I spoke, and only to speak about that which I was confident I knew. Which was often problematic, because a lot of what I was supposed to be speaking about was numbers, and my brain has a tendency to go blank when I see an Excel spreadsheet.

TRIO launched softly and quietly, with limited distribution and not a ton of original programming. After a couple of years, a new president was brought in to lead the network, and I began working directly for her. In Lauren Zalaznick, I found a mentor with an almost supernatural sense of creativity, who shared my love of pop culture and appreciation for weird and wonderful people. We organized our schedule into three or four tent-pole programming events, and the channel became best associated with one called *Brilliant but Canceled*, about shows that had been critically acclaimed but canceled before their time. We produced an original documentary and series about the subject and ran cult-favorite shows like *Freaks and Geeks*, *EZ Streets*, and *Action*. As part of "TRIO Uncensored" we produced a documentary called *The N-Word* (yes, *that* N-word) that went on to win a Peabody, which is an award that does not come with a red carpet but is very coveted among those who work in television.

Oh, and maybe best of all, Lauren shared my enthusiasm for *Battle of the Network Stars*, which we quickly acquired and reran in its entirety. If you happened to watch it, you will undoubtedly be amazed by Howard Cosell's commentary, which ran from racist ("Tim Reid can't swim because he's black") to sexist ("Just look at Joyce DeWitt's chest!").

TRIO was barely available outside of DirecTV and not even big enough to receive Nielsen ratings, but we generated enviable amounts of press due to our quirky mix of programming, and we tried our damnedest to convert it into ad dollars and distribution. I didn't know it then, but I was in something of a boutique Bravo boot camp. When Universal—our parent company—merged with NBC, I heard rumblings that TRIO was headed for the dumpster. Those rumblings were confirmed when Lauren got the job running Bravo and TRIO became a victim of its own making: brilliant, but canceled.

Lauren told me she wanted me to come with her and run current programming at Bravo, a network I'd never really watched but was having a major moment with the success of a show I'd desperately wanted to buy for TRIO, *Queer Eye for the Straight Guy*. Bravo was seriously gay-friendly, with shows like *Boy Meets Boy* and *Gay Weddings*. I guess that didn't make it gay enough for me, though, because I had my heart set on running programming for Viacom's new gay start-up channel, Logo. I was amazed that times had changed so much that I would be considering two jobs involving gay TV. I got an interview at Logo, but no callback. I was disappointed at the time but, in retrospect, I haven't been so glad of anything not happening since not taking that internship at KSDK in St. Louis. Had I gotten that job, my life would certainly have taken an entirely different direction. I don't think I would ever have gotten my own show, and I probably wouldn't be writing this book. So now you know who to thank. Or blame.

PERFECT PITCH

There's no such thing as a perfect pitch. This is a law of the universe that holds true whether you're a bewildered Little Leaguer on the baseball field or an at times even more bewildered broadcast executive in a network boardroom. At least at the network there's no dirt and no tears, or at least not as many.

There's a perception that TV shows are born in a brilliant flash, that an idea becomes a show in a nanosecond. But after twenty-two years in the business listening to thousands of pitches, I can say that the opposite is usually true. There are a lot of cooks in the TV kitchen and everybody wants to add a spice. Or a pile of weird ingredients they grabbed in a frantic quest to appear more cook-like. I have spent an upsetting amount of time (I could've been getting tan during that time!) in rooms with producers explaining show ideas to me and I can't say there's been one singular moment that felt like finding nirvana. Hearing the pitch for *Queer Eye for the Straight Guy* was probably as close as I ever came, but I knew that the show would only go somewhere at a place with more money and more resources. Little did I know that *Queer Eye* would land at Bravo and I'd wind up supervising it when I took over their current programming.

At TRIO and later at Bravo, I've run not only all shows in production, but everything in development as well. "Development" is what happens to 99 percent of pitches that aren't passed on outright. For example, *Flipping Out* was originally pitched as a show called *The WannaBees* about Jenni Pulos and her then husband Chris, two part-time actors who also worked for an obsessive-compulsive house flipper. When that OCD house flipper, Jeff Lewis, appeared on their demo reel, our development team said, "Who's *that* guy!?" and *Flipping Out* was born.

Here's what usually happens during a pitch: People come into your office or a conference room with a document or a DVD or a wannabe star and perform a sort of show-and-tell that's either funny or desperate or brilliant or completely off the mark. Sometimes you know right off the bat that the show they're pitching would never in a million years fit in at the network. In the biz we call that "off-brand." (Though we don't actually call it "the biz.") Sometimes we get pitched things we are already doing, with a slight and often awful twist (e.g., *Real Housewives of the Trailer Park, Real Housewives of Appalachia, Real Housewives of Compton, Real Housewives of the Bayou . . .*). But even recognizing the great possibility that on any given day I may be about to listen to yet another *Real Housewives of Somewhere* presentation, I still live for that gut feeling of excitement I get when I hear something that is fresh, unique, and on-brand.

Ugh! I just yawned while I was typing, which is fitting because I have a terrible habit of yawning during pitches, which has got to be the worst possible trait for someone with my job. Once I took a pitch from Charlize Theron at 6 p.m. on a Friday at the end of a long week and congratulated myself on swallowing several teeny yawns, not realizing that they would get together inside me, combining into one huge yawn that I would be powerless to hold in. When I let one rip, Theron called me on it. Lucky for me, she was more amused than irritated. I'm sure it'd been years since someone had yawned in her beautiful face.

Sometimes pitches can be incredibly entertaining and provide a little window into who celebrities are as people—you could call them "Stars! They're just like us!" moments. I've taken a pitch from Ashton and Demi, who seemed very in love and cuddly at the time. I had a meeting with Naomi Campbell, who couldn't have been nicer and called in to my show later that night. Richard Simmons wore his tank top and short shorts in the winter and shocked a budget meeting as he pressed his face and body against the conference room windows on his way to my office. And what could be better than listening to Ivana Trump talk about her factories and skiing in Gstaad? Certainly not this pitch: A producer had the whole Bravo office in a lather about the HUGE TOP SECRET star he was bringing into the office. I was convinced it could only be J Lo. But the producer arrived for the meeting with only a briefcase, which he opened theatrically to reveal "Madame," the puppet who in the '70s had replaced Paul Lynde as the center square on Hollywood Squares. One memorable pitch took me out of my office and inside the mind-boggling 123-room Los Angeles mansion of Aaron Spelling, where I sat in the "library" listening to his widow, Candy, tell me what she would and would not do on TV. As I munched from a platter of crudités the size of a manhole cover, I realized I was surrounded by leatherbound copies of every script her late husband had ever written. Breathing in the rich smells of leather commingled with aging pages of *Dynasty* and *TJ Hooker* dialogue made me feel appropriately faux-literary as I bided my time until I was allowed into the dowager Spelling's storied wrapping-paper room. It did not disappoint.

But Candy would have had to try really hard to beat my all-time kookiest celebrity pitch meeting. Back when the TRIO network was still afloat, I was in LA when I got a message that Cybill Shepherd wanted to pitch a reality show that she was billing as a real-life *Absolutely Fabulous* starring Cybill and her best friend. We met in her manager's office in Beverly Hills on a hot Los Angeles summer day. I wore flip-flops, khakis, and a T-shirt, which is not unusual office attire for Los Angeles.

It's been my experience that when you take any kind of pitch from a celebrity, they are usually "on." Because in that moment they are their own product, so they are presenting a version of themselves that either they want you to think they are or that they think you want them to be. Sometimes that person can wind up being completely overbearing; other times, they can be charming. With Shepherd, it was somewhere in between.

Cybill was dressed to the nines, made up, hair done, and with her best friend, who was similarly upbeat and well packaged. In a nondescript, steaming office, they were cheerful, engaging, and flirty. Very flirty.

"How *old* are you, Andrew?" they cooed. "Are you *Jewish*?"

"Um, yes?" I stammered. I felt like Dustin Hoffman in *The Graduate*. But Dustin only had one Mrs. Robinson, and he wasn't gay.

"We LOVE Semitic men!" Cybill exclaimed.

Her friend agreed. "We love them!" she nodded.

I was uncomfortable, and it was so boiling in that office that the internal gaydars of two sophisticated, well-traveled LA ladies had apparently completely short-circuited. I wondered if I should just come out to them right then before they tried to titillate me into picking up their show. Cybill said she was baking. She kept fanning herself and lifting her hair off the nape of her neck into a loose pile on top of her head.

"Do you mind if I slip off my shoes?" she asked, not waiting for a response before letting her dogs out. She certainly didn't need to explain needing to let her feet breathe—I was the one in flip-flops. I was starting to groove on her casual style as she told me about the real-life madcap situations that she and her pal got into in real life, and how that would translate to a hit show. Blind dates! Motherhood! Menopause! It was pretty much a pitch for a reality version of her successful CBS sitcom *Cybill*. Not a horrible idea.

Suddenly, though, Ms. Shepherd did have a horrible idea. A very, very horrible idea. "It is so fucking hot in here," she announced, "that I think I have to take my shirt off."

I've been told that I cock my head a lot on *Watch What Happens Live*, particularly when someone says something weird or outrageous (which is a lot). Well, I'm pretty sure I sprained my neck with the extreme cocking I did at her suggestion. Cybill was squealing with laughter as she asked her broiling friend if she was up for joining in this game of pitch-tease. Big shock: Her friend was into it. I thought maybe a better idea was to turn up the air-conditioning, but for perhaps the first time in my life, and for reasons I still can't comprehend, I kept my mouth shut. Maybe I had heatstroke.

They proposed a deal: They would take their shirts off, and then I would follow suit and take off mine. I should remind the reader here that there were *other people in the room*. Other people who were certainly as hot and sweaty as me, but nobody was making them take *their* shirts off. Not that I wanted to see any of them without their shirts. Not that I didn't want to, either. You can see how this was becoming weirder by the second, and although I was already pretty sure at that point that we weren't going to buy this demented version of *Beverly Hills AbFab Theater*, I had to admit I was curious to see how this would all play out. And I *was* hot. And by "hot" I mean that I was sweating-like-I-was-going-through-menopause hot, not hot like ready to bang the *Moonlighting* lady.

"Okay," I said, and off came my shirt.

There I was, sitting across from Cybill Shepherd, famed star of *The Last Picture Show* and *The Heartbreak Kid*, who was now wearing slacks and no shoes and a black bra. The curiosity that had been percolating moments before abruptly evaporated. Now I just wanted my mommy. Or Dan Rather. Cybill's friend was also wearing a black bra. And these ladies were lovely, but I really, really did not want to see them in their dainties. They continued to pitch me the show, the two bra-clad Mrs. Robinsons and me, naked to the waist.

"If this is the first meeting," I wondered to myself, "what would happen if we got into business together?" Would our meetings eventually involve full frontal nudity? Was it a ploy to make their pitch stand out, or could it be that they were just excruciatingly hot? Were they acting out the "parts" they would be playing on their madcap reality show? Cybill was on a tear about the inability of actresses her age to get parts and how that would play out on the show. It was still very hot in the room, but I was not really concerned with the temperature or the show anymore. I wanted out, and I think Cybill noticed.

"I have another idea!" she screamed. Okay, I thought. Maybe she was saving her best idea for last? I sat back, ready to hear her out. "Let's take our pants off!" she said. Of course. "We'll go first and then you do it!" They cackled, thrilled by their latest suggestion.

There were so many problems with this suggestion, the most urgent being that my casual attire that day went beyond flip-flops and a T-shirt. I was not wearing any underwear. Listen, judgy: I was in LA, the pants were soft, it was warm, and I didn't want to be constrained. Also, I was probably out of clean drawers, and you know how much a hotel charges to do your laundry. These are the myriad excuses of a freeballer, I know, and at that moment I gravely regretted my decision.

"NO! I CAN'T!" I immediately yelled, way too quickly and way too defensively. Their eyes immediately broke out in knowing twinkles. I surmised that because of my speedy response, they were now convinced that I had a big, raging, Semitic, double-cougar-induced boner. Which I did not.

"WHY, Andrew?" said Cybill. "Are you that shy? Why won't you take off your pants? What's stopping you?"

"I just . . . can't," I said. Now I was embarrassed. I sounded, and felt, like an ashamed child. Let's be clear: I wasn't ashamed that I didn't want to take my pants off. You shouldn't have to do that in a pitch meeting, or any other type of business meeting. I just couldn't believe that I wasn't wearing underwear and that it was now going to become a freaking point of discussion in my freaking television pitch meeting with freaky Cybill Shepherd.

She pushed and prodded. "Come on," she said. "What's it gonna hurt?" And with that, I was worn down. Busted.

"I'm not wearing underwear," I sighed, just softly enough for her to hear. The game was over.

Flashing her trademark Cybill Shepherd grin, she finally dropped the subject. Which would have been fine, except I was still shirtless and the ladies were still in their bras. I quickly finished our discussion and we put our clothes back on, awkwardly. Then I ran out and looked for a sink to wash my hands, because the whole thing had made me feel dirty, like I'd done something I wasn't supposed to. In retrospect, it's pretty clear that she and her friend were just proving in the room how fun and wacky their show would be. It was kind of a genius idea, but we didn't wind up buying it. And you can bet that ever since that day, if I'm in a pitch meeting, no matter what the thermometer says, I'm wearing underwear.

☺

All this talk of freeballs brings me to a different kind of pitch altogether, but one that was just as nerve-racking.

I've always maintained a pop-culture bucket list, filled with things I have simultaneously dreamed of doing, while also never actually thinking that I would get to. But through the success of

my show, which I realize is lucky enough in and of itself, I've had
the fortune to experience some dream-come-true moments, including an appearance on Letterman and getting to be the grand mar-
shal of more than one parade. (Yes, that's a humble brag about
leading exactly two parades.) One of the toppers had to be when I
was asked to throw out the first pitch at a St. Louis Cardinals game.

When the opportunity first presented itself, I was as excited as
I'd been when I was a twentysomething B-52s go-go boy. It was
big. My family had Cardinals season tickets, I'd witnessed several
play-off and World Series games at Busch Stadium, and many relatives to this day call me "Bird" because of my devotion and love
for Cardinals mascot "Fredbird." Now I of little coordination was
asked to throw a baseball in front of thousands of St. Louisans and
my entire family.

I spent a few months polling everyone I knew who knew anything about baseball about how to throw the perfect pitch, or at
least how to get it over the base. I discovered early that the main
goal of a layman throwing a pitch was to not bounce the ball—the
ultimate in celebrity-pitcher humiliation.

I spoke to several people who'd thrown out first pitches in
their career. Jerry Seinfeld told me to stand on the rubber in front
of the mound. This, he said, was because I wouldn't be prepared
for the height of the mound. While hosting an event for Bravo at
the Kentucky Derby, I asked fellow St. Louisan Bob Costas his
advice. "Whatever you do, do not throw from the mound. If you
do, you'll bounce the ball. Throw from the front of the mound."
Clearly, bouncing the pitch would lead to many unthinkable forms
of terror and punishment. I spent many dark days in a YouTube
hole, repeatedly watching a clip of Mark Wahlberg beaning a fan
in the ass with his first pitch at a Red Sox game in 2009. If Marky
Mark couldn't do it, what hope did I have?

My own history started to weigh heavily on my mind. I was no
stranger to baseball-related humiliation, having played Optimist
Baseball for six years growing up in the 1970s. Looking back, I

guess I played to fit in, and because the real party was after the game when everybody went to Dairy Queen for cherry dip cones. (The things we do for a crunchy coating.) Also you got a different color T-shirt every year, and I wore mine like a badge of honor. Yes, I'd dropped every ball hit to me, endured endless strikeouts, and made several game-losing plays, but at least I had those T-shirts. At the beginning of every season, my dad asked me to let him coach the team, and every season I begged him not to. I wouldn't let my parents even *come see me play*, so the idea of my father coaching was problematic, since he wouldn't be attending any games.

In the last inning of our last game at the end of sixth grade, as we played together for the final time as a team before we moved schools and aged out of the league, we were one run down with men on base and two outs. I stepped up to the plate, with all eyes on me, carrying my teammates' hopes and dreams on my little shoulders. It was like a movie where the underdog has one final chance to redeem himself. Unlike my boo, St. Louis Cardinal David Freese, in the now legendary Game Six of the 2011 World Series, I struck out. On the way home—we didn't even stop at Dairy Queen—the mother who was driving us said, "Oh, Andy, you lost the game *again*?"

When I walked into my house I looked at my mom with a heavy heart and eyes brimming with tears. "That bad?" she asked. She opened her arms to hug me and I sobbed into her shoulder, silently vowing never to be humiliated on the baseball diamond again.

So I did not care to bounce the ball at Busch Stadium. I was given an extra final chance at glory, and I wanted a happy ending to my baseball career, tied in a neat Cardinal-red bow. And I wanted that bitch mother of my ex-friend to hear *all* about it!

As per usual, I completely overhyped the event and told everyone I knew. I secured a box at the game with room for thirty family members and friends who flew in just for the occasion, including my old friends Kari, Jeanne, Dave, and Amanda, Isaac Mizrahi (who was in town directing an opera and is a fanatical baseball fan), and, just to make the possibility of humiliation a smidge more emasculating, my Bravo boss, Lauren Zalaznick, a lover of both baseball *and* completely overhyped events.

The day of the game, my sister Em arranged for me to throw baseballs with a high school coach who would warm me up and critique my throw. Outside of a brief game of catch with Matthew Broderick that I shot for *Watch What Happens Live* ("Don't throw from the mound," Matthew sternly advised, between takes. "Oh, and you want the catcher to *catch* the ball.") I hadn't done much in the way of ~~rehearsing~~ training—but as is often the case, I was unrealistically optimistic. The coach told me that I looked okay, and he deemed me ready to throw—from in front of the mound, just like everybody said. I felt strong and coordinated (only later would I learn that he told Em I was so bad that he rolled the ball to me because he was worried I couldn't catch it). When I got home, my dad asked me to show him my form. I indulged him so that his dream of coaching me doing baseball-related things could also come true.

"You look like you're *pushing* the ball," he warned. "You have to follow through." I was sure he was right, but I had no idea how to make my arm not push, and now I was getting confused. My mom went to YouTube and pulled up George W. Bush throwing out a first pitch to show me how it was done. It was probably the only time anyone in my family used W as an example of doing something right. Ready or not, it was time to go.

At the ballpark, I was given a jersey that said "Cohen" on the back with the number 68, the year of my birth. You don't see many Jewish baseball players, so on top of everything, I felt special to be representing. I left all my VIP spectators to watch me from the box as I headed to the field with my thirteen-year-old nephew Jeremy, my coworker, Bravo exec Dave Serwatka, my boss, Lauren, and her son Dale. And then a pregame event unfolded that changed my game plan.

There was a mass of Little Leaguers doing I Don't Know What on the field, but it involved pint-sized hurlers throwing strikes from the TOP OF THE MOUND. These little pissant punks were showing me up before I even had the chance to humiliate myself! I looked at Lauren aghast. She'd taught me plenty about TV and I needed her help on the field. She tried to console me, though she agreed that my hands were tied and I simply could not pitch from the front of the mound without sacrificing my dignity.

My nephew was incredulous. "What is the big deal!?" he shouted. He didn't get why I would care one way or another *where* I threw the ball from. (Easy for him, when he was the kid in the family who got all the hand-eye coordination.)

As I looked out at my family and forty thousand St. Louis Cardinals fans, Lauren explained to Jeremy, "Andy is having really bad flashbacks to being a gay kid in Little League who dropped balls and continually sucked."

I actually *hadn't* been thinking of that, but was sure to thank her for putting it top of mind, both for me and for my only nephew, just in case there was any danger of him ever looking up to me. We were interrupted by the Cardinals' PR director, who informed me that in a short while I'd be introduced and throw my pitch, and then they'd bring out Bob Gibson to throw his.

Wait. "BOB GIBSON?!" I asked? "Bob Gibson is throwing a baseball?"

Bob Gibson is one of the great pitchers in all of baseball and a Cardinal legend, and he would be throwing *after* me. My heart sank.

Time was running short and the PR guy introduced me to then Cardinal right fielder Joe Mather, to whom I'd be throwing my pitch, and I quickly fell in love. He was tall like a building and under his Cardinals hat was a full head of gorgeous gingey hair (you know I love a ginge, right?). He had no idea who I was or what a Real Housewife was, nor did he care. Nor should he have. I was just grateful for the distraction.

"Go over to Fredbird," the publicist instructed me, ripping me away from my future boyfriend-in-my-head. Ever resilient, I joked with Fredbird, the mascot for whom I was nicknamed, as the announcer introduced me. Then came the very best part of the night: running, in slow motion, to the mound, framed by the Gateway Arch, as the crowd cheered. I caught a glimpse of the Jumbotron; a shot of the back of my Cardinals jersey was on-screen and I looked legitimately like I belonged. Even though the name said "Cohen" and the guy inside it didn't really have any idea how to do what he was about to try to do. It was my finest moment. Except that I still had to make that effing pitch.

Once I got to the top of that mound, I knew it was all downhill from there. I took one last look at my family a million miles away in the stands, and then just got it the hell over with. The throw was, um . . . well, it was *very* high and *very* outside. That is me being kind to myself. But Joe Mather took several steps—maybe a leap or two—and caught it! It was nowhere in the vicinity of the plate, but it did not bounce and it was caught, and suddenly that seemed to be all that mattered.

After the pitch, Joe Mather ran to the mound and we took a picture together. Then, as the two of us jogged in slow-mo away from each other, he toward the dugout and I toward—I don't know where the hell I was going, but it wasn't into the dugout—the six-foot-four Gingey baseball god called out, "Hey, Andy!"

I turned to him and we locked eyes. We were still running away from each other in slow-mo, but yeah, our eyes totally locked. "If you ever need a baseball player . . . call me!" he said. Then he was gone.

My heart fluttered. I DID need a baseball player! I needed him! But I never called him, because I am not a fool and I know he wasn't saying what I was hearing. Clearly, he meant if I needed a baseball player for a TV show or something. He was pitching himself to *me*! *S* to the *woon*.

In an insane twist, Bob Gibson pitched from the front of the mound and his ball definitely bounced. No matter that the man was in his seventies with a bum shoulder. I pitched better than he did. It's as simple as that, and no one can take it away from me.

When I got to my friends and family, Isaac Mizrahi proclaimed it the "gayest pitch in the history of baseball." I turned to my mom and dreamily told her about Joe Mather's good-bye "offer."

"Oh, that is RIDICULOUS!" she howled. "That guy is STRAIGHT! GET OVER HIM!"

And of the pitch? What did my mother think of The Pitch? "Well . . . at least you didn't hit the DIRT." And there you go: I had succeeded simply by not failing spectacularly. I'm sure there's a deep metaphor somewhere in there for anyone who ever has to pitch anything. Maybe it's this: There are no perfect pitches, just try not to hit the dirt.

BRAVO

You've probably seen me with a sheaf of blue index cards in my hands, which my guests on *Watch What Happens Live* or *Housewives* reunions clearly regard as some sort of dangerous weapon. These are viewer questions, and they rightly induce fear. The questions can be rude, invasive, and divisive. (And I mean that as a compliment.) They are what make our discussions interesting. Oh, and I enjoy the freedom that in most cases Andy C. is not asking if anybody was or was not in fact a prostitution whore; Brenda B. from Skokie is. Since turnabout is fair play, I have put some of the questions most frequently asked of *me* since I've been on Bravo on some blue cards and handed them over to my editor, and she has chosen a batch for me to answer here.

Q: How did you end up on the air? Did you just green-light your own show?

A: I hear this question a lot, often put exactly like that. Usually, I just say: If I could just green-light my own show, don't you think I would be hosting *Andy Chats with Susan Lucci While a Parade of Shirtless Gingers Slowly Walks By*?

Short answer: No, I didn't green-light my own show. A chain of coincidental-but-totally-connected events at Bravo have led me to where I've always wanted to be since using that hairbrush as a mic in the backseat of my uncle's car.

Long Answer: It all began when I started sending detailed and gossipy e-mails to Lauren Zalaznick about behind-the-scenes shenanigans on *Battle of the Network Reality Stars*, the first show I concocted as head of current programming at Bravo in 2004. *Rumor has it that Trishelle from* The Real World *hooked up last night*, I'd write. *Richard Hatch has ideas for how the format of this show could be better—he's oddly competing while suggesting twists to the challenges.* Lauren told me I should be blogging for the Bravo website.

For me, my blog became the silver lining of the bomb-shaped cloud that was *Battle of the Network Reality Stars* (more on that later). I envisioned it as a dialogue with Bravo viewers about everything from interviews with the *Project Runway* judges about why they'd eliminated Santino the night before, to, eventually—after readers got to know me a bit—what *I* had done the night before. In the early days, when I was still learning, sometimes I'd lose touch with my journalistic roots and I would be a little too creative in my reporting online. When Heidi Klum made a controversial remark on *Runway* about a design making a model look "plus-size," I hastily blogged that no, no, no, Heidi didn't mean it. Except the problem was, I didn't know what Heidi meant, and moreover, she did not appreciate me speaking for her. I also blogged about rumors that two designers were hooking up. This, I was later told, did not go over so well with the live-in lover one of the designers had back home. "You caused a lot of trouble," Santino told me. I felt pretty awful.

(Of course my mother was constantly up my ass about the blog. "No one liked Wednesday's blog. You got ONE comment! People don't like when you write about things they don't care about. You write about Oprah too much. Are you AWARE of that? Are you MONITORING the comments?" No, I wasn't monitoring the comments. Clearly, my mother had it covered.)

Being a blogging network exec somehow made me "credible" enough to get invitations to be a pop-culture-commenting windbag on various CNN shows, *Weekend Today*, and once even *The View*. This wasn't exactly how I'd imagined getting on TV all those years earlier, but I relished the opportunity. My best buddy, Bruce Bozzi, is a restaurant guru—he helps run the Palm Restaurant empire, which his grandfather founded—and he became my de facto media coach, watching every single appearance I made with a critical eye.

"Okay, here's the deal," he'd say. "That was good. But you sat with your legs wide open. You need to cross the legs!" That was a big one, but it was nothing compared to what I did with my head. "Again with the *head-cock*! You did that whole section about the Academy Awards with your head tipped like your brains were about to run out! But the outfit was great." Of course he would think that: Bruce always told me what to wear when I went on TV.

During Season 2 of *Top Chef*, Lauren decided to create a live webshow to "air" on BravoTV.com after each episode, with me as moderator. She viewed it as an extension of my blog, and I viewed it as a fun lark and an opportunity to learn something about hosting. Every Wednesday night, I would schlep to CNBC headquarters in beautiful Englewood Cliffs, New Jersey, to interview the chef who had just been eliminated at Judges' Table, along with one of the judges who had just done the eliminating plus a famous chef or a *Top Chef* Season 1 alum. The show was named after our Bravo tagline: *Watch What Happens Live*. We didn't have much of a set, studio, staff, or audience, and I loved every low-rent second of it.

The year 2007 was a big one for Bravo. Everything just jelled. With *Project Runway* and *Top Chef*, we had two new hits, and suddenly we weren't just the *Queer Eye* network anymore. Kathy Griffin won an Emmy, *Work Out* had an intense second season, and *Sheer Genius* and *Flipping Out* premiered. Everywhere I went, people wanted to talk about our shows. Many people like to leave their work at the office, but I like to drag my work around with me everywhere, and I couldn't have been more pleased. When the season of *Top Chef* ended, I continued schlepping out to Englewood Cliffs to do *Watch What Happens Live* on the Web as an aftershow to *Top Design*.

Meanwhile, back at the Bravo offices, when the second season of *The Real Housewives of Orange County* took off, we decided to add a reunion, but we needed a host. In a production meeting one day, programming chief Frances Berwick and Lauren asked if I'd want to try a TV version of the webshow for the OC reunion. They were asking me if I wanted to host a show on TV! I did that thing where I pretended that I couldn't possibly do such a thing for about two seconds before I did that thing where I pretended like they had finally talked me into it. My answer was "Eff yes!"

If you watch that reunion show today, you will see me stiffly reading from a teleprompter with a velvet jacket, a Jewfro, and teeth so white they look like a little sheets of paper. (I'm guessing I'd either overwhitened my teeth or overtanned the day before.) You'll also see me having loads of fun with the viewer questions ("Lauri, how do you feel about being compared to a transvestite?"). Despite the bumpy parts, I didn't completely bomb, and the ratings were good. Good enough that my bosses decided I would get several more shots that year, hosting the dramatic Season 2 reunion of *Work Out* (one of the trainers, Doug Blasdell, had suddenly passed away during production, so there were many tears), plus reunions of *Sheer Genius* (I got to ask former Charlie's Angel Jaclyn Smith questions on television!), *Top Chef: Miami*, and *Flipping Out*.

Pretty soon, I was hosting all the reunion shows, and producer

Michael (*Who Wants to Be a Millionaire*) Davies called me up and invited me to lunch. I picked the Palm, of course, and over steaks he told me in his so-charming-as-to-be-nearly-intoxicating British accent, "Wot you should be dewwwwwing is hosting a television show, full-time, Guvnah!" (I may be exaggerating his accent a wee bit.) Whether Michael was blowing smoke up my ass or not, for the first time in my career I believed that I actually *could* do what I'd dreamed of as a CBS intern. I believed I could make the transition from behind the scenes to on-air. I was still making appearances as a pop culture pundit on any show that would have me, and I was still getting notes from Bruce critiquing my appearances. He said I'd gotten my head-cocking at least partly under control, but I needed to watch my interrupting ("It's not dinner at the Cohens'. You can't talk over the anchor!"), keep my legs closed ("Andrew, you were essentially serving up your crotch on that last appearance!"), and to always wear socks, and shoes. ("If I live to be a hundred, I will never, ever get over that you wore flip-flops on the *Today* show! It's *the* Today *show!*")

In 2008, *Watch What Happens Live* moved to Rock Center and broadcast as the online companion to Bravo's final season of *Project Runway*. By then we'd added cocktails to the mix and even booked some non-Bravo celebrity guests to join us. In early 2009, Michael Davies came to Bravo and pitched the idea of bringing the show to the network in late night and moving its home to a small studio he owned in SoHo. Frances and Lauren asked if I'd like to give it a try for twelve weeks at midnight. This time I just said, "Eff yes!" without all the humble bullshit. I met with Davies—again at the Palm—and told him I wanted to keep the format spontaneous, interactive, and simple; the only actual structural beats to hit would be a poll, three "Here's What" items to discuss at the top, a game, and a Mazel and a Jackhole of the Week.

We used my own furniture (a rug, a few chairs, and a bunch of tchotchkes) to decorate the set (aka "the Clubhouse"), which is modeled after my den in my apartment.

So, my show actually happened gradually and organically—from e-mails, to a blog, to online, to reunion shows, to live at midnight, and then 11 p.m. And had the show failed in that midnight slot? I promise you it would've been canceled. Because if there's one thing I know from my day job as a network executive, sometimes no matter how much you personally love a show, if it is wounded and bleeding, you have to put it down.

Hosting a live, televised interactive cocktail party from my "den" is as fun as it looks—maybe even more. We play games involving cocktails, blindfolds, and wigs. We make up words (e.g., *para ejemplar*, "Ramotional"). We acquired a pet turtle, named Tramona, who was really into costumed roleplay. One night, we had a blackout on-air right after I gave Patti LaBelle crabs—the crustacean, eating variety, not the pubic type. Another night, the producers secretly changed my copy in the teleprompter and before I

Holly Hunter looks on as Ralph Fiennes and I role-play Harry Potter *in our PJs. In other words, another insane night in the Bravo Clubhouse!*

realized what was happening, I was obliviously introducing a surprise our booker had orchestrated for me, an appearance by one of my all-time faves, Marie Osmond. (Yes, I welled up—a bucket list moment.) We have a small team, much smaller than any other TV show I'm familiar with, and while we work hard on this informal-seeming little show of ours, we try never to let it *look* hard, and I think that's part of what people like about it. It's also a bit of a throwback to the days when a late-night talk show meant a host and a guest in cool-looking chairs, tossing back a few drinks over a conversation that is neither premeditated nor preproduced. Anything can happen, and I love it best when anything does.

Q: Is there a Bravo show that is actually more successful than you expected it to be?

A: Yes. Believe it or not, I thought that *Top Chef* was destined for the disposal before it was even made. With fashion thriving on Bravo in the form of *Project Runway* and *Queer Eye*, Lauren Zalaznick was adamant that we come up with a show that did for food what we'd done for fashion on *Runway*. When I say adamant, I mean that she declared it the singular mandate of my department. I'm not what you'd consider a foodie, having once thrown up after being forced to eat a pea, and I had a stomach full of peas when I contemplated what might happen if our as-yet-unborn cooking show didn't work.

Top Chef came to be as a collaboration with Dan Cutforth, Jane Lipsitz, and their team at the Magical Elves, already our partners on *Project Runway*. Throughout the show's development and production, we debated our central dilemma: how to make an engaging cooking competition when no one at home could taste the food. It was so easy—and interactive—to critique a dress on *Runway*, but is it fun to hear somebody talk about a scallop being too salty? We formatted the show around two challenges—one fun, fast, and skill-based, and the other unexpected, over the top, and often engineered to highlight inter-chef drama.

Days before we were to begin production on Season 1 of *Top Chef,* I found myself in a position that no TV executive ever wants to be in, and one I'm embarrassed to admit I have lived through several times for one reason or another: We didn't have a host. (For a head judge, Bravo exec Dave Serwatka was pumped about someone who was a newbie to TV: Tom Colicchio, whom Dave called "a chef's chef." Tom was wise and direct and pulled no punches.) Not having a host—or a guest—for a show that is days away from production is a very specific kind of hell. It is a hell involving a merry-go-round of just-out-of-reach names and looming failure spinning around your brain while beads of sweat trickle from every nook of your body.

We had our eye on Padma Lakshmi, an Indian American model/actress/writer/presenter and then wife of Salman Rushdie. You couldn't find a more intriguing combination than that. We began speaking to her, and if you know Padma, you know that she loves to talk, so those discussions went on and on. Bravo loves its beautiful, articulate former-catwalk mavens, and Padma was that and more: She was gorgeous, a world traveler who loved food, had hosted food shows, and knew a lot of chefs. She'd even written her own cookbook, *Easy Exotic.* But she didn't want to be on a reality show. We sent her *Project Runway.* "Look, it's Heidi Klum! She did it!" we prodded. She warmed up, we started negotiating, and after a few back-and-forths, we thought we'd landed her. Then, the week before shooting, Padma decided to do a miniseries in India. We were fucked.

With Padma out, I started telling all my friends, and probably some random passersby on the street, that we were looking for a host of what was going to be an *amazing* new show. Full disclosure: At this point, I don't know if I believed that, but I know I lost more sleep every time Lauren e-mailed me saying, "Who is our host and don't we start shooting in a few days?"

With (near-literal) moments to spare, I got a call from a publicist at Sony Music who'd represented Billy Joel for years. She said she heard through Marcy Blum, Padma's wedding planner (go figure), that I was looking for a host. She begged me to meet Billy Joel's wife, Katie Lee. (Blum planned the Joels' wedding as well.) "She's a total foodie, she's gorgeous, she *loves* food. She's kind of green and this would be a huge break for her, but she's a lovely person and you will have a positive experience with her. Can we bring her in?" Katie Lee Joel was as advertised. We hired her.

We learned a lot, and fast, in the first days of *Top Chef* in San Francisco. On the night of the first elimination challenge, the chefs had completed their dishes and were ready to serve the judges—but we needed to get a shot of the finished plates for the "food porn" footage that we show before the entrees are dissected by the judges. While we were taking our time and making sure we had the shots we needed, Tom stormed back to the "video village," our makeshift control room where producers watch the action. "What's going on?" he demanded. "The dishes are getting cold! This is completely unfair to the chefs."

It seemed like a bad harbinger. I turned to Jane Lipsitz and said, "Is this show going to be a total bomb?" The show's rules were amended that night, and to this day, chefs are required to prepare *two* dishes—one for the judges and one for the food porn. That night, like so many spent on the set of *Top Chef*, stretched on into the next morning and Katie Lee Joel sat waiting to say *Top Chef*'s now-famous dismissal line—"Pack your knives and go"—to the first chef eliminated from the competition, poor Ken Lee. As is still our custom today, the judges and chefs faced off and essentially stared each other down before Katie Lee was to deliver the line. As the director let the chefs "marinate" in the moment, we heard a loud thumping noise coming from the set. Nobody could figure out what it was. Was someone pounding on a door somewhere? Was a piece of equipment failing? Finally the audio guy realized what he was hearing. "That's Katie's *heart*!" he screamed. I love a host with a big heart, and Katie Lee felt so bad about having to send anyone home that hers was pounding hard enough to be heard in the sound mix.

The show was a hit, but sadly, viewers didn't connect with Katie. She was beautiful and incredibly nice, but she was also very young and at the time not directly associated with food, which hurt her credibility as far as viewers were concerned. And, possibly to overcompensate for her youth and sweet Southern accent, we had directed her to appear stern, detached, and robotic on-camera—Klumesque, shall we say. As much as we try to act like we know what we're doing in TV, everything we ever do is basically an experiment. This one didn't work.

By Season 2 of *Top Chef* we'd parted ways—amicably—with Katie, and Padma was back in the fold, having completed that so-called miniseries in India, which, with every passing minute, I become more convinced never even existed. Seriously, Padma, if you're reading this, I've checked YouTube and I can't find even one clip of this "Indian miniseries."

Q: What's been your biggest flop at Bravo?

A: When I started at Bravo in 2004, I inherited some great shows, such as *Queer Eye for the Straight Guy, Celebrity Poker, Blow Out,* and *Show Biz Moms and Dads. Project Runway* was just in post-production and I loved it right away. I was also enamored with a new show that would become the first I'd supervise and shepherd from birth at Bravo: *Battle of the Network Reality Stars.* And can I just say to everyone at Bravo: Thank you for giving me another chance.

The show combined two things I adore, a nostalgic (and personal favorite) brand plus reality stars. We hired Bob "The Bachelor" Guiney, notorious *Apprentice* baddie Omarosa, and party girl Trishelle from *The Real World* to be our sideline reporters. Then we cast alumni from reality's greatest hits, including *Survivor, The Amazing Race, Project Runway, American Idol,* and *Big Brother* to compete. We even threw in someone from *Showdog Moms and Dads* to boost the kitsch factor. I absolutely could not envision a future in which this brilliant show could be anything other than a runaway smash. But my crystal clear vision was actually more like tunnel vision, because Frances didn't share the passion Lauren and I had for the project. But I persisted. I mean, what's not to love about Charla, a little person who had kicked ass on *Amazing Race*, going head to head against the surgically reconstructed winner of *The Swan* in a jousting duel? That *happened*, by the way. Charla lost, but not before almost re-rearranging Rachel's face (again).

We shot the show on the campus of Pepperdine University in Los Angeles, exactly where the original *Battle of the Network Stars* was filmed. We revived its logo and outfits including teeny Speedos and big, fat sweatbands. I was in a sea of modern pop culture meets seventies camp with a strong undercurrent of irony, and I was loving every minute of it.

Watching the reality stars, I observed something that I tell everyone to this day: They are exactly as they appear on-screen. If Omarosa is portrayed as a raving bitch on-screen, it's most likely because she has moments when she's a raving bitch. If somebody was a slut in a hot tub on *The Real World*, you might hear a story on-set about them being slutty in, you guessed it, a hot tub. You get the idea. When people ask me what the Housewives are like, I tell them to watch the show. The same can be said for the stars of every other Bravo show as well, whether it's the fun of Rachel Zoe or the intensity of Patti Stanger. You get what you want from them because they're just being themselves, as opposed to an actor who might be crazy fun in a bunch of comedies but be a droll bore in person.

Despite her doubts surrounding the show, Frances was good enough to put the full complement of Bravo's resources behind it, and *Battle of the Network Reality Stars* premiered amid a nationwide marketing blitz in magazines and billboards and on the sides of buses. And it was a complete flop. A total stink bomb. And it was all mine. I learned a great lesson with that one, which was not only to embrace your mistakes, but to analyze the hell out of them to figure out why you made them. What I found out in that case was what Frances had predicted and had been trying to tell me all along: that the show might've worked on another network, but that it was the totally wrong fit for Bravo. Today I have the poster for the show (featuring various reality stars in a tug-of-war) up in my office just to remind me: It is better to fail spectacularly and learn from it than it is to never fail and learn nothing.

Q: How in the hell did *Being Bobby Brown* ever happen, and why have all traces of its existence vanished?

A: If any show on Bravo embraces the "truth is stranger than fiction" premise, it's the story of *Being Bobby Brown*. Brown had allowed an Atlanta-based production company to follow him and his family with the intention of creating a docuseries about Bobby's comeback. The company showed Bravo some footage, which was at once funny and shocking because it featured the former New Edition singer and his megastar wife, Whitney Houston, in some compromising and uncomfortable situations. I had idolized Whitney for years, and even though it could be painful to see her this way, more raw than ever before, as a fan I could still see the incredible light within her shining through. She was a superstar. We licensed the footage and attempted to make nine airable episodes out of it—no small feat, given the complete lack of narrative in what had been shot. There was no sense to be made out of the couple's life—they seemed to live out of random hotels in Atlanta and may or may not have been completely high for the duration of shooting. Houston's agent and family were horrified by the entire spectacle, but Whitney agreed to participate for her love of Bobby— or "bah-BAY!" as she called him.

The show was a big, surreal hit, and when the run ended, Dave Serwatka and I flew down to Atlanta the day after Thanksgiving for a lunch with "bah-BAY!" and—small world alert!—his attorney, future Atlanta Housewife Phaedra Parks, to discuss the possibility of a second season of the show. The unspoken issue was that Houston's people had made it clear that Whitney was saying *"Hell* to the *no"* to a second season, and without her, Bravo didn't want the show. Although the title suggested that Bobby Brown was the star, Whitney was a huge part of its success. People tuned in to see the "real" Whitney, circa 2005, and visor askew and potty mouthed, she never disappointed. After discussing all the things that Bobby had coming up in his life that he felt would make interesting episodes with or without his wife on-camera, he finally cut to the chase with startling clarity.

"How many episodes would Whitney have to appear in if you picked the show up?" said Bobby.

"Well . . . um," I stammered, "let's say we did ten episodes. If we did ten episodes then I'd say . . . she'd have to appear in . . . maybe at least nine of them?" As the lunch wound down, Dave and I realized the series was done. But just before we left the table I had a last-minute Hail Mary brainstorm.

"What about a *Being Bobby Brown* Christmas special?!" I asked. "Can you picture it? You and Whitney picking out a tree and buying presents for Bobbi Kristina! And your Pops carving the ham?" Brown loved the idea and it was shot two weeks later and rushed to air. It turned out to be the most whacked-out TV Christmas event since Chewbacca tried to return to his home planet in time for "Life Day" in the *Star Wars Holiday Special*, with guest stars Harvey Korman and Bea Arthur. Whitney and Bobby had a massive fight the day of shooting and locked the crew out, and when they finally did appear, they seemed influenced by something stronger than just the holiday spirit. The reason you won't ever see a second of that show again is because Houston's people made sure that much like the *Star Wars Holiday Special*, *Being Bobby Brown* would only be seen once. When she died tragically just as I was finishing this book, Joe Caramanica wrote about the show in his

New York Times appreciation of the star: "She looked not just lean but gaunt, and she was both a robust and erratic presence. It was the sort of reality that rarely makes it to reality television." Happily for Whitney, her legacy is not this show but her great music and golden voice.

Q: Tell the truth, have you and Jeff Lewis ever dated?

A: Let me start by saying that stepping into the world of *Flipping Out* to shoot a reunion is a nutso experience. You are actually entering Jeff Lewis's life, which is to say, the life of a high-profile house flipper/interior designer who happens to suffer from OCD. We usually shoot in whatever home Jeff is living in at the time, where his maid, Zoila Chavez, is puttering around in her uniform and full hair/makeup, bitching at "Yeff" under her breath. It really is what it looks like on TV.

Viewers think Jeff and I have a "Sam and Diane" dynamic, and we do get a huge kick out of each other and love to push each other's buttons. We fell into that rapport when we met for the first time, for lunch at Arnie Morton's in LA, just before we were to go into production on the first season of the show. He had two goals at the lunch: First, he wanted Jenni Pulos, his assistant and the reason for the show's existence in the first place (I told this story in the last chapter, so check it out if you forgot), to have a producing credit—to which I agreed. Second, he wanted to find out how many millions of viewers he needed in order to be the highest-rated show on Bravo. I kept telling him not to worry about the ratings and that I had no expectation of his show being the highest-rated on Bravo, but he would not let it rest. He assured me he would do whatever it took to make a great show and that he'd essentially never turn the camera off during his entire production period. He lived up to that promise, and one of the reasons that show is so great is that the camera doesn't miss a thing. Meanwhile, I spent much of the lunch

On second thought, we look pretty good together.

staring at his lips and much of that first reunion asking every possible lip-related question I could think of. Have you ever really
looked at Jeff Lewis's lips? They are quite remarkable.

Oh, and we haven't dated.

Q: Is Bravo gay?

A: That is a super-deep question. I am attracted to and excited
by Bravo. I have been in a long-term relationship with Bravo. But
because it is a television network, and not a person, I'm not entirely
sure you can call it "gay." If I had to assign a sexual orientation to

it, I would say Bravo is maybe bisexual, because I think at the end of the night, this fun-loving, freewheeling network would be open to going home with whomever it fancied. During my tenure there, we've always had an abundant population of gay boys and girls swimming in the Bravo pool, no doubt because we've showcased people who are leaders in the fields of food, fashion, beauty, design, and pop culture, where it is safe to say the gay community is well represented. And if you identify Bravo as being "gay" and you assume that was all my doing, I'd like to point out how much gayer Bravo was *before* I even got there. *Boy Meets Boy? Gay Weddings? Queer Eye for the Straight Guy? Manhunt?* All green-lit before my time, by my boss, British flower, wife, and mother Frances Berwick. Of course, not every single show on the network had an obviously gay theme before I got here. Bravo was also showing things like Cirque du Soleil and *Inside the Actor's Studio.* Those are kinda straightish, no?

Maybe the reason some people think of Bravo as gay is because we never shied away from that subject matter the way other networks did, and therefore if you tried to put together a list of some of the all-time gayest moments on Bravo, your head might explode. Because I'm a trained professional, I've come up with a few that are top on my mind:

★ *Queer Eye* guy Carson Kressley deciding to surprise the Fab 5 by getting bare-assed naked at a Straight Guy's house, and the Fab 5 locking him outside

★ *Project Runway* designer Andrae and other homosexual contestants making dresses out of flowers as Tim Gunn critiqued

★ A brigade of Atlanta Housewife sidekicks (hairdressers, event planners, and wig wranglers, oh my!) tromping around the ATL wearing high heels

★ Jeff Lewis and Ryan ending their friendship on television as I try to mediate and not cry

★ Kathy Griffin performing at a Bear Convention in San Francisco

★ *Work Out*'s Jackie Warner "turning" her straight trainer Rebecca

★ Brad Goreski's *Les Miz*–inspired flashmob at his tenth anniversary party

★ *Tabatha's Salon Takeover* star and fabulesbian Tabatha Coffey taking over a gay bar called Ripples

★ The Real Housewives of New York arguing over who got stage time at a gay marriage rally

★ The ubiquitous Dwight Eubanks, from *Real Housewives of Atlanta*, ignoring my protestations and showing me his penile implant on *Watch What Happens Live*

★ And while we're talking about Dwight, I'd venture to say that the fur bikini he claims to have designed for the She by Sheree fashion show finale and the baby shower he threw for Phaedra are in a battle royal for gayest events in Atlanta Housewives history!

Q: Why do Bravolebrities who've been sacked keep popping back up again like whack-a-moles?

A: Bravo is like the mob. Once you're in, you're *in*. I used to love when characters who'd long left *All My Children* reappeared years later (1996: "OMG, *Nina* is back!") and I'd forgive them for their sins of years past (1985: "Nina is so fucking *boring*. Pack your pug nose and LEAVE PINE VALLEY!"). It's with similar warmhearted nostalgia that I love seeing former Housewives show up at Vicki's end-of-season barbecue in Orange County every year. Also, remember that these ladies are all still friends and neighbors, whether or not they've remained on the show. So when a former castmate appears at Vicki's barbecue, it's because she was invited by the lady of the house. And if a current Housewife serves a cease-and-desist letter from her attorney to said former castmate, then throws red wine in her eye, our cameras are bound to catch it.

Q: Just tell us, who is your favorite Housewife?

A: You have got to be kidding me.

Q: OK, you punked out on that. So, who's your favorite supporting player on Bravo?

A: Well, that's an even harder question, because there are so many. Let's examine three notable supporting-player categories on Bravo: Gay Sidekicks, Moms, and Maids.

The gay sidekick, no surprise, is big on Bravo. My favorites are the high-heeled boys in Atlanta: Dwight, Derek J, and Miss Lawrence, each delivering something delicious and fun to the show while brilliantly empowering and entertaining their ladies.

Moms, though, are the real scene-stealers. On *Million Dollar Listing*, Josh Flagg's grandma Edith is a grande dame, a Holocaust survivor with wisdom coming out of her little toe. She keeps Josh in check, and I'm proud to see a woman like her on our network. Jill Zarin's mom, Gloria, has a special place in my heart. Drily hilarious and sage, she was the ultimate pint-sized Jewish mom jetting in from Boca. Not since Jimmy Carter has the state of Georgia produced a peacekeeper like Kandi's Mama Joyce on *The Real Housewives of Atlanta*. And Miami's Mama Elsa has it all—one-of-a-kind style, winning wit, wise words, *and* she can tell the future, because she's a witch. She told me she wouldn't fly to New York from Miami to appear on my show, so we sent a couple of staff members in a car to pick her up and drive her 1,288 miles to SoHo. Who cares that she told me, "Dandy, you are incapable of love"? I'm proving that wrong by putting it in print that I love YOU, Mama Elsa!

I'm sure Alice from *The Brady Bunch* would be pleased to see cleaning ladies so handily stealing the spotlight on Bravo. Have you ever met a maid like Jacqueline on *Million Dollar Decorators*? She's chic, she's French, she loves to smoke, and she covets her boss's leather pants. And I was heartbroken when Rosie left LuAnn's employ in Season 3 of *RHNYC*. This was a lady who seemed to be the glue that held the Countess's brood together, and when she moved to be closer to her own family, I selfishly wished she'd decide her own children were doing all right and come back to us. But you know that the woman who owns my heart is the woman who loves her *telenovelas*, the lady who was so nervous about not understanding my English during our first *Flipping Out* reunion that she got overheated and had to leave the set: It's Jeff Lewis's maid, Zoila. And by the way, she may have been nervous back then, but now, between her on-camera charisma and the face-lift Jeff bought her for her birthday last year, she could host the damn thing and look amazing doing it! Hey, that's not a bad idea . . . *te amo*, Zoila!

You may have noticed that I have left out a very important sidekick group: dogs. Well, keep reading.

Being manhandled before the launch of Season 2 of
The Real Housewives of Orange County

THE HOUSEWIVES

This is the point in the book when housewives take over my life. Sure, I'd always worshipped divas. But housewife divas? I only knew them from the soaps . . . which I guess means I actually knew them pretty well. The *Housewives* franchise was going strong before I realized that my youthful days of watching *All My Children* had not been misspent, but incredibly *well* spent. I had unknowingly groomed myself for career success!

Before I go in deep about the ladies, I'm going to tell you a story about their dogs. Why? Because the biggest divas of all do not have two beautifully waxed legs, but four furry ones, and their antics encapsulate one quality I find so endearing about the Housewives—the absurdity. And I love being in the middle of it all.

Before Bravo, I'd never paid any attention to pets—my sister and I had a puppy for exactly twenty-four hours, returning home from school to find it gone, sent to "a farm" by my clever mother, who'd looked into her future and seen fifteen years of taking care of it with no help from us. We were devastated, but not scarred enough for me to remember the banished creature's name. My life proceeded happily from that point on in an almost completely petless fashion, with the exception of my brief crush on Tammy Faye Bakker's outrageous dog, Tuppins. Then came Dina Manzo of the New Jersey cast and her hairless cat, Grandma Wrinkles, and I was shocked awake from my pet-related apathy. Grandma Wrinkles was impossible to ignore, and that is because she was one of the ugliest animals I'd ever seen. When Caroline Manzo reported that old GW stank like bacon, I became mildly obsessed—from afar. A bacon-scented hairless cat named Grandma Wrinkles? As they say, you cannot make this shit up. When Dina eventually brought the animal to the Clubhouse, I fell in love. More accurately, I fell in love with hating her. Because while she didn't leave fur everywhere—how could she?—I swear she left a faint oily spot where she rested her scaly body on the lap of one of my favorite suits. Kind of like bacon does to a paper towel. While remaining disgusted with the cat, I have grown to admire her mistress's eternal devotion to her, despite how positively unappealing she is on every level. Even after Dina left the show, Grandma Wrinkles and I stayed in touch. (Thank God for e-mail, because I plan never to literally touch her again.)

Of course, I am not averse to all follicularly challenged animals. You know who I am talking about: Sir Giggy Vanderpump, Lisa Vanderpump's alopecia-stricken Pomeranian, the ultimate Beverly Hills pampered pet, with his own canopied lounge by the pool and a wardrobe fit for a miniature drag queen with expensive taste and a love of pills. Giggy became an instant sensation, and even I couldn't help but go nuts over that dog on *Watch What*

Happens: Live, featuring him on the show more than many human Bravolebrities. Even when Giggy's not with me, he's there—his framed picture sits over my shoulder on the show.

On New Year's Eve 2011, a new kind of TV history was made when I officiated—live—the first televised wedding between a dog and a cat. Lisa and Dina stood by as Grandma Wrinkles and Giggy committed themselves to holy matrimony. I'm sure the American Family Association let out a big "I told you so" in seeing that gay marriage led to exactly what they'd feared, unions of hairless animals of different species. And to tell the truth, at the last minute, I'd had doubts about going through with the whole thing. During the wedding rehearsal, I asked the obvious question we'd all overlooked due to our hysterical obsession with the housepets:

"Is this going to be stupid?"

"Well, it's not going to be *smart*," producer Caissie St. Onge replied.

Our ratings for the show peaked at 12:15 a.m., at the exact moment of the wedding. And while the Wrinkles-Vanderpump "marriage" was over faster than Kim Kardashian's, it taught me something important: Don't question the stupidity of a stunt you're going to do on your show fifteen minutes after you've dropped a big ball of wigs from the ceiling to ring in the New Year. Stupidity is sometimes what it's all about.

Giggy became so popular that he started a Twitter feed, @Giggy thepom, and I'd find myself in a meeting, or on a date, as my Black-Berry buzzed with a fresh tweet. From a hairless Pomeranian.

From @Giggythepom to @BravoAndy "Oh woofee!
Mistress and I saw next week's episode but I'm not in it
enough! I look cute though!"

From @Giggythepom to @BravoAndy "Rum Tee Tum, you
moved my picture in the Clubhouse. Mistress and I aren't
happy!"

Giggy's complaints about the placement of his photograph became a constant every week when I went off the air. If it was moved in the slightest, that "dog" would "notice" and I would hear about it. And the "dog" would rile up his followers to flood my Twitter with comments. Around the time Giggymania reached its fever pitch, the New York Housewives were returning for their fourth season. My BlackBerry buzzed.

> From @realgingerzarin to @BravoAndy "Annndy! It's me, Ginger! Follow me!"

It was Jill Zarin's dog, Ginger. Ginger had always been a mainstay of the New York Housewives and what I'd call a yippety dog. And while I've been known to profess my love of ginger people, Ginger Zarin was just not my cup of tea. I used to rib Jill about how much I didn't care for her Chihuahua and she'd jab back that I was going to one day fall in love with Ginger and beg to adopt her. I had my doubts.

> From @realgingerzarin to @BravoAndy "OBSESSED yet uncle @bravoandy?"

> From @realgingerzarin to @BravoAndy "Good morning Uncle Andy! Have a nice weekend! I know you will obsess over me someday!"

Now I don't know if Ginger was tweeting for herself or if she was having someone else do it, but whoever it was seemed to have a poor grasp of how obsession works. Because it is rare that a person knows someone, or some dog, for four years and THEN becomes obsessed. It's usually the opposite.

> From @realgingerzarin to "Ask @BravoAndy where my picture is in the Clubhouse? Sad?"

From @realgingerzarin to @BravoAndy "Follow mommy
@JillZarin and follow ME @realgingerzarin."

Um, who was supposed to be obsessed with whom again? I
wondered if I would seem crazy if I contacted my attorney about
taking a restraining order out on a canine because I was being
stalked by a dog on Twitter.

I didn't have the heart to block @realgingerzarin, but I ignored
the tweets and I never followed her. I had to draw the line somewhere. When Jill was booked on *Watch What Happens Live*'s one
hundredth episode, the night of *RHNYC*'s fourth season premiere,
she insisted on bringing Ginger even though I told her I was concerned that the dog would yip and yap through the show (unlike
darling Giggy, who always seems . . . sedate . . . and was possibly
born without a voice box). So, Ginger arrived dressed in what looked
like a miniature Madame Butterfly outfit—a doggy kimono!—which
Jill announced was "in honor" of the recent (devastating) earth-
quake in Japan . . . I did not even know how to respond to that
one. I still don't. During that show, Jill presented me with a framed
picture of Ginger for the Clubhouse, further exacerbating my
dilemma. What exactly were my obligations regarding this portrait? Did I dare risk the wrath of @Giggythepom by replacing his
photo with Ginger's? I try never to play favorites with Housewives,
but wasn't I allowed to prefer one Housedog over another? Was it
really that big of a deal? Days later, in a long e-mail from Jill about
some issues she was having with Bravo, she dropped this:

"Even Ginger asked me, 'Mommy, why is Giggy (whose show
is not in cycle) on WWHL and mine isn't? Why doesn't Andy
like me too?'"

At first I thought that Jill (or Ginger) was joking, but the rest
of the e-mail conveyed a pretty sincere tone. In my reply, I noted,
"I am at a serious loss for words about your dog being jealous
about my affection for Giggy. There are 30 dogs on Bravo."

After that exchange, I did not put the photo of Ginger on my set. I just couldn't.

Then, later in the season, the undeterrable Jill gave me an incredible oil painting of Ginger dressed as Queen Elizabeth. This could have been considered passive-aggressive, given that Giggy is a Brit and Ginger seemed to be mocking his monarch, but the portrait was actually too hilarious to not feature on the show. It was amazing! Maybe Ginger wasn't so bad! Jill was thrilled and said we could keep it for as long as we wanted, and I probably would have left it on the set forever, because I really did admire it. But after Jill's contract was not renewed for a fifth season of *The Real Housewives of New York*, we got a call asking that we please send the portrait back. And who could blame her for wanting to repossess it? Ginger never looked better or seemed more interesting than she did in that painting.

Even though I may not love every Real Housepet of every Real Housewife, I do love that all of their mommies anthropomorphize them by dressing them to the nines and setting up Twitter accounts for them and taking them to nicer restaurants than I can get into. The absurd doggy drama juxtaposed against the absurd but real human drama—now that's television.

Back in Beverly Hills, Adrienne Maloof got a German shepherd from her husband, Paul, as a surprise birthday present at the end of Season 1. But Adrienne quite possibly realized that there are no designer totes or cute outfits for German shepherds, meaning that they are not good accessory dogs. So for the opening of Season 2, she brought in a ringer—a mini-schnauzer named Jackpot. This made Giggy *very* insecure, and I made matters worse—with my wicked old button-pushing tendency again—by running a pup popularity contest on *WWHL* asking viewers whether they preferred Giggy or Jackpot. Jackpot won.

From @Giggythepom to "OK @BravoAndy I am not
coming out, ever."

For male dogs, these two were really acting like a couple of bitches! I got the silent treatment from Giggy for weeks after that poll. It was kind of nice to have more time to interact with actual people. But I couldn't let the bad blood go on between us, so I had the brilliant idea of commissioning *Mad Fashion* designer Chris March to make me a Giggy costume for my Halloween party on the show. Chris is a genius, so I trusted him implicitly and never even looked at the costume until I was getting dressed and made up for the live show. I looked like I was in blackface with a decapitated grizzly bear on my head, and my hands were swaddled in huge furry paws that made it very difficult to sip my cocktail, which I desperately needed for hydration because the costume was a sauna, and I was shvitzing like crazy. Worst of all, the costume, the heat, and maybe the cocktails made me kind of delirious/crazy/woozy, and I felt the inexplicable need to punctuate my comments

with weird little barks, which didn't sound at all like Giggy. I sounded like GINGER!

Succumbing to heatstroke in a dog costume on national TV, I had to wonder: How the hell did I get here?

Let's start from the start, shall we?

☺

One afternoon in early 2005, Amy Introcaso-Davis, then head of development at Bravo, hovered in my office doorway with a VHS tape in her hand and a glint in her eye.

"Watch this," she said, handing me the tape, "because it's coming your way." Amy's team frequently passed ideas in various stages of development to the production department, which I headed.

"It's called *Behind the Gates*," Amy explained.

Scott Dunlap, an advertising exec from a gated community called Coto de Casa in Orange County, had picked up a camera and shot some footage of a few of his neighbors, who all happened to have big boobs and big blond hair. I know that sounds blunt, but WOW did it ever describe these women. Amy and Frances Berwick were intrigued and commissioned a development reel, which means Bravo pays a production company to do some more shooting in order for us to get a better idea of what the show might look like.

The development reel featured the women of Coto de Casa talking about their personal lives and ritzy lifestyles. They showed off their homes, which were like fiberglass castles looming behind big gates that miraculously kept people out but let cameras in.

I didn't discern much self-awareness among these women as they proclaimed how much they detested anything "fake" in people. They all had what looked to me to be a decent amount of silicone up front and very expensive dye jobs that were all the same color. One woman, whose house had a backyard pool with a grotto and waterslide that reminded me of that all-men's Palm Springs resort, talked a mile a minute about her insurance business, which she said was extremely important to her. It felt kind of unreal to hear a woman who looked like she did talking about . . . insurance? Her neighbor and good friend was a former Playboy Bunny whose husband was a pro baseball player and whose son freely admitted that his friends' mothers were MILFs. Another (blonde) told us that every single person in her neighborhood had had breast enhancements. Duh.

The true lives of these women seemed more titillating (sorry, couldn't resist) than anything I'd seen on daytime TV in *years*. These ladies were completely transparent about their vanity and their love of money, and about wanting to have it all while being the hottest and most well-rounded women in the County of Orange. Unabashed and unfiltered, they meant what they said even though they occasionally contradicted themselves (which were, of course, the best moments). If we got this right, I thought it could be a *Knots Landing* for the millennium: hot women in an aspirational town living the high life, marked by drama both extraordinary and ordinary. ABC's *Desperate Housewives* was the biggest show on television at the time. Clearly, people loved watching a show about fictional fabulous friends and frenemies living in the same neighborhood. Wouldn't they love the real thing, too? We changed the name from *Behind the Gates* to *The Real Housewives*, and we were off.

Except that the rough cuts sucked. The confessional interviews where the ladies spoke straight to camera weren't stylized—they weren't well lit, and the women didn't look their best. Something else was missing, too. The women weren't going deeply into their emotions or being honest about what was happening with their friends. And the stories didn't always make sense—what they were saying didn't match the way we saw them acting. Why was Jo bored while Slade was at work? Did Vicki have a love/hate relationship with Jeana, or did she really just hate her? And where was Jeana's husband all the time?

The more we at Bravo asked the producers out in California for answers to fill in the blanks, the less anyone knew. We discussed killing the *Housewives* before they ever hit the air. In fact, we went so far as to put together a budget to how much of a bath Bravo would take if we just cut our losses and walked away. But—thank the lord—we decided to stay with it and start over again. We parted ways with the original producers and sank even more resources into the *Housewives* by shooting additional interviews with the women and even more footage of their daily lives. Then we headed back to the editing room.

Even with this richer material, we had other problems. For instance, the cast looked like a California Implant Pageant where you couldn't tell the contestants apart. I wasn't the only one at Bravo with this issue, and if *we* couldn't keep them straight after watching hours of footage of them, we certainly couldn't expect viewers to be able to. That's when we devised the animated banners and little chapter headings that appear before each person's scene.

Lauren Zalaznick and Bravo marketing head Jason Klarman came up with the idea of playing off the opening of *Desperate Housewives*, where Teri Hatcher and the gang held apples, by having our ladies hold oranges. Just before the premiere, Lauren tacked "of Orange County" onto the title, in case we ever decided to do another version of the show somewhere else. Bravo exec Shari Levine and I initially objected, worried that the "of Orange County" was so CLUNKY. Plus, given the troubles we'd had in the edit of this show, we just knew the chances that we'd ever replicate it anywhere else were zero. (Yes, I am occasionally a massively misguided idiot.)

I held my breath the first time I saw the show intro for the OC *Housewives*. Each of the women appeared in various pieces of "fashion"—that season it was bust-enhancing satiny tops with a big, bejeweled centerpiece (called "skytops"!)—while saying something that was supposed to define who they were. The statements were along the lines of "I love Botox!" and "Everybody has enormous boobs!" and "Here's to not being fake!" (If you're keeping a running tab of how many times I'm mentioning the word "boob," welcome to my world with the *Housewives*. I've talked more about boobs in the last few years than most editors at *Playboy* and way more than any gay man ever should.) Watching that first episode as it aired, I worried that the women were going to think we'd painted them in the most shallow light possible. I was sure they were going to hate it, freak out, and quit. I asked Shari to find out how the women had reacted. She left to make some calls, and after just a few minutes, she returned to my office.

"They absolutely love it." She smiled. And just like that, I knew that the most important element of the show, the only element, was stable. These women were going to go along for the ride. And the ride? It was going to be wild . . .

The reviews were mixed. Tom Shales of the *Washington Post* called the women "fascinating bores," but predicted "sociologists and anthropologists of the future are going to have tons and tons of material to sift through as they try to understand what life was like in the first decade of the 21st century." David Bianculli of the *New York Daily News* hated it: "Not only did I not care about this quintet of California preeners, but I was rooting against them." Charles McGrath in the *New York Times* opined, "Like so much reality TV, it's both educational and grimly fascinating, and leaves you feeling much better about your own life—if for no other reason than that you would never be so stupid as to appear on a show like this." I did say they were mixed, right? I mean, if you stare at that Shales quote long enough, it is practically a rave of the magnitude normally reserved for British mysteries on PBS!

To be honest, I wasn't expecting this type of show to win acclaim from the pros; I was much more worried about the critics closer to home. When Graciela called after the first episode, I had been silently questioning whether I was on to something or crazy. Then she gushed: "Vicki Gunvalson? Are you kidding me? Did you make her up? Obsessed. Lauri? She might be my favorite. She's the Farrah. Is Jeana's son hot? Doesn't she look like Wynonna Judd?"

Back in St. Louis, *The Real Housewives of Orange County* wasn't playing to any standing ovations in the Cohen household. My mom was having none of their self-absorbed nonsense.

"I can't watch those women," Evelyn declared. She refused to budge no matter how many times I implored her to give it another try. She only tuned back in the following year for the reunion show and that was because I hosted it. And her comments still weren't exactly positive.

"Well, *you* looked okay," she allowed. But "THOSE WOMEN!??" Evelyn would never be swayed by OC.

The first season—only seven episodes—did okay in the ratings for most of the run. Then suddenly, just before the finale, it started popping. Viewers who'd begun watching only to confirm that they found the women repellent somehow became invested in their stories—which proved to be more universal than anybody initially thought.

That first season we established guidelines and rules of thumb for making the show that we still follow today. Though we shoot a lot of footage for each season, we don't shoot the show like *The Real World*, where cameras follow the stars around 24/7. For Season 2 of *Real Housewives of Beverly Hills*, we shot 1,270 hours of footage to make twenty 44-minute episodes—or a ratio of approximately 85 hours of footage for every 1 hour used. Why do we shoot that much? Because we're looking for those elements that make the perfect storm of a *Real Housewives* episode, namely, real humor, conflict, emotion, heart, and something totally unexpected—let's say, a wig pull. Our producers find out what the women have coming up in a given week, and they pick and choose which situations to document. They keep tabs on how the ladies are feeling about each other and what happened the last time they were all together, so that no jarring or confusing gaps are left unexplained. When the ladies meet a friend or another housewife for lunch, the restaurant is called in advance and cleared for shooting. The housewives are not told what to say or how to think—all the footage is unscripted. The drama comes from the casting. We do not cast wallflowers—we want women with a point of view, plenty to say, and the confidence to say it in the presence of equally outspoken women. What started as a possible one-off experiment became an ensemble drama with story lines as complex as anything anyone could ever write.

At this point, we knew we were on to something. Plus, we had at trick up our sleeves that we didn't even realize was there at first. Amy's team had another show in development called *Manhattan Moms*, which featured two women that we absolutely loved, Jill Zarin and Alex McCord. They didn't know each other, but they would soon enough. Jill was a fast-talking Upper East Side yenta type. (Her mother, Gloria, would castigate me years later for using the term "yenta," but I always meant it with love.) Alex and her Australian husband, Simon (proud owner of the glossiest red leather pants mankind has ever seen), were from a completely different mold: outsiders striving to be insiders who were breeding their kids for overachievement. We thought we had the seed of a decent show on our hands, but with the success of *The Real Housewives of Orange County*, it occurred to us that it might be smart to turn *Manhattan Moms* into *The Real Housewives of New York City*. (If I didn't thank her at the time, I would like to now publicly thank Lauren Zalaznik for her stroke of brilliance in adding a location to the original franchise title. It wasn't clunky; it was genius.) The mere thought of a *Real Housewives of New York City* series gave me goose bumps, because I knew firsthand that women in New York were nothing like our Orange County ladies. Only the packaging and themes of the shows would be similar. And once we realized that our format could work somewhere else, producing a wildly different show depending on where it was set, we could not stop thinking of the possibilities. And indeed, every series has its own flavor: OC is cul-de-sac normality. Atlanta is campy and over the top. Jersey is hot-tempered and clannish. DC was thoughtful and provocative. Beverly Hills is image-conscious and *this* close to Hollywood. Miami is spicy and tele-novelic. New York is aggressive and controlling.

We set out to cast more women in New York and fell into the method we still use today—ask the women themselves to be our talent scouts. In this case, Jill Zarin became a great resource for us. In addition to Ramona, she brought us several other women in her circle, all of whom would have been perfect. But for one reason or another, women kept falling out—one cosmetics company executive couldn't get her boss to agree to her appearing on the show, while another couldn't convince her husband to go for it (both common obstacles that wind up quashing would-be wives). We passed our start date with two roles still to fill, so we started shooting with just Jill, Ramona, and Alex, knowing that footage would be unusable if we could not nail down the final cast. Finally, we told the producers and the women that we were canceling the show before it ever began if we didn't get two more cast members. And then the reality TV gods smiled upon us, orchestrating a fantastical event that changed the face of the franchise.

It was a summer Saturday in the Hamptons—*Super* Saturday, to be exact, when a major shopping fund-raiser to fight breast cancer coincides with a big polo event. All you need to know about Super Saturday is that it's a madhouse. On this particular Super Saturday afternoon, two desperate people—both desperate for something *more*—met at a place that is a magnet for desperate people . . . the polo tent in Bridgehampton.

Bethenny Frankel was in a fight with her boyfriend, and despite a splitting headache, she'd forced herself to go to that tent to network. She wanted to brand herself as a celebrity chef and she was searching for a photographer to take her picture, hoping that that picture might land somewhere and lead to something. She was looking for anything that might get her noticed and get her face out there. She was in a vile mood and, like I said, desperate.

"You skinny bitch! Look at you! Where'd you get the VIP bracelet?" There was no mistaking the nasal honk of Jill Zarin across the noisy tent.

Bethenny had met Jill several times out and about on the New

York social circuit. They were just casual acquaintances, but that was all about to change forever. Jill had brought one of our casting producers with her to the polo tent. With the fate of her show on the line, Jill wanted to help. Jill, as we now know, is big on helping.

"I'm doing this show—we already started filming a little bit but we need someone else. It's about housewives and moms. We need another housewife," she told Bethenny.

Bethenny didn't think she fit the bill. She wasn't a housewife or a mom. She was a celebrity chef, or at least she wanted to be one. Jill's husband, Bobby, brought over the producer. Bethenny shut down. She had nothing to say. But then her boyfriend, Jason, went into action. He opened up to the producer about his kids and his life with Bethenny. He was selling it; he was selling her.

In the car ride home, Jason encouraged Bethenny to do the show, but he also made it clear to her that he would have no part of it. Bethenny thought she had everything to lose—she had an endorsement deal with Pepperidge Farm and a diet/cookbook coming out. She'd already been a finalist (and lost) on *Martha Stewart's Apprentice*.

"If I do this show, and it does badly, I am officially the biggest loser ever. I will have been on *two* reality shows," she would later remember telling Jason. But perhaps against her better judgment, she agreed to let the producers put her on tape.

Back at Bravo, when I watched a tape of Bethenny, I was against casting her, even though I thought she was really funny. Simply put, it seemed lame to me to have someone who'd already been on one reality show turn up on another. Also thanks to Jill, we had another woman on tape, LuAnn de Lesseps, who seemed a bit dry, but I couldn't resist the fact that she was a countess, and spoke about her title without a hint of irony. Her husband's family had given America the Statue of Liberty! I lobbied for the Countess, and she was in. We continued to debate about Bethenny, and although I still had reservations, her acerbic wit and willingness to risk it all convinced us to offer her a contract.

My guess is that if you're reading this book, you're the kind of person who knows that the rest is Housewives history. Jill and Bethenny established themselves as a well-heeled Laverne and Shirley and *RHNYC* was a big hit, in part because the viewers loved their friendship.

Of course, it wasn't all one big happy sorority party. I placed an important call to my parents in St. Louis. "You have to watch this!" I urged them, certain that *New York* would engage them in ways *Orange County* never could. Evelyn was duly amused and an instant habituée. Can a Jew say "Hallelujah"? My mother became wholly invested in the women, their clothes, where they ate, and how they spoke to each other. We began comparing notes like we'd always done with *All My Children*.

"I do NOT have a good feeling about THAT COUNTESS," she'd say. "Your father just can't STAND the sight of Simon. He has to LEAVE THE ROOM when he comes on! Actually all of them make him very nervous. He gets upset—you can't believe it!"

"I just can't get over that people speak to each other this way, in public places," Dad said. "They make me very nervous, Andy." Mission mostly accomplished!

A few years later, weeks before we began shooting Season 3 of *RHNYC*, I went with a friend to finally check out Bridgehampton Polo for myself and stepped right into a steaming pile with Jill Zarin!

"I am so fucking mad at Bethenny. You have no idea how horrible she's been to me. I am letting it all hang out this season. It's not gonna be pretty, Andy."

You know I'd be lying if I said I didn't love a good brouhaha, but I also knew that viewers liked seeing these two *together*. How would a ruptured relationship play on the show? Without trying to control the situation, I gently suggested to Jill that maybe they could work it out before the season started. To my utter chagrin, that failed to happen. All during filming I heard reports from the field: an awkward encounter at a fashion show, Jill playing LuAnn an old nasty voice mail from Bethenny, phones being slammed down—everything but a reconciliation. "No!" I thought. "These women are ruining everything. For us and for themselves!" I had a terrible feeling that the crack in this beloved friendship wouldn't resonate with our audience and that it would spell the end of the show and doom the spin-off we were planning with Bethenny.

It turned out viewers were enthralled, and that fractious third season did better than the previous two. There was something weirdly relatable—or maybe cautionary—about two good friends calling it quits, possibly forever. And watching the other women play two ends against the middle and scurry back and forth across enemy lines was simultaneously painful and entertaining. (It was enter*paining*!)

The next *Housewives* edition to premiere was Atlanta, which would go on to become our highest-rated of all the cities in the franchise. We'd been sitting on a casting tape for a show called *Hotlanta* for a while, featuring a group of affluent black women with energy and attitude. I was excited about the idea of doing a show featuring rich African Americans, a concept I hadn't seen on TV since *The Fresh Prince of Bel-Air*. The *Hotlanta* women became *The Real Housewives of Atlanta* and all I could say was, "BAM!"

Linnethia "NeNe" Leakes was an instant standout, telling the camera even then, "I walk into a room and my eyes are popping and my lips are busting and BAM!" But every time I watched the tape I became more confused by Kim Zolciak. I didn't understand her role within the group—first of all, and most obviously, she was white. Just as obvious, her blond mane was a full-on wig. She looked like a country singer to me and seemed more Nashville than Atlanta. She just didn't feel Bravo, which lots of analysts crunching numbers tell us is watched by the most upscale and educated audience on cable—lots of urban women and their gay best friends, along with hip suburban moms. A fair number of straight men get hooked on the Housewives, too, after their wives cajole them into watching. (My theory: They love having the green light to gawk at hot women with big knockers getting into catfights.) Boy, was I wrong about Kim!

New Jersey was next. We threw out a casting net in three locations but were immediately drawn to the women from Franklin Lakes—featuring the original five Wives, all of them as Jersey at it gets. It was the first time we considered using women who were related to each other, and the intense family bonds added a whole new dynamic. Amy Introcaso-Davis, a Jersey girl herself, made several trips to the Garden State to rendezvous with the women. These ladies weren't about to enter into this show lightly or quickly and had many questions about the process and ramifications, questions unlike any we'd heard in the past. For instance: "Has anyone been audited as a result of this show? Or wiretapped?" From the beginning, Caroline Manzo was their leader; everyone in the room seemed to defer to her. Teresa Giudice, an old friend of the Manzos whom we were eager to cast, dropped out of and then back into the show multiple times before we even started shooting. We never got a straight answer about why she kept changing her mind, and at some point I just stopped asking.

We shot the season and it was on the shelf for at least a year before it actually aired, which sometimes happens. We're kind of like air traffic controllers, making certain all the different programs are lined up for prime landing and takeoff spots. I first met the Jersey ladies in person a few months before they were about to finally debut, when they came to the Bravo offices to meet our PR team. I rarely meet Housewives before their seasons are wrapped and in the can. I get to know them on tape, just like everybody else. (After all, it's not a real "set" of a show I'd be visiting, like stopping by the *Top Chef* kitchen; If I went on-"set," I would be busting in on what is essentially someone's real life. So, I wait.) At that first meeting, the tension in the room was palpable. Remember, for them, all the drama you see in a season has already happened months before in real time, so when the show finally airs, it is like a post-traumatic flashback for them. The Jersey women hadn't all been together since the infamous Teresa table flip, which had happened over a year earlier, even though viewers wouldn't see it until the season finale. Grudges, hurt feelings, and resentments had been marinating for months by the time our PR team started discussing the launch plan for the show.

"You see what you're in for, Andy Cohen?" Dina Manzo taunted me. "Are you ready for this?" Dina and her sister Caroline call me "Andy Cohen"—always both names. By this point, I considered myself an old hand at Housewife-wrangling, and I thought I did, indeed, know what I was in for. I thought wrong, of course. There was so much venom in that room that day, we could've shot the reunion right then and there. The only thing missing would have been the hideous Teletubbiesesque set. If you haven't figured it out yet, there's nothing I like better than sitting atop a powder keg in a roomful of loose cannons. That's why I love my job. But making stars—Bravolebrities, if you will—out of everyday alpha women (and men) means that my role as producer can be particularly intense and unpredictable. In fact, I don't feel like just a producer. I'm often a shrink, or a cheerleader, protector, peacemaker, and referee. I work with a team of really sharp people, including Shari Levine and Christian Barcellos, who are basically making an entire documentary every week, and my day-to-day contribution to the series includes screening multiple cuts of every episode and giving editorial notes on the show (change the music, hold on a shot of someone's reaction to something, explain in an interview what was happening in a scene, etc.). When I'm not concerning myself with those fine details, I'm involved in casting, tracking stories with the production companies, and mapping out how they'll play over the season, and the offscreen drama of picking up and negotiating the Housewives' contracts between every season.

Yes, negotiating with a Real Housewife is a story unto itself, and one whose nitty-gritty details must remain confidential. Suffice it to say, the process can be tense and fraught with emotion. In the early, uncharted territory days, the New York women used

Bethenny to do their collective bidding—they fancied themselves akin to the cast of *Friends*. She once called me from Jill Zarin's closet to demand more money on behalf of the group in exchange for . . . something I can't even remember now (more episodes? a reunion?). On *Watch What Happens Live*, Ramona's tendency toward outbursts inspired the term "Ramotional," and she's always been that way. Before Season 3 of *RHNYC* could start, in a highly unusual move, Ramona insisted on accompanying her lawyer to the Bravo offices to negotiate in person. She arrived dressed to the nines, sporting sunglasses indoors. It wasn't long before she decided that she didn't care for the direction in which things were heading and Ramotionally stormed out of the room. That was the end of Ramonagotiating in person. Luckily, we were eventually able to hammer out a deal that looked okay to Ramona, with or without her Pinot Grigio.

While I don't usually interact with the women while they're in production, on rare occasions I am asked to step in. For instance, a couple of years ago, NeNe tried to get out of joining Kim and Kandi on the last leg of their (classic!) Tardy for the Party Tour. She'd committed to riding on the tour bus, and the other ladies were going to meet up with them in Miami afterward. It was a potentially great way for all the women to come together at the end of the season. We really wanted NeNe on the bus.

"I don't want to fight with Kim," NeNe confessed.

I asked her to go on the bus and told her to do what she wanted once there. "Just go have fun," I said. "Don't fight. People love seeing you and Kim having fun together—you're a great team."

Ultimately, NeNe decided to take the bus with Kandi and Kim, and, of course, just as they were pulling out of Orlando, she got in a massive fight with Kim that lasted the entire four-hour drive to Miami. Now, I'm sure you think I was happy about that, but I was really sorry that Kim and NeNe ended up fighting, because I knew that it wasn't what NeNe wanted. I can't imagine that's what Kim wanted. And that was the fight that caused the final rift in

Kim and NeNe's on-again off-again friendship. The two have barely spoken since, and I really miss seeing them together.

One of my hopes for the women is for them to come across as fun and interesting, to be happy, and to do well as a result of the show. The Housewives can also make serious money, especially when they use the show—with Bravo's blessing—to brand themselves, the way Bethenny did with her Skinnygirl margarita empire, or Teresa with her Italian cookbooks. But, as it does for anyone, fame can have its own price, even though the prospect of fame is what draws most of the women to participate. In my not always successful role as counselor and guardian, I tell the women never to read what people are saying about them online. Not one of them has listened to me. I can't say I can blame them—imagine becoming suddenly famous and knowing that complete strangers are writing and commenting about what you said or did months ago. And once they've looked, it's hard not to look again, as fans' opinions can change on a dime: One minute they hate you for calling someone a "Chinky Chinky Chinaman" (Ugh. See: Vicki, *RHOC* Season 2), and the next they're crying with you as you send your daughter off to college.

On the night of the *RHBH* series premiere, I begged Camille Grammer to ignore what people were saying about her; having already seen the shows, I knew she was in for a rough season and told her as much, but I promised that the viewers would get behind her toward the end. I checked in with Camille a few times during that season and she was miserable. Her voice was heavy and she sounded despondent. At a time when she was going through such a low point in her life, the fans' comments hurt her even more. I tried to convince her to poke fun at herself as a defensive strategy, but that's hard to do when you just don't feel like laughing at anything. In the meantime, she was labeled "the most hated Housewife in history." But by season's end, when Camille showed her true, vulnerable self after learning that her husband, Kelsey Grammer, had been cheating with a twenty-nine-year-old flight attendant, the fans could finally empathize. Camille was vindicated, and relieved.

The advice I give the ladies most frequently and emphatically is "Just be real." Be who you are and own it. I certainly have tried to live my life exactly this way, and though I didn't grow up to be a Housewife, it has otherwise worked for me.

My biggest problems with Housewives occur when they try to alter their personas and control how they appear. It's like they're trying to produce themselves, and it never works. The camera catches it all. What it caught in Washington, DC, was—literally— one for the history books.

When we decided to extend the *Real Housewives* franchise to Washington, DC, the country had just elected its first African American president, and we were interested in exploring the nexus of society and race among women in a place where proximity to political power, as well as money and an amazing shoe closet, dictates one's status. My fantasy was that this group of Housewives would disagree—okay, maybe even fight—about affairs of state rather than affairs of the heart.

As we started filming, it seemed like our wish had come true; the women were indeed talking about race and politics and Washington insiders. But then the latter discussion became all too loud during the Thanksgiving weekend of 2009, when Michaele Salahi, a cast member, and her husband, Tareq, attended President Obama's first state dinner in the White House, allegedly without an invitation.

What the Salahis were and what they wanted to be had been a topic of much debate and discussion among the other cast members long before the White House debacle. Michaele was a real character, kind of a bubbly space cadet who was a former makeup counter salesgirl longing to be one of the society ladies whose faces she painted. She was zany, untrustworthy, likable, and fragile all at once. Her husband, Tareq, reminded me of an incredibly litigious used-car salesman whose suits needed a good dry cleaning.

We always suspected he was taping phone conversations with Bravo and the show's producers, constantly collecting "evidence" and picking enemies.

When the Salahis told our producers that they were invited to the White House for the state dinner honoring India, no one had reason to question them. One of the first scenes we'd shot with the Salahis was a polo match featuring the ambassador from India and a friend of theirs from the State Department. I've always thought that the unexpected is the single greatest advantage a docuseries holds over any scripted drama or comedy. The axiom "truth is stranger than fiction" reigns supreme at Bravo. But therein lies the rub: You can't predict or prepare for the unknown. We had been filming the DC cast members for months by the time our crews followed a giddy Michaele and Tareq through their preparations for this gala evening. And we shot plenty that day: Michaele trying to figure out how to pin herself into her elegant red sari, Michaele looking for the invitation that may or may not have existed (was she acting?), then the two of them climbing into the limo and heading toward 1600 Pennsylvania Avenue. Since the production crew didn't have credentials for the dinner, they left after filming the Salahis' arrival at the White House gate. We only learned the following day—along with everyone else in America—of the alleged "gate crashing" incident. I was on vacation in Indonesia, perusing the *New York Post* online, when I noticed a blonde on the cover and idly thought, "Huh, she looks just like that woman we cast in DC." Then I checked my e-mail, which was filled with frantic messages from Bravo: *Call if you get this!*

Speculation that the Salahis had used the state dinner as a stunt to be cast on the show was rampant—and ridiculous. The series wasn't being cast at the time the Salahis' "invitation" "arrived," it was being *wrapped*. The dinner happened in the final two episodes of a nine-episode series. But this was much more than a tabloid media firestorm. It was a federal case. Not figuratively, but again literally. It ignited a huge debate over national security, the competence of the Secret Service, and, to my great frustration, the ethics of reality TV. I eventually came to believe the Salahis' situation could be likened to being told you might be on the list for a club, then showing up and winging it with the doorman to see if you'll be let in. In this case the club was the White House and the doorman was the Social Office, who must've been enchanted by Michaele's beautiful red sari. Whatever the reason for the slipup, they got in.

The press went after Bravo as hard as the couple; we were excoriated for "rewarding" the Salahis' behavior by putting them on the show and making them more famous. During the months between the state dinner incident and the series debut in August 2010, I told anyone who would listen that being on this show isn't always a reward—and that the verdict on that is up to the individuals who choose to be on and those who choose to watch. I found myself having to defend my position in private as well as in public. I just wanted everyone to wait and give it the chance it deserved. Anderson Cooper, who is a friend and a fan of the Housewives, told me that he considered the Salahis repugnant whores for attention, and he wasn't giving them any of his. He wasn't alone. My mom was utterly repulsed by the Salahis. "You have to cut them out, Andy, they're HORRIBLE! Vile people!" she scolded. "The show is good, though!" I protested. This was the first time the public would have any significantly preformed opinion on any Housewives cast members before the show even premiered. And those preformed opinions were ugly.

We had set out to do a show about, among other things, what people in Washington will do to get closer to power, and in the Salahis we had an extreme example. We aired the show, and the other women forever resented the Salahis for turning it into their own private circus. When I heard reports, more than a year later, that Tareq had reported Michaele missing, my heart lurched. I worried that something terrible had happened between these two seemingly desperate souls. I had to laugh when it turned out she had merely run off into the "Open Arms" of the guitarist from everybody's favorite eighties rock band, Journey. Now *that* would have made a great episode.

After the DC finale, we premiered *The Real Housewives of Beverly Hills*, a location I initially objected to because it seemed almost redundant—hadn't we already done it with Orange County? Wrong again. It was a huge hit, and people loved seeing a show about really rich people who were really, really rich! Of course wealthy people had been on all our other series, but since the show is a reflection of reality, many did not stay wealthy. Overextension, downsizing, liens, loans—it all happened, in almost every city. The Beverly Hills women, though, lived in football-field-sized mansions. We had succeeded with our casting, too—the women all had real connections to one another, and did I mention that they were really, really rich? The world of the Beverly Hills Housewives was so fun and frothy and pink and fantasy-like that I thought we had a real-life *Dynasty* at last. That this show, of all the franchises, would turn so tragically dark surprised no one more than me. The ladies, as it turned out, were hiding a terrible secret.

When our producers at Evolution Media in Burbank started trying to cast various women in Beverly Hills, no one was interested at first. Finally, one woman wanted in, and she was our tipping point, giving us the biggest competition we'd ever seen to get on a Housewives show. Soon we had a line of Bentleys outside the production company and a lobby full of fur-wearers with similar faces (I'd later learn they all shared the same surgeons), as five hundred women tried to become Beverly Hills Housewives. For the first time, I started hearing from publicists and agents and potential Housewives themselves. We had established actresses wanting to get on, and even Sumner Redstone's girlfriend at the time applied. The company put 122 women on tape, submitted 22 to Bravo, and then we all narrowed it down to 5.

When we told Lisa Vanderpump she was in the running, she gave us a taste of her shtick: "Hold on a minute. I'm having sex with my husband but I'm going to push him off so I can talk to you." I saw in her the potential for a narrator, someone Joan Collinsesque to lay down the rules of Beverly Hills. (Indeed, her intro would later declare that she "made the rules in Beverly Hills.") Lisa's neighbor, Adrienne Maloof, couldn't decide whether to do the show and asked executive producer Alex Baskin, "If you were me, would you do the show?" He replied, "No, and I'd be making a huge mistake." Adrienne was in. Through Adrienne, we found Taylor Armstrong, whose daughter went to Adrienne's kids' school. The two used to meet for coffee after dropping off the kids. We put an offer out to the Richards sisters, Kim and Kyle, who had a competing offer from another channel to star in a docuseries with their sister Kathy Hilton. Over Thanksgiving break 2009, while we were dealing with the Salahi mess, Kim and Kyle were wrestling over whether to be Beverly Hills Housewives or 3 Sisters.

Just before production began, Kyle was looking through her address book to see if there was anyone else she knew who'd be perfect for the cast. She came across Camille Grammer's name, not realizing she was helping to cast her eventual arch nemesis. Grammer seemed indifferent and nervous about the prospect, but she came in the next day and shot an interview with Evolution. The production company thought her husband would never let her do the show in a million years. Imagine their shock when Kelsey Grammer himself called the casting director, expressing his full support of his wife's participation and saying that he would do whatever he could to make it happen. His wife was still on the fence when producers Douglas Ross and Baskin visited their Malibu compound.

"These guys seem like nice guys—they seem like we can trust them," said Kelsey, briskly dismissing her concerns. In the meantime, Kelsey had enlisted Adrienne and Paul to get Camille to do the show. (In hindsight, it appears that Grammer may have been trying to keep his wife busy with the show while he moved to New York to have an affair.) His campaign worked, and we had six Housewives.

During that first season, the Armstrongs' marriage seemed tense and very business-oriented. Taylor bragged about her husband's wealth, saying, "He's richer than Texas," and threw a $60,000 birthday party for their five-year-old daughter. I should mention that if someone says they're going to throw a $60,000 birthday party for their five-year-old, as Taylor did, we're going to be there, for sure. But we never suggest that people go on shopping sprees, or spend money they may or may not have, or pretend to own a mansion that's not theirs.

On the show, Russell appeared cold and distant to his wife, and he told producers that though he didn't love how it was edited, he loved the show. His biggest complaint that season concerned a dinner that had been shot in Lisa's wine cellar in which her friend Mohamed accused Russell of stealing $15 million from him. He was upset about this potentially airing, and to his delight the scene never made it into the show (not because of his complaints, mind you.) He boasted at the end of the season that his business was up "900 percent" since the show started airing, and he told producers at Evolution that he was interested in buying their company.

What I didn't know was that by the end of Season 1, Taylor had already confided in her castmates about alleged physical abuse by Russell. It became kind of an open secret, and though I only found out after we'd wrapped, I can't say that I was surprised. The whispers in the cast were that Taylor was on her way out of the marriage and would be before we shot more. By the time we rolled on Season 2, the women were having frank and difficult conversations with Taylor about her life with Russell, but they were mainly happening off-camera. Meanwhile, Russell sent Camille and the producers a letter threatening to sue anyone who said anything defamatory about him on the show. But at no time during production of that season did Russell ask to be taken off the show.

We'd planned to wrap that season with a party we'd shot at Lisa's restaurant, Sur, where all of the friends were seeing Taylor for the first time since she'd left her husband. Days after that party, Lisa and Kyle were awakened at 6 a.m. by a phone call from TMZ chief Harvey Levin with the news that Russell Armstrong had been found dead, an apparent suicide. At that moment, I was on vacation (I always seem to be on vacation when bad things happen), but nonetheless on the phone with Bravo exec Christian Barcellos discussing a crisis with the Jersey Housewives when an e-mail popped up on my BlackBerry with the TMZ.com report that Russell Armstrong had hanged himself. I was stunned. Speechless. I could barely say the words to Christian, and immediately thought of Taylor, and especially of their daughter Kennedy. Next came thoughts about the position we were in. What should Bravo do? The suicide raised many questions that nobody ever even dreamed would come up. We had to figure out what we should do with a show in which Taylor and Russell's story played a big, dark, and real part.

I spent the next several weeks pacing around with a phone to my ear, rewatching the first eleven episodes of the series, which was due to premiere in a month. The conversations—with Evolution, the women, our lawyers, our PR people—were exhaustive and deliberate. We had serious decisions to make that would affect a family already going through the most difficult time imaginable, and we were weighing matters of taste and protocol. Should we delay the show, or should it air at all? Should we keep Russell in? What do we do about this domestic abuse story line, which ran throughout the season? The producers fought to stay the course and keep the show on the air. They'd felt no one involved with the show had done anything wrong, and not to air it would imply otherwise. The producers were asking for the chance not only to tell a story they felt was important, but also to combat the many lies that they felt were going out unchallenged.

The media were—no surprise—having a field day, and they grabbed on to what I consider to be the easiest hook they could: that reality TV had killed Russell Armstrong. The man was in serious financial trouble, and his business associate killed himself within twenty-four hours of Armstrong's passing, but according to

HLN, I had blood on my hands. As we at Bravo internally debated about how to proceed, we said very little to the press other than the truth: that we were discussing all options relating to the show. I guess that was too boring to believe, because there was a massive amount of misinformation being reported and re-reported: that I was doing an hour-long interview with Taylor about the suicide, that we were filming a special suicide episode of the show, that we were or were not airing specific scenes involving Armstrong. Armstrong's family spoke out, pinning the blame on Bravo, then saying he'd been murdered, and then indirectly implicating Lisa Vanderpump.

The life of a Housewife is fraught with myriad small crises—from a costar's household staff making fun of her on-camera to a castmate's accusations on Twitter about plastic surgery—but here was a major crisis to put all others in perspective. The women were being attacked from all sides and they were scared—they didn't want their reputations to be ruined or the show to be blamed, and all desperately wanted to do the right thing. The problem was, Emily Post never wrote any instructions on how to handle this kind of situation.

Evolution Media called a meeting with the women at Adrienne's house. Within minutes, the press got word of the "emergency meeting" that would determine the fate of the show. In fact, its purpose was to calm the hysteria. At Adrienne's house, the conversation veered all over the place. These women are insiders. They're plugged into your TMZs and Radar Onlines and have friends at the LAPD, all of whom were floating multiple conspiracy theories. Some said it was murder, others that he had committed suicide because he was hiding a gay lover, another that he was in Brazil, alive and escaped. The women wondered why news of the business partner committing suicide wasn't being reported; they felt it explained the depth of financial ruin Russell faced. They knew that he'd left a suitcase full of unpaid bills next to his body. Some of the women said that the Armstrongs had passed themselves off as people of means for years to enhance their image; it wasn't just for the show. Despite how terrible they felt for Taylor and Kennedy, they all felt that nothing anyone had done or not done could have changed the decision that Russell Armstrong had made to end his life. Nonetheless, Lisa thought the show should be delayed. Camille thought it shouldn't air at all—she'd been the one to out Russell's physical abuse on the show.

I reached out to Taylor every way I could, but never heard back. Alex Baskin spoke with her many times and she was adamant that every scene be shown, that if people were really going to understand what happened, and connect with the story and maybe make a change in their own life if necessary, they'd need to see all the events as they happened. She didn't want to keep silent anymore.

My mother, of course, was very upset and kept sending me press clippings and editorials. "What are you going to DO?" she pleaded. "I will watch it, but will anyone else?" As for me, I was having a hard time seeing the forest for the trees, worried that the outrage in the media was too loud for anyone to watch the series without being disturbed by the noise. My colleagues were more levelheaded.

Finally we decided, as we had with the Salahi scandal, to move forward and let the show speak for itself. If people could tune out the tabloid noise, they would see a very raw, real documentary about a circle of women trying to figure out how to help a friend who was in danger and who was going—by her own admission— off the rails. But we knew we had to be very sensitive—the press was all too ready to accuse us of exploitation no matter what we did, but we were mostly concerned with how our audience would feel. We wouldn't use any scenes including Russell Armstrong to promote the show, and we edited out scenes with him in the early episodes, feeling that it was wrong to show him so soon after the suicide. We cut small mentions of Russell. We cut lines that weren't funny anymore or that took on a new meaning, like Adrienne saying, "I could kill my husband, he bugs me so much." We cut a scene in the season premiere of Taylor lingerie-shopping and a friend noting that her husband would die when he saw her in a certain outfit. There was a scene in the third episode illustrating how cold Russell and Taylor's marriage was, and we cut it. He did eventually appear, though, and the reason was that we felt we'd do him a greater disservice by cutting him out entirely—you humanize him by seeing him instead of just hearing that he's a bad guy. In the end, what we had, unfolding throughout the season's twenty episodes, was an honest depiction of what happened to a woman in the midst of an unhappy marriage. She found the strength, with the support of her friends, to leave. It was real life.

For all the campy fun and pure escapism that the Housewives embody, more than once I've had to grapple with the difficult truth that reality TV captures real life not only in its lighter moments, but in the darkest times as well. No amount of wealth, beauty, or fame can immunize you from misfortune, tragedy, or despair. I do not believe to this day that Russell Armstrong killed himself as a result of the show.

My experience in reality TV is that the truth always ends up coming out. It might take some time and patience and even skillful reading between the lines, but it will be there. Leeches, grifters, pretenders, and manipulators are always exposed or expose themselves. Flawed people and flawed relationships are laid bare, whether it's a controlling husband, a conniving friend, or an insolent and ungrateful offspring. Viewers are invested in the truth, whether it's sweet or sordid, and the Housewives never disappoint, just as they never fail to provide equally honest moments of deep loyalty, tender vulnerability, and unself-conscious self-parody. There will always be those who disagree, but I know that while the root of this show is entertainment, it's also laced with social commentary, and whether we're getting to know these pretty people or their pretty little dogs, their lives are undeniably real. And sometimes real life isn't very pretty at all.

REUNIONS

T he Clayton High School Class of '86 has reunions every five years, and I go back to St. Louis for every one. Most of us are still in touch, so there's never that shocking moment when the music dims, everyone gasps, and we all whip our heads around to see the formerly nerdy chess club president walk in looking super-hot with the quarterback of the football team. There are no drinks thrown, no damning evidence suddenly produced with an accompanying shriek, no old feuds suddenly boiling over at the bar. I would describe these gatherings as "sweet." And that's one of the reasons there won't ever be a *Real Housewives of St. Louis*. I've seen that show and, trust me, it's nice, but it wouldn't make good TV.

The same cannot be said for the reunions I host on Bravo. Allow me to quote Whitney Houston from *Being Bobby Brown*: "Aww HAYALL NO!" At first, the concept behind reunion shows was to tie up loose ends and avoid the following season turning into a rehash. They were also a way to extend the seasons of shows that were getting good ratings. But what started as a little jaunt down Memory Lane has evolved into a smoldering high-speed pileup on the Autobahn, and I'm equal parts horrified, mesmerized, and—mainly—excited. After all, I'm not only a producer, host, and boss, I'm also a superfan.

The reunions on Bravo started with *Project Runway* and *Top Chef*, and even though we were dealing with relatively down-to-earth personalities like fledgling designers and young chefs, you may be shocked to learn that these initial get-togethers were dramatic, drunken—and sometimes very ugly. The first *Top Chef* reunion featured Tiffani Faison running to the side of the studio to throw up, contestant Ken Lee threatening original *Top Chef* host Katie Lee Joel, and chef Stephen Asprinio calling Candice Kumai trash. At the time, I honestly wondered: Was this the most repulsive or the greatest thing I'd ever seen on TV? The answer, possibly, was yes to both.

The first OC *Housewives* reunion occurred without me, and for that maybe I'm grateful: Today it looks as primitive as the first episode of *The Simpsons*. The women gathered in Vicki's backyard and sat on her tall, wobbly outdoor furniture, reminiscing directly to the camera. The next season, I hosted, but we still didn't get the setting right, moving the proceedings into an antiseptic, football-field-sized studio where we sat far apart from each other on director's chairs that made my butt hurt. When the women entered the studio, Jeana asked if the big fancy studio meant the show was a big hit. It was.

The set for the first *RHNYC* reunion was perfect. We convened at the Russian Tea Room; the women were seated close to each other on couches, surrounded by old New York City glamour. We positioned the biggest adversaries on either side of me. That season, like others that would follow, it was Jill and Ramona. I squeezed into the middle, which I've learned is always the best seat in the house.

The Housewives see the reunions as a last chance to rewrite their own story, and at the heart of it, isn't that what all reunions are really about? You go to your twentieth determined to leave an even better impression than the last time, to have people say, "That person looks great/has their shit together/has really changed . . ." It's a manipulation of sorts, but a manipulation that goes both ways. While the Housewives are trying to manipulate each other and (especially) the viewers, I'm trying to manipulate them into spilling their guts on television.

The Housewives both love and dread the reunions, and I can't say I blame them. They typically take at least eight hours to shoot, because we let all the women talk and talk (and talk) until they feel they've had their say. This is when they have to face the harshest jury—the viewers—who fire direct, often angry, questions and opinions. Even though the Housewives have signed up for the show and everything that entails—and though they keep coming back for more year after year— answering intensely personal questions and getting roasted for your behavior on national television would be a grueling experience for anyone. It's probably not unlike throwing your hat in the ring for public office, knowing that there's a chance Matt Lauer is going to show up with that pic of your butt you drunkenly tweeted.

Often a Housewife attempts to use the reunion show to reposition her "character." Sometimes, as in the case of Camille Grammer at the first *Real Housewives of Beverly Hills* reunion, it works. She was sincere, vulnerable, and owned everything she'd said and done during the season. Viewers who'd been hard on her all season now saw a likable person beneath the boasting about the nannies and square footage.

As much as the women are trying to say their piece and reinvent themselves, the reunions can serve a larger agenda for Bravo: They can be a determining factor for deciding who stays, who goes, and when to pull the plug on a series itself. I'm sure that one of the reasons the DC Wives were so forthcoming at their reunion was that in their minds, the pickup of their show was in jeopardy and they had to deliver. And deliver they did, but their instincts were correct: The show was in jeopardy, and even a lively reunion ultimately couldn't justify another season. In the end, the Housewives shows are still about telling the women's stories, and if the story being told has no chance to grow or change, then it can't go forward.

After the fourth *RHNYC* reunion, the chatter on social media about the women's nasty negativity was so loud and strong that it not only reinforced what the producers and Bravo had been worrying about all season, it freed us to make our boldest move thus far: not renewing the contracts of Jill, Alex, Kelly, and Cindy.

QUESTIONS I CAN'T BELIEVE I ASKED ON NATIONAL TELEVISION:

* Sonja, was your vagina rude to Kelly?
* Camille, was the real reason you used a surrogate to keep your figure?
* Danielle, what did you think when you heard Teresa say that Steve was just interested in you for blow jobs?
* Alexis, do you think God approves of your plastic surgery? You've taken what he did and changed it.
* Adrienne, I know you are too humble to reveal your net worth, but Lisa, how much do you think Adrienne is worth?
* Teresa, you said that you formerly had big hair—do you consider what's going on now not big?
* Taylor, would you ever consider having your lip implant removed?
* Gretchen, he was dating Jo, he's been with Laurie—is there something in you that feels at all weird about getting sloppy thirds?
* Cat, do you feel uncomfortable around black people?
* Lisa, do you have any poor friends?

✱ Sheree, do you think you've gone too far with toning your arms?

✱ Teresa, you said that your husband is more of an ass man. After you got your new bubbies, did he change his opinion?

✱ Tamra, you're going to sell your implants on eBay?

✱ NeNe, Angela from Great Neck, New York, wants to know why would you, at your age, wear clothes that show your old gals sagging?

✱ Danielle, your ex-husband says you were married to a big Colombian cocaine dealer, were a paid escort, were a raging nymphomaniac, had a bob job, had an eyebrow lift, and are a pathological liar. Comments?

Each woman brings a different MO to the tapings. Besides Pinot Grigio, Ramona requires a very clear idea of the day's schedule—when breaks and lunch are. Vicki winks at me throughout the taping, no matter whether someone else is talking about something funny or serious. (And I do love a wink.) Kim Zolciak is constantly trying to take away my blue cards full of prying questions—"Give me those evil blue cards!" Alexis from *Orange County* had a wonderfully absurd evidence-presenting moment: After a revelation that fellow Housewife (and soon-to-be-former-best-friend) Peggy had dated her husband years earlier, Alexis piped up just minutes later with her phone triumphantly in hand, announcing that Jim had just texted her to reveal that Peggy had been a stalker. I love that she thought that would settle it!

Normally, I am a relatively laid-back guy, even at work. But when it comes to reunions, I am a man on a mission, to get the story behind the story, to answer the pressing questions that every viewer wants to know, to confront the women and get them to confront each other. I was fully prepped for this role after years of shit-stirring in St. Louis, first with my family and then with my mini–Real Housewives of Clayton High, Jackie and Jeanne. It's cathartic to get everything out on the table, and if I have to pry and prod a little bit to make it happen, I will. To say I never take any joy or glee in the drama would be as much of a lie as these ladies sometimes try to get away with. So, no matter what, if I see a Housewife getting mad, I'm going to keep poking at her. If I see her get emotional, and I see an in, I'll keep going down that road. That's my job. Sometimes I even have to evoke Dan Rather, picking the threads of a story apart until I unravel the shroud and find some truth hidden beneath—okay, maybe I'm taking myself a little too seriously here. But what about the time I tried to get Kim to either say she had lost her hair to cancer or admit she was lying? Let's revisit, shall we?

> **AC:** Welcome back to the Atlanta Housewives Reunion Special. Mertise from Oakland e-mailed, "Kim, is that your real hair or is that a wig?"
>
> **KZ:** You know, I really want to talk about this. And NeNe, I want to address something to you from an emotional standpoint. I got very sick, I don't want to cry but (starts tearing), but I got very sick. It's not something (starts crying) that I would ever choose to do. Almost three years ago, I lost twenty-five pounds, my hair was falling out and nobody knew why and they said, "Kim"—it was a friend of mine, who was a doctor, and he said, "Kim, I got to be honest with you, I mean I'm ninety percent sure you have cancer."
>
> **AC:** So you had cancer.
>
> **KZ:** (nods) I wouldn't choose to walk around with a hairpiece EVER. Nobody would, and for you to say that, NeNe, you knew. I mean I got really skinny, I was sicker than . . .
>
> **NeNe:** That I knew what?
>
> **KZ:** That I was . . .
>
> **NeNe:** I didn't know that you were sick, that you had cancer; that was the first time I ever heard that.

KZ: I mean I was used to having beautiful hair, that's what I was known for; that was my signature growing up.

NeNe: Let me go on the record to say, I never knew that you had cancer. Had I known that, things would have been different. I thought you wore the hairpiece for style. I don't have a problem with it, you do. I mean if that's what you want to wear, that's what you do. I NEVER knew you were sick.

AC: And are you cancer-free now?

KZ: You know, they found that I did not have cancer, that I had some other problems.

AC: So you didn't have cancer?

KZ: No, I did not. I lived about three weeks. I remember sitting in a Chili's waiting for my test results and it was terrible and they were like, "You are healthy this way, but we got some other stuff going on." Which is not what I want to talk about but there was some other stuff. And it's been almost three years and my blood work's great and it changed my life. I'm just happy to be here.

AC: Okay. So you DIDN'T have cancer.

KZ: No I did not. Thank God.

Did that make sense? Besides the sitting-in-Chili's part? You might wonder: How hard is it just to establish whether a person did or didn't have cancer? But if you're wondering that, you may not have watched many *Housewives* reunions. Talking in circles was never more predominant than at the DC *Housewives* reunion, where Michaele and Tareq Salahi simply refused, over and over, to respond directly to a question, as if it was everyone else who was nuts for even asking. Forget the hours we spent going around and around like a Ferris wheel dissecting their infamous night at the White House. Listening to Michaele "answer" the question of whether she was or was not ever a Redskins cheerleader would drive a levelheaded person as insane as, well, Tareq and Michaele Salahi appeared to be.

Andy Cohen: Laura from AZ wants to know, was Michaele ever a Washington Redskins cheerleader for the NFL? There have been a lot of conflicting reports.

Michaele Salahi: The Redskins in the nineties, uh, well, no, in the eighties, I had worked with, and they came to me at the millennium.

AC: You had cheered with them in the eighties?

MS: Not as a full-time cheerleader. I was kinda, I went out in one or two games. I went and fluffed it and did their promotional—they had a show called *Redskins Sideline Report*. Then in the millennium Terri Lamb had come to me and said would you be interested in joining the alumni? And I said, no not really, to be honest—

AC: Well, why would she—?

MS: It would hurt me to join it. Because I would have to divulge my age.

AC: Okay.

MS: And she said, well if I made you '91 would you join the alumni? So for the last seven, eight years I've been paying dues, and I've been a part of it.

AC: So Terri Lamb, who is in charge of the Redskins—

MS: Still a good friend—

AC: —cheerleaders, she says that you weren't a cheerleader in the eighties. Or the nineties.

MS: Right, because well, I'm on the roster. I'm on the roster, so I don't know. I still have the roster and—

AC: But, I mean, I read the Diane book [Diane Dimond's *Cirque Du Salahi: Be Careful Who You Trust*]. She, in all her research, has no record of it.

MS: She can't find our answer. She can't find that I am or that I'm not.

AC: Your brother—your brother apparently said you were not a cheerleader.

MS: Right, well, he didn't know—

AC: The head of the Redskins cheerleading organization said you were not a cheerleader.

MS: Yeah, but my—I wasn't a cheerleader.

Stacie Scott Turner: And you didn't have the roster. The roster?

MS: I do have the roster.

SST: That—well, no, not in the book.

MS: Yeah, well, the thing is, Terri and I have the roster, but Diane interviewed Howie—

AC: Hold on. But you just said to me—hold on.

Mary Schmidt Amons: They're saying no!

AC: You just said to me that you weren't a cheerleader, that's what you just said.

MS: No, I've gone out two times. I was never an NFL cheerleader out of our league. I never said that.

AC: So, what does that—you hopped on the field twice? On the show you said that you were a Redskins cheerleader.

MS: Right, because that's what I've been told to say by the alumni.

MSA: (sigh)

MS: So, when they said—

AC: It's a circle. It's a circle.

(general groaning)

MS: No, so, no, was I a cheerleader? Yes. Did I go out two times? Yes. Does that constitute as a cheerleader? I don't know.

So, was she ever a Redskins cheerleader? By the end of it, I neither knew nor cared.

A great Housewives reunion, for me, is when tempers flare

and friends, enemies, and—my favorite relationship moniker—frenemies alike lay it on the line. All my voyeuristic thrill buttons are pushed by witnessing such direct, intense encounters from just five feet away, for instance Bethenny telling Alex and Simon to their faces that they're social climbers, or NeNe lunging at Kim in the first ten minutes of the first Atlanta reunion.

Actually, that first Atlanta reunion was an interesting case: great television and delightful for me as a network executive, but not all that fun for me as a host and a person, now that I think of it. NeNe Leakes was initially the one who made that reunion happen; at the time *Atlanta* premiered, it wasn't a given that a reunion would follow every season. We didn't build it into our schedule and didn't assume there'd be a demand for one with every series. I got a voice mail from NeNe (the first time I'd ever had contact with her directly) saying, "I'm begging you to do a reunion, Andy. I want to confront Kim. I am so mad at the things she's been saying on the show about me." NeNe had spent months and months stewing in her anger as she watched the show. She felt she had been slandered. So, who were we to deny her the opportunity to set things right?

The tension, as the women were getting settled into their chairs, was as thick as an expensive weave. I hadn't experienced anything like this level of hostility before. Normally, my job during these marathon tapings is to keep everybody's energy up and get them motivated to reveal everything. With the first Atlanta reunion, I quickly realized my job might be to block a punch. Within ten minutes of shooting, while I was probing Kim about her secret-identity sugar daddy, Big Poppa, NeNe went ballistic and looked like she was about to swing at Kim. As NeNe kept yelling at Kim to "close your legs to married men, trashbox," I wavered between amusement and actual fear.

I think this is honestly the appropriate response to a Housewives reunion. It's like getting the giggles at a funeral: You know it's not the time to laugh, but you can't stop. I get that sensation a lot during reunions—I think viewers do, too—and the editors often have to

Am I smiling because I'm scared, amused, or both?

cut away from my smiling face. How can something so occasionally mortifying also be so hilarious? It's the women's personalities, their turns of phrase, the pressure-cooker setting, the sharpness of their accusations versus the tenderness of their feelings, that contribute to making it seem like theater of the sublime, at once dramatic and comedic. Oh, and they're all in cocktail attire with big hair.

When that first Atlanta taping was over, I was honestly worried about the outburst—I didn't want the show to be too negative. We cut back on much of NeNe's tirade but left enough in that you got a taste of the moment. The ratings were huge.

First reunions are always intense—there's all that expectation and anxiety around a major event the women haven't experienced before. I've already mentioned my preview of the New Jersey Housewives reunions when I met the ladies for the first time in the Bravo offices. Dina looked at me that day with terror in her eyes. All she knew about me was that I was an instigator, and she didn't want to be instigated. I told her not to worry, that we were just having a professional meeting—the reunion was months away. But as the meeting progressed, the tension among the women erupted into screaming matches. I kept telling the women, "This isn't the reunion—save it for then!" To which Dina replied, "Are you really ready for this, Andy Cohen?" I thought I was.

We usually tape the reunions a few weeks before the finale airs, and we solicit as many questions from viewers as we can leading up to the event. We knew at the time that the *RHNJ* table flip—arguably one of the greatest *Housewives* episodes ever— would be big, but we didn't know it would be one of the highest-rated episodes still in the history of the franchise and generate countless parodies from every corner of pop culture. We went into the taping with high expectations that the tension among the women would translate into something extraordinary. And here's a lesson: I've found that the reunions I anticipate the most wind up somehow falling flat.

The whole setup for the New Jersey Season 1 reunion felt like a comedy waiting to happen. We had two very pregnant participants—Jacqueline and Teresa. Because Jacqueline's due date was a few days away, we had to shoot close to her hospital and wound up in a small commercial studio somewhere in the middle of Jersey; to be more precise, amid abandoned railroad tracks and empty warehouses. If anybody had wanted to get rid of *my* body, there would have been no lack of places to stash it, as long as someone else wasn't already buried there. When I walked in that morning, I took one look at the set and turned to Bravo exec Christian Barcellos, my on-site producer and partner-in-crime at almost every reunion, and declared it the ugliest we'd ever used.

How to describe this set . . . a chessboard-style black-and-white-tiled floor; the tackiest white sofa and loveseat flanking what was to be my chair, a wide white baroque throne with wings; a big white filigreed coffee table topped with a massive, funereal flower arrangement in the shape of New Jersey; and a background resembling an endless Teletubbiesesque blue sky with several large chandeliers hanging from nowhere. Christian, usually a pro at making last-minute lighting tweaks that magically transform the feel of a set, said, "Well, it does feel like a cross between *The Avengers* and *Heaven Can Wait*, but we're working on making the blue darker." When we sent a preview picture to Shari Levine at Bravo HQ, she e-mailed back: "I can't stop laughing. That is the funniest thing I've ever seen." The New Jersey Housewives always ride that line between over-the-top and leopard chic—it's part of the fun of the show—but this set was like New Jersey on a bad acid trip.

Despite the god-awful set, we thought it would be a great show: Tension had been high among the ladies *for over a year* and the confrontations were bound to be epic. When I walk into a reunion taping, the first person I look for is Christian, who's always ready to brief me on the moods of the various ladies. And on that day it went something like this:

I especially enjoy the flowers in the shape of New Jersey.

"Danielle is sequestered on the other side of the building, far from the others. They won't run into each other. She's ready to go and in a great mood. You need to go talk Caroline off the ledge—there's something that's been going on between Dina's family and Danielle since we wrapped and Caroline is furious and freaked out.

"She wants to speak with you. Neither she nor Jacqueline nor Dina will mention what's going on, and Dina is threatening to walk off the set if anything gets ugly and if this *thing* gets brought up. We don't know what *it* is. Jacqueline looks ready to give birth—we have a nurse on the set—but she, Caroline, and Teresa say there's more about the book surrounding Danielle's past they want to expose. They're nervous but fired up. Teresa's in there, making jokes and in a great mood. Go say hi to Danielle first."

Good morning to you, too, Christian.

I sat down in my heavenly throne knowing that we had all the ingredients, or "ingredientses" as Teresa might say, for a bang-up show. I do remember it well, but mainly for the long, painful silences. Nothing happened. Dina and Jacqueline froze and totally clammed up. I pushed and prodded, but the more I tried to get them to reveal their feelings, to admit how they really felt about each other, the further in the other direction they went. As their castmates looked on in shock, they essentially said they were willing to give Danielle another chance. If you'd seen the season that preceded this discussion, the sentiment seemed completely unreal, unbelievable, and of suspicious motivation. Then, Teresa and Caroline, obviously frustrated with their costars but not willing to climb out onto any limbs themselves, basically let Danielle off the hook. It was only in the last five minutes that Caroline confronted Danielle with a cryptic, "You are garbage. What you did to my family was so terrible . . ." For years people have asked me what the hell Danielle had done to that family. Well, finally, here is what I know: The allegation was that Danielle had somehow gotten involved in a matter involving Dina's custody of her daughter, Lexi. Danielle, of course, denied it, and, to my knowledge, the matter went no further.

The next day, Sirens Media, our producers of *RHNJ*, called to say Jacqueline and Caroline felt like they had more to say and were even suggesting that they do a "do-over" to get out their feelings for Danielle. The truth was, they didn't want us to use the footage of Caroline crying about Danielle and the secret issue.

Another shot? A do-over? There are no do-over reunion shows! In happier news, Jacqueline's baby, Christopher, was indeed born two days later. And as far as I know, nobody welcomed him to this world with a New Jersey–shaped flower arrangement.

Another highly anticipated reunion turned into a snore with Season 2 of *RHA*, which had been a fever-pitch rage-fest all season long, full of wig-pulls, controversy over Kim's debut single "Tardy for the Party," even warring fashion lines (there isn't enough tape stock in Japan to satisfy my love for discussing She by Sheree). But when I got to the set that morning, I encountered five very shut-down Atlanta Housewives who had taken some sort of vow of silence. Two days before, I'd had my one and only cross conversation with NeNe Leakes. I actually don't know that I'd call it a "conversation," and "cross" may be too polite a word; she actually called, screamed at me for five minutes, and hung up. She was torrentially unhappy with the finale, which she'd just finished watching in preparation for the reunion show. It was the big She by Sheree fashion show and she didn't like how she was portrayed, nor did she care for the epilogue cards about each of the women at the end.

The lack of agita during that reunion was causing *me* agita, with the women not playing along with the questions, not backing up things they'd said during the season, and refusing to call each other out regarding obvious issues. The only one on-set getting any shade from the women was me. At one point I turned to NeNe and asked, "What'd you do with NeNe?" During the break, I chastised them: "You know what, this is so BORING. I don't want you to fight. I could give a shit whether you fight or not, just be *yourselves*. Don't clam up." But, with the exception of Kandi, the women never opened up, and the viewers were pissed. ("Why were the women so SHUT DOWN?! They decided to stop talking at the REUNION? What is with them?!!") Again, those expectations that a huge, drama-filled season equals a huge, drama-filled reunion show will get you every time.

Of course, as you know, it's not always stony silence—far from it. The New York reunions are unique for their frenetic, unwieldy energy. The *RHNYC* women have this uncanny ability to talk over each other at peak decibel level; it's like being trapped in an Evelyn Cohen echo chamber. When they go at it, there's no interrupting them. And yet, as loud and nasty as they got, there was something that always amused me about watching Jill and Ramona fight over almost anything, be it a tennis match, RSVPing to a party, or what happened in front of a step and repeat. Watching any Jill vs. Ramona kerfuffle is like indulging in a slushie—it'll give you a headache, but that won't stop you from enjoying it. There is something so primal about the atmosphere the New York women create that I remember breaking for lunch at Season 2's reunion at Cipriani and feeling that it might be perfectly acceptable for me to strip off my clothes and eat raw meat with my bare hands. (Note: I quickly decided against this.)

One of the most common questions people ask me is, "How do you *deal* with those *women*?" The main answer is that I am crazy about them and the show. These women are funny, they are earnest about what's important to them, they dress to the nines for every occasion, they often only take themselves seriously, and most of them recognize the simultaneous gravity and sheer absurdity of the end-of-season forum. It is like a courtroom of manners and etiquette and they're the overdressed star witnesses. And me? Even as I'm caught in the cross fire during an intense exchange, my producer-brain is parsing what they've said and determining if we're getting what we need to make an exciting TV show, whether it'll be enough content for two parts, and if the fans will feel like they got enough drama, excitement, news, and fun. I'll admit that I've had my moments when I was too exhausted to listen to one more word, or if I did, I would simply lose it, but I never crossed that boundary. Not until minute 45 of the *Real Housewives of New York* Season 4 reunion taping. Allow me to relive my shame.

The morning had started out intensely, with Jill asking anyone who would listen whether she was in the "A Position"—not a term anyone on any reunion set had ever actually used, but which in her mind meant seated beside me. I knew from *Watch What Happens Live* that she was big on seating placement: "I would like to request to sit next to Andy," she'd tell our booker, as though there were tons of other options on our tiny set. Needless to say, she wasn't pleased to discover that LuAnn and Ramona had already been assigned seats on either side of me.

In the final moments before we started rolling tape, Alex arrived on-set and was also annoyed about the seating arrangement. She was supposed to sit on the far end of the couch, the same position she'd had for every other reunion show. "I don't want to sit here. Can I sit further in? I'm always on the end. I'm tired of being on the end!" I told her to think of herself as the voice of reason on the end, which she very often was, but she still wasn't happy.

With all the talk about "Where am I sitting?"—as if these grown women were little kids at a birthday party table before cake—by the time we got rolling I was already a little spent, and you can see it on my face at the top of the show when Alex and I curtly greet each other. That was as quiet as things got, though, because once we were off to the races, I was in the middle of a pack of wild beasts roaring and screeching simultaneously over each other. I tried to get them to quiet down, or at least speak one at a time, to no avail. It was as if they couldn't hear each other. Or me. Unfortunately, it was the only reunion show taping my parents had ever attended. They stopped by on their way to a matinee of *Book of Mormon*.

"Please let each other speak! One at a time!" I begged.

I had the Countess to my right, and I tried to appeal to her respect for etiquette and called for decorum. No one listened. I moved on to sporadically telling them all to "*Shut* UP!" Nothing.

To give you an idea of the scene, read this mini-transcript really fast and imagine everyone speaking at once:

> **Jill:** You can give it but you can't take it.
> **Ramona:** I can take anything, whatever you want to give to me. You just said . . .
> **Kelly:** You don't want to encourage that kind of behavior.
> **Ramona:** . . . my husband, inferring whatever.
> **Jill:** No, go ahead . . . what about your husband?
> **Ramona:** Nothing. He's a great man, I'm very lucky. I wish you had a great husband like mine because I know you don't.
> **Countess:** You know what . . . I love Bobby.
> **Kelly:** I love Bobby!
> **Jill:** Were you there? WERE YOU THERE? Because I got . . .
> **Ramona:** Get a life! Get a life, loser!
> **Jill:** Lowlife!
> **Andy:** Shut up!
> **Alex:** Shhhhhh!
> **Andy:** Shut up and let me ask about it, okay? You guys are acting like beasts today!

A half hour into shooting and I was yelling at grown women, telling them to shut up, something I could not have pictured myself saying to anyone just an hour before. Oh, and it wasn't working. Finally, I screamed at the top of my lungs, "SHUT THE FUCK UP!!!"

And they did. We all apologized to each other and moved on. Hours later, as we dissected the situation that led to me yelling at them—almost like an instant reunion for the reunion—they agreed that me yelling "STFU" was the only thing that could have actually gotten them to do it. When we took our next break, I remembered that my poor parents, who'd come to New York hoping to see their son in action, making them proud, had instead witnessed me dropping an F-bomb to a bunch of ladies in cocktail dresses. Luckily, they were on my side.

"It was all you could do to SHUT THEM UP!" Evelyn said, herself screaming.

"I think it was the right—and only—thing to do, Andy," my dad quietly agreed. They skedaddled out of there in a hurry, and at the time I wished I could have scurried right along with them.

Still, probably the most heated and most talked-about reunion of all was at the end of *New Jersey*'s second season, which was the first time all the women had been in a room at the same time with Danielle since the first reunion. The second season of that show was essentially fourteen episodes of Danielle vs. the other women. The uneasy feeling as we were getting settled at the Atlantic City Borgata was even worse than it had been for the Jill vs. Bethenny reunion of *RHNYC*. I knew going in that Teresa's temper was intense, but I wasn't expecting much more than raised voices. I was wrong.

The pot boiled over about an hour into the morning, when Danielle—totally off-topic—accused Teresa of not visiting her new nephew in the hospital, tipping off that she'd been in touch with Teresa's sister-in-law. (Yes, Melissa Gorga, who would later go on to become a Jersey Housewife herself.) Teresa lost it, stood, and got in Danielle's face. I didn't know what to do. I had, like everyone else reading this, seen Teresa flip an innocent table on national television. Being a nice Jewish boy, I've never been in a physical fight in my life, and so if you rewatch a clip of it, you can see how completely awkward I am in trying to hold Teresa back, and indeed am eventually overpowered completely by the Italian Stallioness, who hurls me like a Raggedy Andy doll into my chair as Danielle walks off the set.

I spent the next fifteen minutes going back and forth from backstage to the stage, trying to calm both women down. Danielle was worried I wasn't going to protect her as I weakly defended my not-quite-yeoman's job, kind of sounding like my dad defending an action that my mom considered weak. "I got up . . . I helped . . . I'll keep protecting you," I muttered. She kind of, barely, bought it. (I did mean it, though; I would never in a million years allow anyone to put her hands on anyone else while I was there. And I now probably had the bruises to prove it.) When I got back to the set I pleaded with Teresa to just stay seated. "Just please do not get up off the couch. That's the rule. Don't get off the couch." She nodded, but just as viewers sometimes wonder if Teresa processes what's being said to her, in that moment I was not completely confident she wouldn't get up again. At that point I didn't contemplate that my ass had been kicked on-camera. I was way more concerned as a producer that the whole thing would dissolve into chaos and that we wouldn't have a show at all.

When I returned from Atlantic City that day, I went straight over to my friends Mark Consuelos and Kelly Ripa's house for a drink. They wanted to know what had happened at the show. "I don't really remember—there's too much noise in my head. I think I got pushed." That push, when it aired, was replayed time and time and time again. An unintended consequence of learning that it was one of our highest-rated reunions to date was the ability to calculate just how many people all over the world had seen me get roughed up by a girl. When Teresa next appeared on *Watch What Happens Live*, I made her wear a seat belt during the show, as a joke. And because I was a little bit scared.

Danielle's walk-off wasn't unique. Walk-offs (or the threat of them) are common currency on reunion shows. They're like a labor strike, with each side waiting for the other to blink. When Simon van Kempen joined us for the first *RHNYC* reunion, the other women threatened to walk off because they wanted *their* men to appear as well. The fact was that Simon had played a big role that season, so it seemed right to invite him. When Simon walked on, nobody walked off, and I thought we'd narrowly averted a huge crisis. Then, later on in the taping, Ramona became so upset that I'd brought up Alex's nude photo controversy, which had erupted while the season was airing, that she walked off then, instead. At the time, I naïvely thought we'd have to get very creative in the edit to try to hide the fact that Ramona was no longer on the set, but after the show, I took one look at Christian and realized that it might have been the best thing that could have happened. It was all very theatrical. After that, we had a virtual parade of walk-offs in most of the franchises—not because of any encouragement from me, but because the Housewives look to each other for behavioral cues. At this point, though, angrily toddling off in your sky-high Louboutins seems very 2009, so I always beseech the women to just stay put.

At the end of the day, true emotion is the main ingredient behind a great reunion. Kandi is someone who "goes there"—she is an emotional woman who feels things deeply. Other women wipe fake tears in order to build sympathy. I won't name names, of course, but review the contents of your DVR and judge for yourselves. But, truth be told, the line between real and fake (tears, not boobs) can get a little murky. In 2011, I was interviewing Slade Smiley on the Season 6 *Real Housewives of Orange County* reunion. Slade is a serial dater of OC Housewives, an incredible character whom we couldn't make up if we tried—not even his name! Slade has appeared and reappeared on that show, most recently as Gretchen's boyfriend. In this interview, Slade was saying that he loved Gretchen so much that he would let her go if he knew she was going to have a life surrounded by wealth, because that's what she really deserved. He seemed like he really meant it, and Gretchen was silently weeping (or acting like she was weeping and doing an expert job of it). I was looking at Slade and I could see that his eyes were watering, a cue to me that he was in the zone where he could potentially really break down and cry, which is always interesting. So I started thinking—in a moment of half puppeteering and half producing—that it would be really something if Slade actually broke down. We'd never seen the man get emotional like that, and I thought it would lend a new dimension of depth to him and the show. Usually during an emotional interview I try to lock eyes with whomever I'm speaking to and let them know that I am there with them feeling it all, which I usually am. And when I feel something, my eyes tend to get a little glassy-looking. (I have very dry eyes, so this is, in fact, semi-common.) My face usually registers a look that I assume mirrors my feeling of empathy and conveys to whomever I'm speaking to that we're on this journey together. At least, that's what I've always thought. Now that I've seen myself on TV, I know that that look is also similar to the way a baby looks when it is pooping or moments away from wailing. In either case, it sometimes allows whomever I'm talking with to emote along with me. But in the case of Mr. Smiley, he wasn't going there. I was so in the moment, though, that before I knew it, I realized that I had actual tears running down *my* face. In my peripheral vision, blurred though it was by a cataract, even more tears ready to spill out, I saw the camera pointed directly at me, and I dissolved in terror. *I cannot be seen on national television weeping for Slade. I'm the only one crying on this set!* At that thought, I started surreptitiously dabbing at the tears on my cheeks, wondering what Slade—who was still talking—must be thinking. Then I started simultaneously laughing and trying not to laugh, over my self-induced tears for Slade Smiley, which was even more inappropriate than the crying had been a moment before. After all, the man was still pouring his heart out to me.

I guess that's why these reunions are so universal: You laugh, you cry, and then you laugh again. What these women are living out on TV are just exaggerated versions of our own lives. Sure, many of them have money and houses with big closets stuffed with furs and jewels and shoes to-die-for, but in the end, the things they wrestle with are the same things we all wrestle with: love, family, friendship . . . betrayal. Who hasn't longed for an opportunity to set the record straight or to finally just say how they've really been feeling? Maybe next time I head home for a high school reunion, I should try to lock eyes with a couple of my classmates and get them to spill their guts about things they thought they were long over. Hey, now that I'm thinking about it, shouldn't I have gotten the invitation for my next reunion by now? Maybe it's lost in the mail. Clayton High School Reunion Planning Committee, call me!

☺

In 2009, NBC broadcast a special celebrating the best sketches from *The Women of Saturday Night Live*. They shot one original sketch, written by Paula Pell and Emily Spivey, which was a brilliant parody of pretty much every *Housewives* reunion show we've ever done. Shooting this sketch, surrounded by my favorite hilarious women, on a re-creation of that horrible *RHNJ* Season 1 set with Tina Fey, Cheri Oteri, Kristen Wiig, Maya Rudolph, Nora Dunn, Ana Gasteyer, Molly Shannon, Rachel Dratch, Julia Louis-Dreyfus, Amy Poehler, and Laraine Newman was one of the high points of my career. If anyone had told me I'd get to play myself on *SNL*, I would've said they were high.

> *Andy Cohen sits in a gorgeous overstuffed chair flanked by the ladies: MOLLY, MAYA, TINA, and NORA on one side and ANA, RACHEL, CHERI, and KRISTEN on the other side. They look amazing: hair big and coiffed and they are dressed outrageously to the nines. The set is perfection, blue background, chandeliers, candelabras.*

ANDY

Hello everyone, I'm Andy Cohen, and welcome to
the *Women of SNL* reunion show. I am thrilled to
be a part of this gathering. I'm such a huge fan of
all of you, so this is truly an honor. Here with me
today is—

CHERI

You bet your ass it's an honor.

[They all chuckle daintily.]

ANDY

Exactly! An honor. Thank you, Cheri.

[As Andy introduces the ladies, we cut to each one of them as
they smolder to camera.]

ANDY (cont'd)

Let's welcome Molly Shannon, Maya Rudolph,
Tina Fey, Nora Dunn, Ana Gasteyer, Rachel
Dratch, Cheri Oteri, Kristen Wiig, and, joining us
from Los Angeles, Julia Louis-Dreyfus, Amy
Poehler, and Laraine Newman.

[Cut to: Amy and Julia and Laraine.]

AMY/JULIA/LARAINE: (ad-lib hellos)

[Cut to: Int. Real Housewives of SNL set.]
[They all ad-lib hellos.]

ANDY

You all have had such wonderful years at *SNL*. I
wanna catch up on your lives since you left. Nora
Dunn, let's start with you. You look amazing.

NORA

Thank you, Andy.

ANDY

Has it been difficult for you since your divorce
from the Count?

NORA

I am a Countess, but I am not going to discuss the
Count.

[Cut to: All the ladies looking uncomfortable.]

CHERI

She don't wanna talk about the Count!

NORA

I want to talk about my new exercise video.

ANDY

Oh, yes, you have an exercise video.

NORA

It's fantastic, Andy. All the exercises are designed
for you to do while you're doing other things, like
getting your legs sanded or going to the opening
of Billy Bush's new restaurant. It's called "The
Classy Countdown to Fitness: Working Out with
the Countess."

KRISTEN (O.S.)

Maya could use a classy workout.

ANDY

Uh, somebody over here said something. Was
that you, Kristen? What did you say?

KRISTEN

I said Maya is not classy. And she knows it. She is
not classy, because she is not.

MAYA

Don't! You. Even. Begin to.

[Maya fumes at Kristen.]
[Cut to: All the ladies looking uncomfortable.]

ANDY

All right, let's talk a little bit about what went on between you two.

KRISTEN

I was leaving the SNL after party and as I was heading to my car she was hiding in the shadows and reached out and pulled my weave.

MAYA

I didn't pull your weave!

KRISTEN

Oh, yeah? Well, who pulled my weave, then? Who pulled my weave? A ghost? A hobo? 'Cause I've got it right here. Look at this, look at this . . .

[Kristen pulls out a hunk of hair.]
[Cut to: The ladies gasping.]

ANDY

Wait a minute, wait a minute, is that the actual weave piece that you pulled out of her head?

MAYA

No, because I did not pull her weave! Why would I pull her weave? If I'm gonna pull a weave, wouldn't I pull my own weave? Andy, I am no weave-puller. It's insane!

[Cheri gets in Maya's face.]

CHERI

You pulled her weave! You know it, Andy knows it, and the weave knows it! You're garbage. Garbage.

MAYA

That's it.

[Maya storms out. Rachel gets up to console Cheri and Kristen.]

ANDY

Maya? Maya? *(To an imaginary producer)* Is she coming back?

RACHEL (à la Caroline Manzo)

You're just giving her what she wants. You just gave her what she wanted. She's not worth it. Look at me, Kristen. Look at me. Remember, we're fambily. Fambily. Look at me. Fambily.

[Cut to: Maya backstage being hugged by her hairdresser and makeup guy (James and Eric). She has more makeup applied with an airbrush.]

ANDY

Rachel, you were really the peacemaker there.

RACHEL

Well, you know, Andy, we on SNL are one big happy fambily, and when you mess with my fambily, you mess with me. Don't mess with my fambily. Period. You mess with my fambily? You lose.

ANDY

Molly Shannon. What's been happening with you?

MOLLY

Well, Andy, I've been so busy traveling all over the country promoting my cookbooks, as you know. My low-fat cupcake cookbook, and low-fat medications, and also my book of low-fat cocktail recipes.

ANDY

And you invented your own signature cocktail, right?

MOLLY

Yes, I invented my own signature cocktail. It's vodka, a little bit of shaved ginger, and then a different kind of vodka. It's called the Molly, and it's not just a drink, it's a lifestyle.

ANDY

Great. I know Cheri had a bunch backstage. Good, Cheri?

CHERI (drunk)

Oh god yes! They were so freaking delicious that I lost my purse!

KRISTEN

So loud.

ANDY

Now Ana, you've been very busy.

ANA

Yes. I've been working very hard on my skin care line. It's called "About Face," and three percent of the profits go to my charity, which does provide books to women at the beach on vacation, so I'm very proud. It's a great skin care line and it's made with an array of really great spermials.

KRISTEN

That must have been easy for you to get.

ANDY

Wait—what, Kristen?

KRISTEN

I just said it must have been easy for Ana to get spermials.

[Ana and Kristen fume at each other.]

ANDY

Now Tina, what's been happening with you?

TINA

Amazing, I'm doing amazing. My dance single is dropping in December 2014.

ANDY

I understand you cut a record with . . .

TINA

Bruce Willis's music producer. It's amazing. We share the same car dealer. It's called "I Wanna Spend Some Time Witcha."

ANDY

Can you give us a little taste?

TINA

No, Andy, stop! You're putting me on the spot!

[She immediately goes into the song, to camera. She is singing with a track.]

TINA (singing):

Put down your keys baby
Stop looking at your mail

Cuz cuz cuz baybeee
I wanna spend some time witcha

[Maya comes strolling back out and pointedly stalls herself in front of Tina for a beat or two. Track keeps going a sec, as Tina sits down, annoyed.]

ANDY

Oh good. Have a seat, Maya. We're glad you're back.

MAYA

Are we?

[Maya holds up her hand and does a pulling motion.]

KRISTEN

Hey! Did you see that, Andy? Did you see that? She's pretending to pull my weave! That is proof!

MAYA

You're insane.

[Maya and Kristen glare at each other.]

ANDY

Maya, why did you come back out?

MAYA

It's boring back there, plus I wanted to ask Kristen a question.

ANDY

Okay, Maya. Go ahead.

MAYA (softly)

Why did you choke my dog?

KRISTEN

What?

MAYA

Why did you choke my dog?

KRISTEN

I didn't choke your dog! I was hugging your dog and he wiggled and got tangled up in his halter top!

MAYA

She choked my dog till he passed out, y'all!

[Cut to: Ladies' reactions. Cheri loses it.]

CHERI

You pulled her dog's weave! You know it, the dog knows it, and everyone that was at that dog's birthday party knows it!

[All of them ridiculously arguing.]

ANDY

You know what? I think now would be a good time to throw to Amy and Julia and Laraine in Los Angeles. Hi, ladies!

[Cut to: Amy and Julia and Laraine. They sip glasses of champagne.]

AMY AND JULIA AND LARAINE

Hi!

[Cut to: Int. Real Housewives of SNL set.]

ANDY

It's so good to see you! Tell me what you ladies have been up to.

[Cut to: Amy and Julia and Laraine.]

AMY

Well, as you know, we couldn't be there today because you all have a restraining order against us.

[Cut to: Int. Real Housewives of SNL set: The ladies all wave.]

ANDY

You ladies do look great! LA is really working for you.

[Cut to: Amy and Julia and Laraine.]

JULIA

Well, Andy, we've been all over Southern California promoting our jewelry line of eco-friendly clip-on earrings, because we're all so environmentally conscious. And of course our sex tapes.

AMY

Yes, it's been so fun promoting our sex tapes. I have two sex tapes.

JULIA

And I have one sex tape, but I'm currently working on another. So two sex tapes.

LARAINE

Yes, and I told them in no uncertain terms that they're not to make sex tapes on my property.

AMY

Too late.

JULIA

Way too late. Can I just say something, Andy? Whatever we did to you guys, it was so not intentional.

[Cut to: Int. Real Housewives of SNL set.]

ANDY

You hit us with your limo.

NORA

On a closed course.

KRISTEN

Your limo ran over my weave.

[The ladies are all getting teary.]

RACHEL

We have to get past this! We are a fambily. And we will always be a fambily. It's time to make amends.

ANDY

Don't you think part of all this is about being funny people? To be funny, don't you have to be a little bit crazy?

[They all turn on Andy. Rachel stands. Andy stands. Rachel pushes Andy. Several of the ladies go over and turn over a table. Several more ladies storm off. Tina stands and begins to sing her song.]

TINA (singing):
I wanna spend some time witcha
I wanna spend some time witcha!

ANDY

Stay tuned! We'll be right back!

OUT

Jackhole of the Week

BravoTV.com

SINGING MUNCHKINS

People sometimes ask me if my life is different now that I'm on TV. Here's the extent to which things have changed: Sometimes I can get into a great restaurant, sometimes people want to have their picture taken with me, and sometimes people come up to me and say something that they perhaps intend to be nice or funny, but that leaves me feeling . . . sweetly bludgeoned. Something like: "You are cuter than I thought you would be!" Or, "The Housewives are the end of civilization!" It also took becoming kind of famous for me to realize that I'm actually kind of short. Just like with my wonky eye, I didn't consider myself a shrimp until I went on TV and read a flood of comments about my height online. (I'm five nine, by the way, which *might* make me taller than Seacrest, but don't tell him I said that.)

Usually, though, I forget that anyone knows who I am. But something happened in 2010 that made me realize that I had indeed become something of a public figure. And I wouldn't mind giving this moment back. It involves a terrible storm, Diana Ross, and a bunch of Munchkins singing. And I know what you're thinking: Didn't *The Wiz* come out in 1978?

The story really starts my senior in college, on Academy Awards night—the gay Super Bowl. That night I was bored to tears: *Dances with Wolves* cleaned up, winning award after award. I hadn't seen the movie and I never will. Then finally, somewhere along that evening's endless march to the obvious Best Picture result, there was a performance that gave me an Oscar® boner!

Since then, I've watched the moment online so many times that I know it by heart. It begins with a black-and-white clip from *The Wizard of Oz*. Judy Garland is in Kansas, plaintively singing "Over the Rainbow." A few lines into the song, another voice joins in, and a glorious duet erupts, as Miss Diana Ross appears onstage in a white sequined dress. Slowly, the Judy clip dissolves and it's all Diana. The music swells, and Diana says, "Sing with me, Los Angeles . . . *sing along!*" as images of the audience appear behind her on a massive screen. Jessica Tandy is singing. Lovebirds Tom Cruise and Nicole Kidman are singing. Slowly people in other cities appear behind Ross. And they are singing, too! *The world!* Tokyo! London! Moscow! Diana is leading a live, global sing-along of "Over the Rainbow"!

It would be hard to create a moment like this today—we're all so jaded and steeped in irony—but that number was pure, glorious theater. At the end, Ms. Ross struck a pose that suggested she might've just brokered world peace. It was her signature move: hands in the air, head back, legs in sort of a lopsided, tilted almost-curtsy. The silhouette was iconic Diana-Triumphant-Showbiz-Lady for whom there Ain't No Mountain High Enough.

I was devastated that I hadn't recorded it on my VCR. I was too enraptured to coordinate the remote. Back then, YouTube was only a futuristic gleam in a young nerd's eye, so I was forced to face the possibility that I would go through life only seeing that clip one time. (So, if I didn't already thank you in the acknowledgments, shout-out to the person who invented YouTube for allowing me to watch this and, naturally, Susan Lucci's Emmy win—and cute pandas—any time I need a pick-me-up.)

Fast-forward twenty years. I'm at my bestie Bruce's place in Los Angeles putting on my tuxedo as another interminable Oscar broadcast is coming to an end. I'm in a hurry to get ready because I'm lucky to have invitations for what I know will be two great parties: *Vanity Fair*'s annual bash and then a more intimate affair hosted by Madonna. I half-watch the proceedings over my shoulder in the mirror as *The King's Speech* wins Best Picture and I work against the clock to sculpt my hair into something less Q-tip-ish. Then I turn toward the TV and see a group of children clad in royal blue and lime green T-shirts trooping onstage and mounting a set of risers. Their mouths are open and they're gesticulating wildly, in a re-imagination of Miss Ross's glorious rendition of "Somewhere Over the Rainbow," but to me it looks like a lip-synched catastrophe.

I cannot lunge for the "mute" button quickly enough. My friends and I are all scowling. What happened to the Oscars being Holly-wood's most glamorous night? Clearly, I'm a fan of a good Oscar sing-along, but my beloved Diana moment featured pageantry and celebrities and formal wear! Kids on risers wasn't doing it for me.

Thirty-six hours later I was back in New York and booked on MSNBC's *Morning Joe*, which I like to think of as a current-events version of *Watch What Happens Live*, serving Starbucks instead of Maker's Mark. This time, I was determined not to indulge too heartily at *Mo' Joe*'s free coffee bar, because in the past I'd guzzled so much that I shvitzed my way through my segments, thus ensur-ing a barrage of "Your upper lip is sweaty" tweets when I left the studio. (Slightly less embarrassing than the time I walked off the stage at *The Wendy Williams Show* to see that I had several hundred tweets waiting. I'd come on to surprise Wendy's special viewer co-host Carole from Mississippi, allegedly a big fan of mine. And at some point during the hysteria of our greeting, Carole's cheek transferred a large swatch of her [very brown] foundation to my cheek, which made me look like Carole had beaten me up instead of kissed me. Suffice it to say that I don't love anything involuntary happening to my face on live TV, but now, with social media, you have to relive the humiliation as various time zones live-tweet the experience in waves throughout the day. But I digress.)

My segment on *Morning Joe* was called "Oscar After Party with Andy Cohen," but it was essentially a pop culture free-for-all. We talked about Charlie Sheen and I referred to his two latest "goddesses"—as he called them—as "whores." The minute it came out of my mouth I regretted it. This was mean, potentially slanderous, and hurtful. I mean, I did think the women might, in fact, have been prostitutes, which is why I used that term, but still. I shouldn't have said it. My mother had raised me better than that. In the back of my mind I wondered if I'd just derailed the whole appearance.

Then Willie Geist asked me for my lowlight of Oscar night. The show had been widely panned as a bomb as far as Oscars went, and I could have chosen from a plethora of lowlights. But, without hesitation, I told him it was the public school kids who sang.

"I don't know why you don't like public school children," Willie joked.

I clarified that I in fact loved public school children. I reminded him that I was a graduate of Clayton High, a fine public school. But then I compared the kids to Up with People, the unctuous choral group from the seventies that performed at Super Bowl halftime shows and the like. Everybody at the table was laughing. Cohost Mika Brzezinski gasped, "Did he really say that?" which is exactly what you want to hear on a TV panel show. Joe Scarborough, thinking he had me pegged, told me, "You just don't want to see uplifting stuff."

"No, that's not what I'm saying, either," I said. "The media twist your words. You are twisting my words. I know how this works." I was joking around, but was also kind of serious. And, it turns out, prophetic.

Joe started to make the point that I was the man who made *The Real Housewives*—meaning, who was *I* to provide meaningful social commentary—but I interrupted him. "If I wasn't going to go out to some parties I would have slit them [my wrists] right then. I was looking for a knife. I was looking for a knife to stick in my eye. It was terrible."

The table cracked up! From the first time I ever succeeded in making people laugh as a kid, I loved it, and as long as they're laughing, I will continue talking. And, of course, the hosts of a *talk show* weren't about to stop me. I told the *Morning Joe* crew that everything had its time and place, and that the end of the Oscars was not the time for nonprofessional singing children. "Those kids ruined everything!" I told them. I further stated that the children lacked appropriate attire for a sacred institution. "They're wearing *T-shirts* at the Academy Awards," I said. "Is this a *telethon*?"

When my segment was over, everyone smiled and shook my hand, and we parted with promises to see each other again soon. I left the studio feeling good. I hadn't over-caffeinated, and I'd not only made some astute observations, but was witty and entertaining to boot.

Back at the office, I saw Lauren and reported that I'd been mildly hilarious on *Morning Joe*. She took my word for it. My mom e-mailed and told me I shouldn't have called those women whores, but that she thought I was "very funny talking about the kids." More affirmation. Then, on my way to lunch, I got an e-mail from Bravo's head of publicity, Cameron Blanchard. I assumed it was just a quick congrats on my appearance earlier. Nope. She was asking if I'd really said unkind things about the kids from the public school.

Apparently, there was already an item on *New York* magazine's website reporting on my rant. I replied that I absolutely had said those things, that they were hilarious, and that every sane person agreed with me. She said I was wrong and that we'd discuss it after lunch. I felt like I was being called to the principal's office. (And that's one of the weirder things about being a "personality" on the network where you are also an executive. I was about to be lectured for crossing the line by a coworker who is now working on my behalf and on behalf of the company for which we both work.)

By the time I got back to work all hell was breaking loose. Our PR department had to explain to me that these kids, whom I had never seen nor heard of before the Oscars, were in fact beloved all across the country. They were apparently America's freaking Sweethearts, viral video sensations who'd also been on *Oprah* and performed at the White House. While I was logged in to YouTube watching an endless loop of Diana Ross's sing-along, apparently everyone else in the country was watching clips of these kids. And everybody but me, Mr. Pop Culture, knew that their appearance at the end of the Oscars was some big aspirational American Dream moment. And now the *New York Post* had sent a reporter to their school on Staten Island—and the *New York Times* was at the airport to greet the kids when they returned from LA—and both wanted responses to my remarks. Of course, the kids hadn't actually heard what I'd said, but the reporters helpfully filled them in.

I felt terrible for the kids and at the same time angry at the moralistic reporting on what I'd thought was just lighthearted cultural commentary. I wondered why anyone even cared what *I* thought of the Oscars or those kids anyway. Cameron told me that I could no longer just babble anything that was on my mind and expect it not to have repercussions. (You might think a pitcher of iced tea dumped over me years earlier would've taught me this lesson.)

That was the day I realized I was kind of famous . . . and I wish I could've enjoyed that moment instead of having it forever tied to the nauseous feeling in the pit of my stomach, growing larger as it became clear that I would now be world famous for being a child-hater. Some people get to bask in the glow of the spotlight, but others of us have it shine on us while we are stepping in poop.

On my show, I always name a Jackhole of the Day, or Week, someone who's done something particularly stupid or egregious, and that night I gave myself the distinction. I didn't even make excuses for myself. I just apologized to the kids and reiterated that I'd gone to public school, too, and that I felt awful about the whole incident. I really did. It killed me that reporters were still going to these fifth graders and repeating the nasty stuff that I'd said. Before it happened, those kids knew as little about me as I did about them, and now they not only knew who I was, but thought I was a big fat jerk.

But the damage was done. The next day the *New York Post* blared, "Oscar Grouch Trashes SI Kids." Perez Hilton posted an item and scrawled, "Shame on You!" on a picture of me (which I realize is still better than an ejaculating cartoon penis, which is what he usually draws on people), and the *New York Times* headline read DID P.S. 22 SINGERS RUIN OSCARS? Even worse, the *Times* called me "curmudgeonly." Me, curmudgeonly!

No one printed any part of my apology, and the stories rolled out all week. I was the ultimate elitist and a self-righteous tool—the *Housewives* dude who would dare trash a wholesome public school choir. The *Times* "Week in Review" put my quote between one from Gadhafi saying "All my people love me" and John Galliano's "I love Hitler" anti-Semitic rant. Oh, and in the same edition an op-ed repeated my "whore" line regarding Charlie Sheen's "goddesses," making my *Morning Joe* appearance a twofer in terms of ill-advised commentary.

When I think about it today, I have to laugh, albeit ruefully: The Oscars, "Over the Rainbow," a kids' choir, bad outfits, and me, all wrapped in an Oz-themed tornado that made me wish a house would fall from the sky and smoosh me. *Could there possibly be a gayer scandal?*

For days, my Twitter feed was an endless stream of now ex-fans telling me they saw me for the arrogant prick that I truly was. Wendy Williams went after me on her show, and I'm sure Carole from Mississippi was upset that she'd wasted her foundation on my cheek. Bette Midler tweeted, wondering what I could've been thinking. *Bette Midler!* If only *she'd* sung the damn song at the Oscars, none of this would've happened. I dared to venture out to a New York Knicks game and a huge mountain of a guy came up to me, got two inches from my face, and yelled, "STATEN ISLAND RULES!!!!" I told him I agreed, but of course I thought he was going to punch my lights out. The longer it went, the more frustrated I became and the worse I felt. But no one felt worse than my mom.

"ENOUGH ALREADY," she yelled to me over the phone. "This is RIDICULOUS! When is it going to END!? Do you have any idea the PROBLEMS that are going on in the WORLD right now? People are mentioning this to me at SCHNUCKS!" (If people were talking about this at Schnucks supermarket in Missouri, then I was in even worse trouble than I'd thought.) "Why does anyone *give a damn* what you said?" She told me—for the five thousandth time in my life—to "WATCH. YOUR. MOUTH." Oh, and she said to "MAKE IT STOP!" Like I had the power to do that all along and I was just letting it go on because I didn't realize I just had to click my heels together three times. (Although if anyone in the world could have made it happen, it was not me, but Evelyn Cohen.)

Since my public apology on my show was completely ineffective, I contemplated a new course of action. I felt like I should know a thing or two about what *not* to do in a situation like this, having been a human shield between countless warring women on numerous reunion shows. Housewives' apologies are often like dinner parties—in that they usually go horribly wrong. The aggrieved only becomes *more* aggrieved, and everything is misinterpreted and relations are worse than they were to begin with. But here I was, walking in the shoes of women who'd stuck feet in their filler-plumped mouths and paid the price. And, sister, I did not like those Louboutins. When Patti Stanger went two steps too far two feet from me on *Watch What Happens Live* (calling gays incapable of monogamy and Jewish men liars), I watched as she made it right. The advice I'd always given the Housewives was to own their words and to say sorry and mean it, but I'd done that already and it made no difference whatsoever. After a lifetime of overtalkative slipups that had been smoothed over by everyone from my mom to my bosses, now it was up to me to clean up my own mess.

Not that Evelyn didn't have ideas. She suggested going to the school and apologizing in person. I told her I was worried that that would generate more attention. I wanted the kids to know I was sincere and not just doing it for appearances. Dave suggested that I donate instruments to the school, which seemed to me like a blatant bid for mercy in the press. And besides, the kids were a chorus, not a band.

I finally just wrote a note directly to the choir director. I told him that adults say stupid things sometimes and that I wished the kids nothing but success. It was, in my opinion, an honest and humble apology delivered the right way.

A couple days later (well over a week after Oscar night), Perez Hilton reported that I had "finally" apologized to the kids and that they were responding. He posted a YouTube video of the choir director reading my note aloud to the kids, who clapped at the end. At that moment, I felt so relieved—the kids, it seemed, had forgiven me, which was all that really mattered. But then the choir director told them that I could've sent a longer note and that I could've shown up in person, but that he guessed it was okay. I thought it was kind of crappy that he was telling the kids all the things I *didn't* do—was that a good lesson on the importance of being gracious? Then I noticed that the whole scene was being filmed by a documentary crew. Oh joy! I could look forward to reliving the whole incident with myself as Ebenezer Scrooge in the eventual big-screen Hollywood version of their story, *Staten Island Fairy Tale*.

The director proceeded to lead the kids in a rousing rendition of the song "Apologize" by One Republic. You know, the one with the chorus: *It's too late to apologize . . . Too laaaaate!* This seemed like a bitchy way to "accept" my apology. At least as bitchy as my comments, if you ask me—but thankfully, nobody did. There *is* such a thing as bad publicity, and I was happy to be ignored for the first time in weeks.

Still, the story would not die. The press posted and re-posted the video, but it wasn't just to gush about how great the kids were. Some said what I was thinking, that this song didn't seem like the adult way to accept an apology. Then people at home started posting comments online saying that the choir director should be ashamed of how he'd handled the apology in front of the kids and maybe what he really cared about was being in the spotlight himself. (I know what you're thinking, and none of the comments were from me. And to the best of my knowledge, my mom does not have a YouTube account.)

Was I happy? Not really. If anyone can understand doing something dumb in the heat of the moment, it's me. We'd all learned valuable lessons, but the last thing I wanted was for this guy to go through anything even remotely similar to what I'd just put myself through, especially at the expense of these kids, so I was happy when I heard that he'd apparently pulled the clip down from YouTube. But you know what's still up there, though? Diana Ross singing "Over the Rainbow." I know because I just watched it fifteen more times.

LIFE LESSONS FROM THE GUY WHO PUBLICLY INSULTS SINGING SCHOOLKIDS

- ★ Never say never—I am the king of proclamations that I later retract. "I will NEVER tweet." "I will NEVER wear one of those polo shirts with a huge polo logo." "I will never write a book."
- ★ Don't poo at work. If you absolutely have to, go to another floor to do it. Or a restaurant nearby!
- ★ Listen to people when they speak to you, especially if you're interviewing them. Then you can ask a follow-up question.

★ Try to remember people. I'm the very worst at this, so maybe I'm writing this here as a reminder to myself.

★ Don't fuck with kangaroos. I was in Australia for *48 Hours* and a nasty—but cute—piece of work knocked one of my contact lenses right out of my eye! Same goes for swans—nasty in a pretty package.

★ My foolproof overnight flight combo is an Ambien with a glass or two of wine. Works like a charm. Speaking of flying, the overnight to London isn't long enough for a good sleep—the day flight is the way to go. Leave New York at 9 a.m., work the whole flight, and land at 8 p.m., just in time for a late dinner with heavy cocktails and you'll be ready for bed and on GMT without any hassle.

★ Keep your sense of wonder, always remember where you're from, and appreciate moments as they happen. I can't tell you how many benefits I've attended featuring amazing performers singing their heart out while the audience is engrossed in their phones.

★ This is the most urgently important piece of wisdom I can give you: Be aware of your breath at all times! Bad breath strikes us all, no matter how rich or famous you are—it can and will happen to anyone! There's nothing worse than getting a big whiff of someone's rotten sulfurmouth at a party. You will never forget that person, for all the wrong reasons!

ALL MY LUCCIS

H ere's what: I'm ending this book right where I began,
with Susan Lucci.

Over the course of the early nineties, a pop culture
seismic shift occurred in my life as I slowly weaned
myself off my ten-year addiction to *All My Children*. I know what
you're asking right now: "WHY!? HOW DID THIS HAPPEN,
ANDY?" Well, let's get you a nice cup of herbal tea to sip while I
explain it to you.

It was a combination of things. First, *AMC* started to get boring. I can only imagine how hard it must be to write incredible
amounts of dialogue and drama every day, but nonetheless, the plot
kinda ran out of gas. At the same time, I was producing stories at

CBS This Morning about a topic that had once been odious to me: CBS soaps. Specifically, *The Young and the Restless*, which had always seemed repellent to me because of its glacial pace and dark atmosphere. But apparently, I was alone in my assessment, because *Y&R* had been the number one soap for eternity.

And that's when the unthinkable happened: I got hooked on *The Young and the Restless*. (Are you FREAKING OUT from that news?) Maybe it was network loyalty, maybe I'd matured, but somehow this show that I'd always considered languid and boring now felt moody, enigmatic, and fascinating. The stories had a slow build that made their climaxes all the more powerful. It was a new way to look at soaps, and after having criticized the show for years, I embraced it. This kind of thing happens to me constantly. Call it self-contradiction, call it flip-flopping, call it bloviating opinionated gasbaggery without foundation that will soon crumble. I prefer to call it growth.

I didn't advertise my switch to CBS daytime, I just quietly started taping *The Young and the Restless*. Which was all well and good, except *Y&R* shared a time slot with ... *All My Children*. If DVRs had existed back then, I probably could have gone on leading this double life for years, but as it was, I had a choice to make. And though it saddened me, I quietly entered into a trial separation with *AMC*.

Regardless of that breakup, I was still dying to have Susan Lucci on CBS. My love for her transcended my allegiance to any soap. But while my heart ached to produce her in a morning show segment like she'd never been produced before, my mind knew it would be unlikely to have such a big ABC star appear on a competitor's morning show.

It had been five years since I ran into her again, in June 1992, Daytime Emmy night. She'd just lost for the twelfth time but received a one-minute-thirty-second emotional standing ovation later in the show as she took the stage to present an award. At the end of the broadcast, she was surrounded by press and fans as she made her way out of the Marriott Marquis ballroom in New York City. I was now an assistant producer at CBS News covering the show. I fought my way through the crowd until we were face-to-face in the frenzy. Grabbing her hand, I said, "You wouldn't remember me, but I'm . . ."

"You're Andrew!" she said. "What are you *doing* with yourself?" she asked. When I told her I worked at CBS News, she turned to her husband and Dick Clark. "This is the boy who took me to lunch when he was a sophomore in college," she told them. "And I said, 'Oh, I'll be hearing from Andrew Cohen again.' And here you are! You brought me that sweatshirt," she added, as though that day were as indelibly imprinted in her memory as it was in mine. I floated on air all night.

A few years later I was at the premiere of a James Bond movie at the Museum of Modern Art. In honor of the film, MoMA had been transformed into a casino, albeit the less fun legal kind. I saw her across the room—tiny and glamorous and glowing. Before I realized what I was doing, I walked halfway over to her. I broke out in flop-sweat. What was I supposed to say? Would she remember me? Would she NOT remember me? The fifty free hors d'oeuvres I'd eaten earlier combined with just the thought of approaching her had me right on the cusp of throwing up, but I knew I'd hate myself if I didn't try to talk to her. I continued right up to her, praying my stomach contents would stay in.

"Susan!" I said. "It's Andy Cohen. I interviewed you for the BU newspaper?"

I was relieved when Susan said, "Of *course* I remember you! Hello!" Then I said, "Hello!" She nodded and smiled. I had nothing to say beyond that, the exact thing I'd said to her the last time I'd seen her. I did an incredibly awkward nod/shrug/bow combo and backed away. I fake-cashed-in my fake-chips and left, convinced that she actually had no clue who I was.

But like any stalker worth his salt, I never gave up on her, and I did finally concoct a reason to get her on *CBS This Morning*. We were doing what might rank as our lamest series ever—which is saying something. This venture was called "Celebrity Secrets." The people involved were neither big celebrities nor were they revealing anything that came close to being a secret. In fact, the only secret revealed by this segment was that morning shows have a *lot* of time to fill. No matter. I used it as an opportunity for another Close Encounter of the Lucci Kind.

I called Lucci's publicist—a new one, I have no clue what happened to the woman who'd made my college dreams come true—and pitched this "Celebrity Secrets" idea. Surely there must be a "secret" that Susan would share with Paula Zahn on our morning show? To my unmitigated joy, they agreed that Susan would do the segment, and after some back-and-forth, we agreed on what unbelievable secret Susan would reveal to the world, for the first time ever, on our show: Susan Lucci Loves to Shop on the Top Floor of Bergdorf Goodman! In my mind, the image of Paula and Susan and Susan's personal shopper strolling through Bergdorf's seemed like Morning Show Gold. In retrospect, I realize a TV star shopping at Bergdorf's was not really much of a secret. Where did people think she shopped?

Many preparations, walkthroughs, and schedule adjustments followed in the ramp-up to the Lucci shoot. *All My Children* helpfully rescheduled Lucci's on-set day to accommodate Paula's interview. Bergdorf's agreed to close their top floor for several hours. I locked in our two best crews and lighting guys to ensure the women would look flawless. I was proud to be meeting Lucci this time as an established TV professional and not an awkward fan. It felt like another one of those out-of-body moments when you can see your dreams and reality meeting.

Then everything went to shit. The morning of the shoot, I got a call from my boss telling me to cancel the crew. "Why?!!" I practically screamed. "Why?!!!" I was given several explanations as to why the whole thing was off. One version was that Paula thought the segment was beneath a newswoman of her stature. Another version was that the executive producer *hated* the series and that this particular non-secret, at Bergdorf's, was beyond his comfort level. I've come to believe the former.

Whatever the real reason, it was then up to me to break the last-minute news to Susan Lucci's camp. And of course, I had to think of a fake excuse to offer them, because of the two excuses *I'd* been given, one version made our anchor look bad and the other made me look like an idiot for coming up with the idea in the first place.

Bumbling my way through an uncomfortable series of phone calls with the publicist, I'm sure I came across as a total nutjob because I hadn't gotten my story straight. I blamed Paula's schedule. I blamed breaking news. I blamed Bergdorf's. I blamed my executive producer. I blamed me. I was a flailing hot mess.

How did this happen? How, in what was meant to be my moment of glory, could I have ended up in the doghouse with my all-time idol? This was like Oprah, but worse. In an attempt to save face, I sent flowers and a very sincere note of apology.

You can breathe a momentary sigh of relief now: This next Susan Lucci story is not humiliating. In fact, she became a guardian angel at a moment when I least expected it. In early 1999, Graciela told me she was getting married. I responded with mixed emotions. I was thrilled for her but also deeply sad that now, officially, she and I could not spend our lives together. I worried I was losing my accomplice. She'd still be around, but it would be different. I knew I couldn't be selfish, at least not outwardly, and I had to find a way to properly send her off into her new life. So I organized what I think was probably one of the first all-gay wedding showers, a chance for all the boys who worshipped Grac to let her go and to show her how much we loved her. The evening was so important to me that when I realized that the date we'd chosen conflicted with the Daytime Emmy Awards, I shrugged it off. Grac was way more important. I'd just have to set my VCR.

I'd spent months planning the gay shower and making a special video. It was a high-tech love letter to Grac featuring montages of her fabulosity. It included celebrity well-wishers I'd grabbed while doing my day job at CBS—everybody from Johnnie Cochran and Sandra Bullock to several cast members from *The Brady Bunch.* Graciela arrived at her event in full Britt Ekland hair, a red gingham dress, and white cat-eye sunglasses. She carried shopping bags, a Barbie phone, and a huge lollipop that matched her skirt. How could I give this woman up?

Among her gifts were a Dollywood poncho, Vivienne Westwood's latest perfume—called Boudoir—fur handcuffs, and red stilettos. The highlight, if I do say so myself, was the video, and as it was playing, I got beeped; it was CBS telling me that Susan Lucci, after nineteen nominations, had finally *won the Emmy.* It was like a hug from above.

When I announced to the party that Lucci had won her Emmy, the reaction was like Stonewall 2. Graciela and I decided that it was some kind of cosmic sign. Susan Lucci was our fairy godmother, sprinkling magical dust over us, saying that even though everything was changing, we would always be the same. Love would rule.

If Graciela was my Dorothy, Susan Lucci was our Glinda that night. And Judy.

As I'd done for so many years in the past, I had prebooked a morning-after appearance with Lucci's people on the off-off-off-chance that she would win this time. Monday, I was up at the crack of pitch black, waiting in front of the CBS Broadcast Center for Lucci's limo, something I hadn't done since the time Joan Collins visited the studio and scared the shit out of me. When Susan stepped out, wearing a Chanel-ish crème suit, I hugged her with as much happiness as if I'd won myself. I felt like finally there was justice in the world, and I wanted her to know it. She had *won!*

On the air, we presented her with a dozen long-stemmed roses, which was thoughtful enough. But unbeknownst to us, she'd just come from *Good Morning America,* where they'd given her *nineteen* dozen roses, one for each year she'd been nominated and lost. And here we were, handing her a dozen roses that would be dead in hours from the Korean deli on Tenth Avenue. Does that not sum it all up perfectly? Susan, amazing actress that she was, acted as if our roses meant more to her than anything. She even wiped a "tear" from the corner of her eye!

On her way out, we hugged one last time and triumphantly posed for pictures holding up that day's newspapers. (*The Daily News* blared AT LONG LAST, LUCCI.) And after so many encounters crammed with so much awkwardness on my end, it felt like the best possible ending to the Lucci-Cohen story arc.

Or so it would have been. But, like characters in our own day-time drama, Susan Lucci and I weren't done.

It was "winter" in Los Angeles, and Lucci's daughter, Liza, was Miss Golden Globe. Miss GG is a yearly fixture at the Golden Globes award show where the (pretty) daughter of a (pretty) celebrity (and sometimes even a pretty celebrity couple) puts on a gown and presents the trophies to the winner. This particular year it was Lucci's daughter, Liza Huber, who would be doing the honors, and the Friday before the Globes, I ran into her, her mother, and their whole family in the lobby of the Regent Beverly Wilshire Hotel, where, it turned out, we were all staying. (This was a one hundred percent coincidence, I promise.)

Of course, my heroine was as radiant as ever, but I wasn't the same Andrew Cohen. By that time, I'd worked with Dan Rather and met more huge stars than I could count. I'd traveled the world, left CBS, and was running programming at TRIO. I was a man, not a kid, and comfortable in my own skin (and with my own eyes). But one slightly cross-eyed look at Erica Kane reduced me right back to a sweaty-palmed nineteen-year-old. No, actually, I was way more nervous than when I'd met her at age nineteen, because over the years I'd lost some innocence and naïveté while gaining plenty of experience in things going terribly.

Of course, no matter how anxious I was, there was no way I

wasn't going to talk to her. I tried to make up for my nerves by raising my decibel level, as though I were in my parents' kitchen in St. Louis. "SUSAN, IT'S ANDREW COHEN. I'M THE KID FROM BU WHO YOU TOOK TO LUNCH!?!?!" I screamed in her face. Again with that? Why didn't I just have it printed on some business cards to hand to her every time our paths crossed?

She was, naturally, lovely and introduced me to her family. I made a huge deal out of her daughter being Miss Golden Globe, then I scampered away as fast as I could before I got the sweats. Later that day, I was on the phone with Lynn, the producer who'd turned down my request to be friends years earlier when I was an intern and who I'd predicted would one day relent. And because we were friends, just like I said we'd be, I knew Lynn was almost as big an *AMC* fan as me. I told her about meeting Lucci in the hotel lobby.

Suddenly, I said, "Hey. If we're both in the same hotel, that means I could *call her room.*" Being struck with this idea was so much like being possessed by the spirit of Graciela that I now felt kind of guilty for not immediately hanging up to make certain that my mischievous old friend hadn't died and flown into my body.

Lynn paused, then said, "Yeah, you could call her room. For what, though? What would you even say?" See, this is exactly why I needed Lynn as a friend. To bring up logical points that I won't listen to.

"Just to hear her voice. I'll hang up!" And that was it. Before Lynn could talk any sense into me, I said, "I'm putting you on hold while I do it." And I did it. I put the call on hold, called downstairs, and asked for Susan Lucci.

"Hold on, Mr. Cohen," the operator said. "We'll tell Miss Lucci you're on the line."

Oh NO! She was having the front desk screen her calls! I know what you're thinking: Of *course* she was. She's Susan Lucci! You can't just *call up* the front desk of a hotel and have them ring you through to Susan Lucci's room, no questions asked! I felt like such an idiot. When the operator put me on hold, I quickly hung up.

Then I realized something even more horrible. The operator had said, "Hold on, *Mr. Cohen* . . ." He had been able to refer to me by name, so the operator wasn't just telling Susan Lucci that someone was on the phone for her, he was telling her that "Andrew Cohen in Room 222" was calling for her. The only way it could have been worse is if the operator had somehow been able to add, "You know, the guy who interviewed you for the BU paper?" Panicked, I picked up my other line.

"She's screening her calls," I screamed to Lynn. "The dude is telling her I'm *on the line*! But I'm not on the line. I hung up!"

"Oh NO!!!!" Lynn was mortified on my behalf. Suddenly, my other line rang. Lynn and I panicked.

"I have Susan Lucci for you now, *Mr. Cohen*." The operator sounded displeased—bitchy, actually. "You were . . . disconnected."

"Ummm . . ." There was no way I could possibly take that call. I was humiliated. "Uh . . . I just got an urgent work call from . . . work," I stammered. "Please . . . please, tell her I . . . I'll call her back!" I hung up.

I spent the next two days paralyzed with the fear that I was going to run into Susan Lucci at the hotel. Just in case I did, though, I had concocted an elaborate explanation: My photographer friend had taken an amazing picture of Lucci and her daughter at some point and I had been calling to tell her that I would send it to her if she was interested. The only issue with that story was that there *was* no photograph. So if I went with that excuse, I would then somehow have to find an existing photo of her and her daughter to send over. And then, to be on the safe side, I would have to somehow befriend the photographer who'd taken it, should Susan Lucci ever meet the photographer, recognize his name, and then bring up my name. It seemed kind of like a long shot, but I literally could not think of anything else to say that sounded *less* crazy. Thank God I never ran into her again that weekend, but I spent a lot of time in my room thinking about how I now had a canceled shoot and crank call on my permanent record with Susan Lucci.

And now, at last, the final encounter—or near encounter, I should say. In 2010 Lucci was booked to appear on my show, *Watch What Happens Live*, to promote her new book. She'd even agreed to a joint appearance with a New York Housewife. It was going to be the ultimate full-circle moment: the queen of the daytime drama with one of our Bravo queens of reality. Then, shortly before her appearance, the announcement came that after forty-one years, *All My Children* had been canceled. We soon got word from the publicist that Susan Lucci might cancel her appearance on my show, which in publicist-speak meant "Susan Lucci is canceling."

I could have gotten involved and said, "Susan! It's me, Andrew Cohen. I'm the kid from BU who you took to lunch!" But it was then and there that I put two and two together. Why would Susan Lucci want to sit next to a woman who was part of the kind of show that might have helped lead to her own show's demise? And though it pained me to do so, I quietly allowed my dream guest booking to slip away. But I was stuck with a haunting question: Was I, in some way, partly to blame for this? Had I helped kill soaps? With *The Real Housewives of Orange County*, we'd begun making real-life soap operas with nonactors, and it had snowballed into something huger than we ever imagined. The media had certainly done their share of speculating as to whether reality programming had chimed the death knell for soap operas. And now my old sweetheart *AMC* would be no more.

But here's the thing: I'm now (sort of) a grown-up and I know that, first and foremost in this world, things change. Many things occurred that led to the end of several daytime dramas, of which *All My Children* was one. The viewing audience had been evolving over the years, abandoning soaps for daytime talk, game shows, and courtroom shows; as soap audiences aged, they failed to gain essential new, young viewers; and the cost of producing a daily show with a large cast of highly paid talent is enormous.

With the *Housewives*, we're doing a real-life version of the format I fell in love with as a kid, running with the baton passed on to us from a television tradition that simply may not be sustainable anymore. By featuring these powerful, outsized, outspoken women in their wildly dramatic everyday lives, we're playing off the idea of *and* paying tribute to indelible characters like Erica Kane.

☺

It's September 23, 2011. I'm in St. Louis for a visit with my parents, and I happen to arrive on the day ABC will broadcast the series finale of *All My Children*. And, as if it is 1984 again, I gather in front of the TV with Em and my mom to watch the show, while my dad and Blouse wander in and out of the room. After more than four decades, this is it for Pine Valley and its residents.

Watching the opening is a montage of flashbacks; my eyes fill with tears. These people are like family that I've lost touch with. One by one they appear as they are today—and, on a certain street in St. Louis, the peanut gallery explodes.

"Is Tad FAT?! He used to be cute!"

"He looks like Mrs. Doubtfire!"

"I can't see BROOKE through her FACEWORK!"

"Brooke *always* had high cheekbones, Mom. She hasn't been touched."

Our favorite characters now have kids, and grandkids. We feel old.

"How did I ever WATCH this DRECK!?"

Erica Kane's last moments on *All My Children* feature her in sequins and a fur shawl and not quite a side ponytail but maybe a side chignon?

"Well, thank God Erica looks PERFECT."

And she doesn't disappoint. Tad is making a toast and he's quoting from the *AMC* bible: "In joy and in sorrow, in sickness and in health, we are . . . all your children."

I am getting choked up and Blouse enters the room wanting to talk about *Guiding Light*.

My dad walks in: "Is that Adam and Brooke?"

"QUIET, Lou!" Evelyn barks.

Erica's last words on the show as she storms after Jackson are "I won't let it end this way."

The show was over, but we left the TV on.

ACKNOWLEDGMENTS

First I want to thank Gillian Blake who not only taught me how to write a book, she ultimately allowed me to include the word "boner" several times within these pages even though she does not find it one bit amusing. Stephen Rubin for reading my treatment a second time and going from hate to love, and for believing more than I that this book wouldn't be stupid. Sara Bershtel for proving that smarties can love the Housewives. Maggie Richards, Pat Eisemann, and Allison Adler, Maggie Sivon, and Rick Pracher for taking the final product and running with it. Simon Green, who motivated me to write this in the first place and guided me through the process.

I would not be in a position to write this book if not for Lauren Zalaznick, who breaks rules and listens to her gut. I am eternally grateful to you, Lauren. Frances Berwick teaches me something every day, plus she's fierce and a glam fairy. Michael Davies is m'producer and m'cheerleader and m'friend, and Deidre

Connolly makes it all happen. My incredible colleagues at Bravo through the years with whom I have found myself in unusual, incredible, and hilarious situations—and who always make me look good—especially Dave Serwatka, Eli Lehrer, Shari Levine, Christian Barcellos, Cori Abraham, Daryn Carp, Anthony McCarthy, Amy Introcaso-Davis, David O'Connell, Ellen Stone, Jason Klarman, Lara Spotts, Lauren McCollester, Jen Levy, Jerry Leo, Cameron Blanchard, and Alana McElroy. I am in awe of every single Bravolebrity for being unforgettable and exactly yourselves. I also want to thank all the amazing production companies with whom I have the honor to work and my former colleagues at CBS News for ten amazing years of memories and fun.

Caissie St. Onge for guiding me to humor and heart, because she has so much of both. Tamara Jones for helping me think about my life thematically, which is difficult. Kari Morris Vincent who was really my first editor, and is a great one. Lorne Michaels and Marci Klein for letting me reprint Emily Spivey and Paula Pell's hilarious words.

My friends give me unconditional love, support, and laughs. Thank you especially to Mike Goldman, Jackie Greenberg, Jeanne Messing Walsh, Dave Ansel, Amanda Baten, Graciela Braslavsky Meltzer, Lynn Redmond, and Bruce Bozzi Jr. for letting me tell our stories in this book. Thank you to Bill Persky for being a great sage and East Coast Parental Unit. Thank you to the very wise Emily Lazar for your thoughts on the treatment and manuscript. John Hill, thanks for being Fender.

My dear friend Liza Persky made an incredible short film with Mary Matthews about my letters from camp that not only served as the basis for the earlier selections, they also motivated me in more ways than you can know during the course of thinking about this book. Thank you!

My family is incredible and I love them very much. They let me play, prank, poke, and pry with them in this book and elsewhere, all the while cheering me on. Blouse, thank you for being amazing and fun. (Smile.)

Thanks to Susan Lucci for taking a strange kid out to lunch at Santa Fe. Sorry I prank called you that time. By the way, do you even remember me? I'm the guy that gave you that BU sweatshirt. Oh, forget it . . .

About the Author

ANDY COHEN is Bravo's executive vice president of development and talent, responsible for overseeing production of such hits as *Top Chef* and *The Real Housewives* and development of new franchises for the network. In addition, Cohen is the host and executive producer of *Watch What Happens Live*, Bravo's late-night interactive talk show. He also hosts the network's reunion specials. He's won an Emmy and two Peabody Awards for his work and lives in New York City.